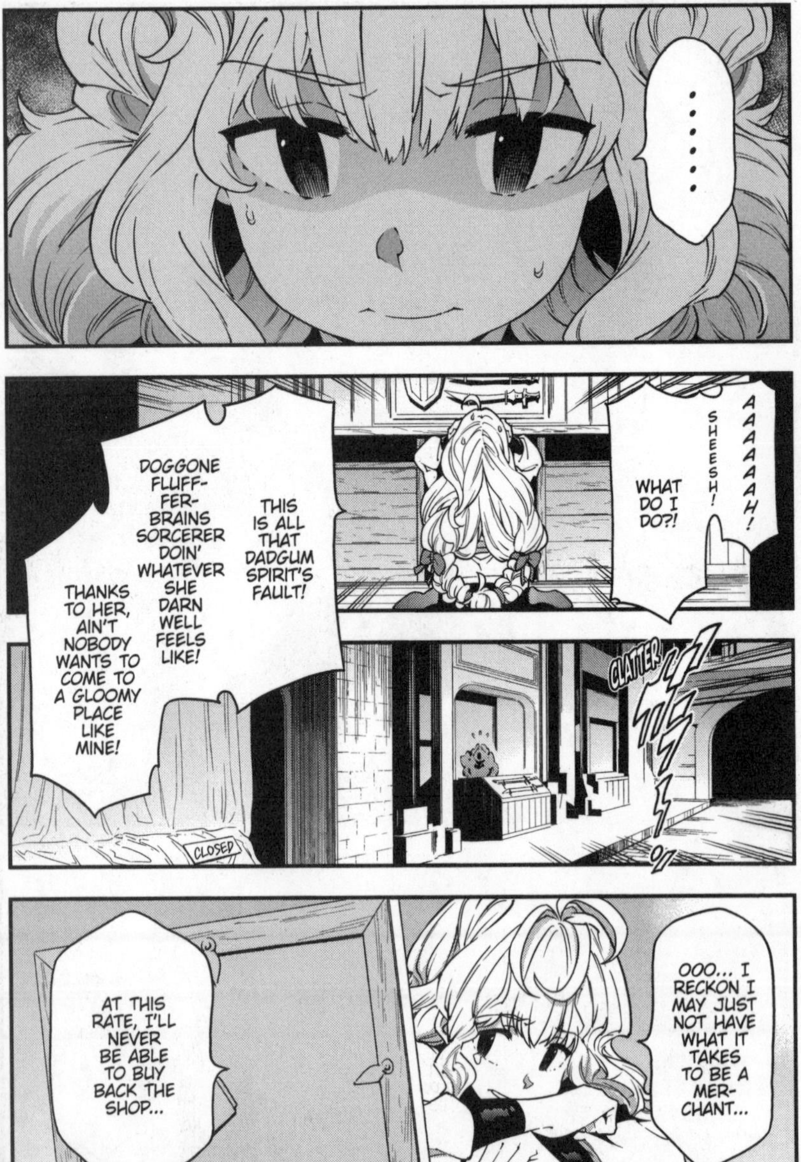
......
AAAAAAAH!
SHEESH!
WHAT DO I DO?!
THIS IS ALL THAT DADGUM SPIRIT'S FAULT!
DOGGONE FLUFFER-BRAINS SORCERER DOIN' WHATEVER SHE DARN WELL FEELS LIKE!
THANKS TO HER, AIN'T NOBODY WANTS TO COME TO A GLOOMY PLACE LIKE MINE!
CLATTER
CLOSED
OOO... I RECKON I MAY JUST NOT HAVE WHAT IT TAKES TO BE A MERCHANT...
AT THIS RATE, I'LL NEVER BE ABLE TO BUY BACK THE SHOP...

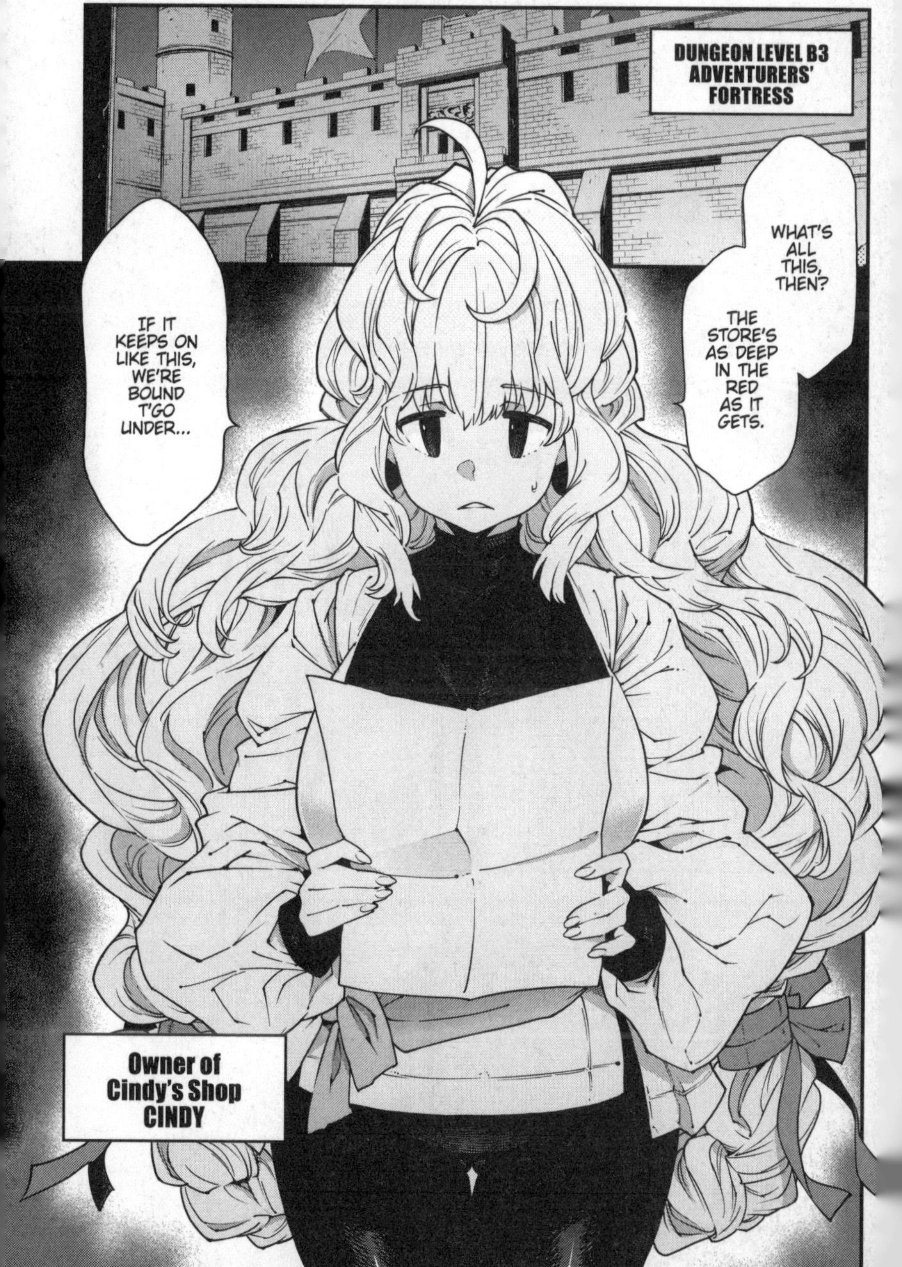
DUNGEON LEVEL B3 ADVENTURERS' FORTRESS
WHAT'S ALL THIS, THEN?
THE STORE'S AS DEEP IN THE RED AS IT GETS.
IF IT KEEPS ON LIKE THIS, WE'RE BOUND T'GO UNDER...
Owner of Cindy's Shop CINDY

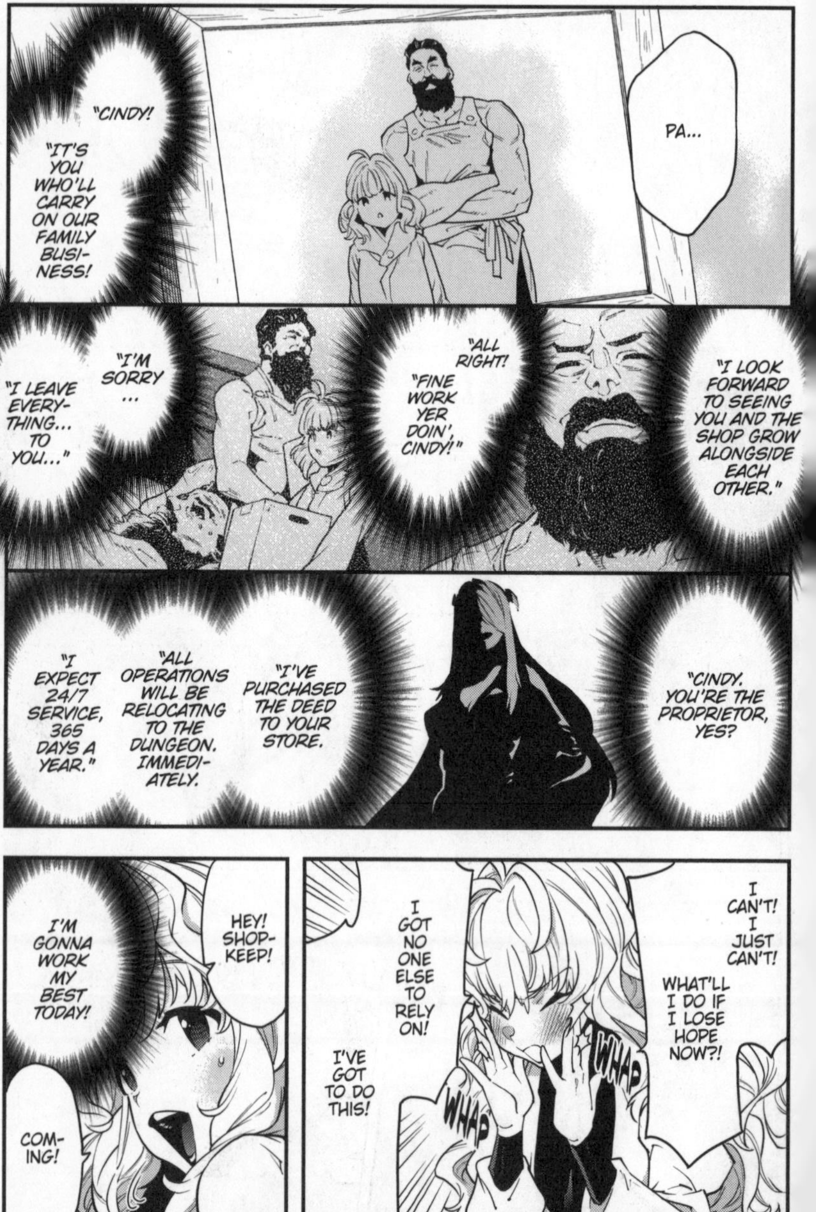
PA...
"CINDY!
"IT'S YOU WHO'LL CARRY ON OUR FAMILY BUSI-NESS!
"I LOOK FORWARD TO SEEING YOU AND THE SHOP GROW ALONGSIDE EACH OTHER."
"ALL RIGHT!
"FINE WORK YER DOIN', CINDY!"
"I'M SORRY ...
"I LEAVE EVERY-THING... TO YOU..."
"CINDY. YOU'RE THE PROPRIETOR, YES?
"I'VE PURCHASED THE DEED TO YOUR STORE.
"ALL OPERATIONS WILL BE RELOCATING TO THE DUNGEON. IMMEDI-ATELY.
"I EXPECT 24/7 SERVICE, 365 DAYS A YEAR."
I CAN'T! I JUST CAN'T!
WHAT'LL I DO IF I LOSE HOPE NOW?!
I GOT NO ONE ELSE TO RELY ON!
I'VE GOT TO DO THIS!
WHAP
WHAP
HEY! SHOP-KEEP!
I'M GONNA WORK MY BEST TODAY!
COM-ING!

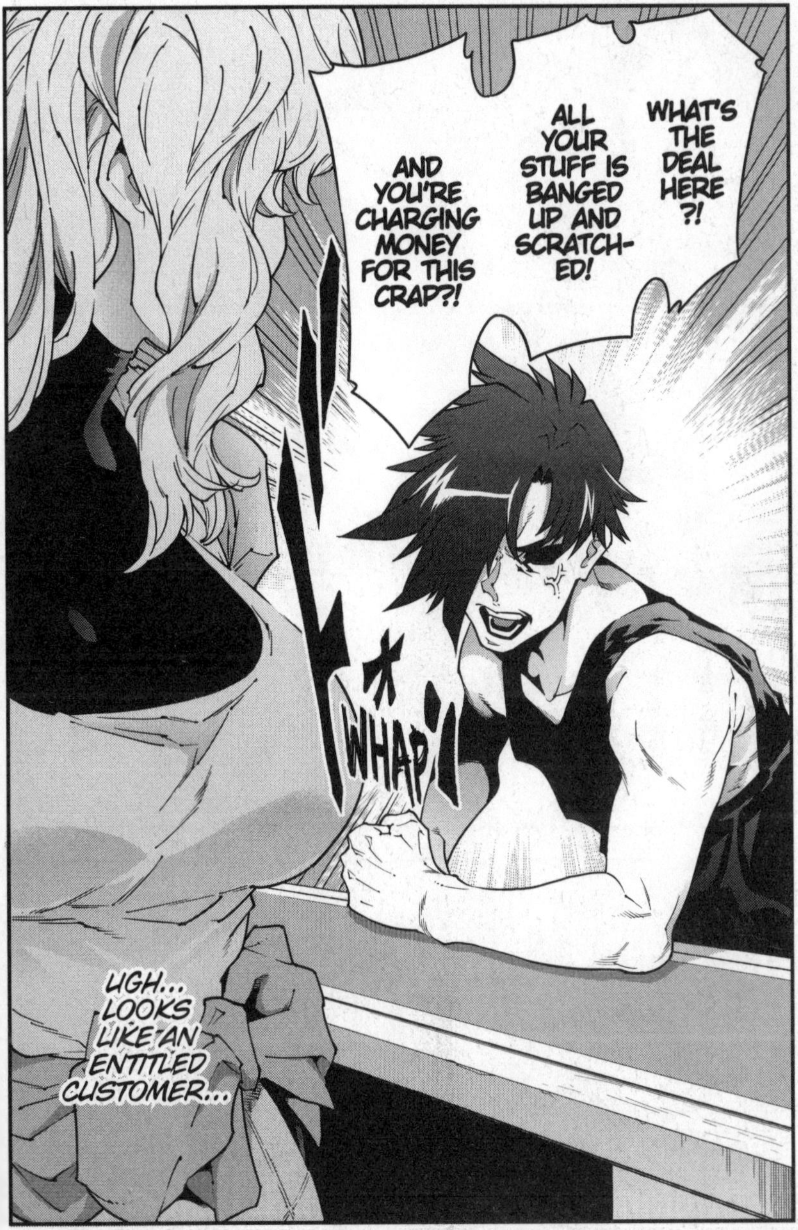
WHAT'S THE DEAL HERE ?!
ALL YOUR STUFF IS BANGED UP AND SCRATCH-ED!
AND YOU'RE CHARGING MONEY FOR THIS CRAP?!
WHAP
UGH... LOOKS LIKE AN ENTITLED CUSTOMER...

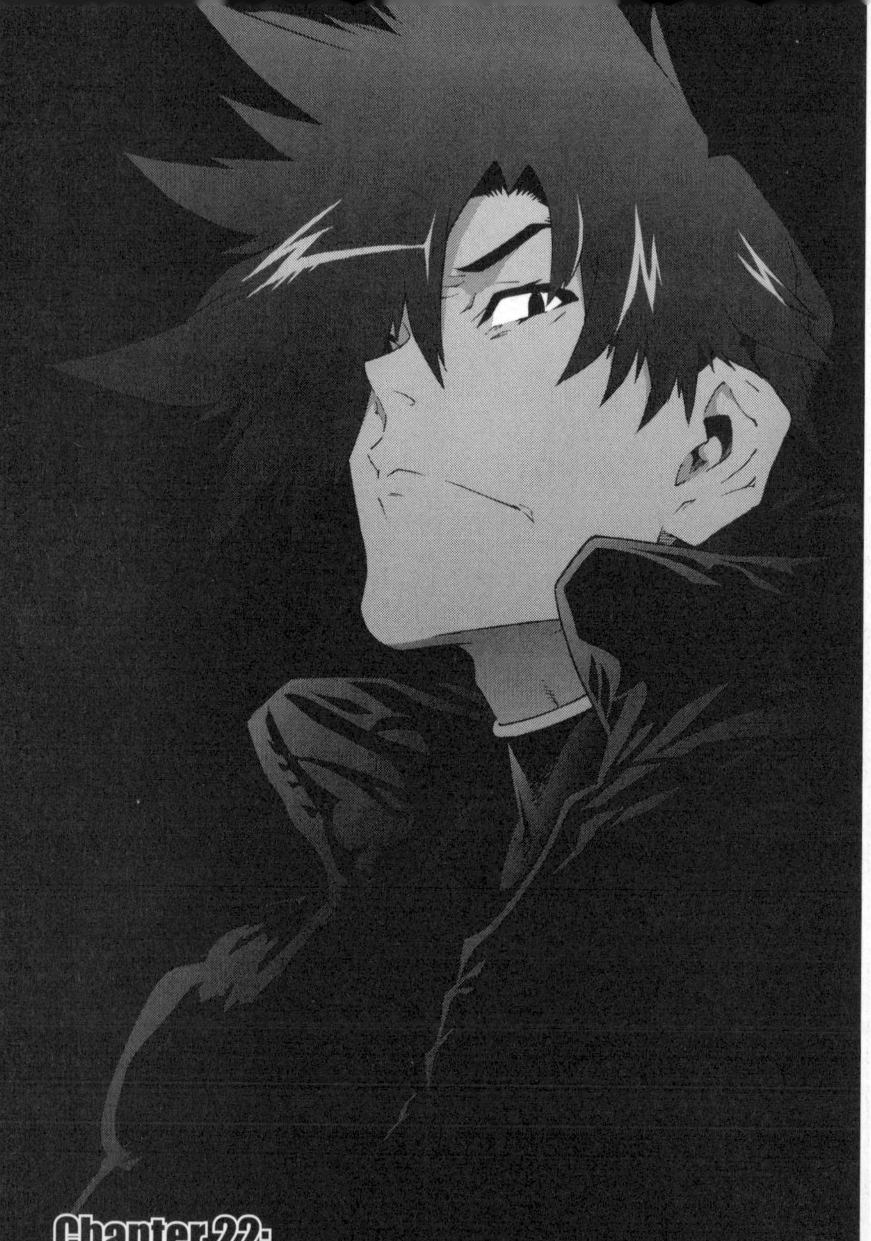

Chapter 22: Earning Money for Someone Else's Sake

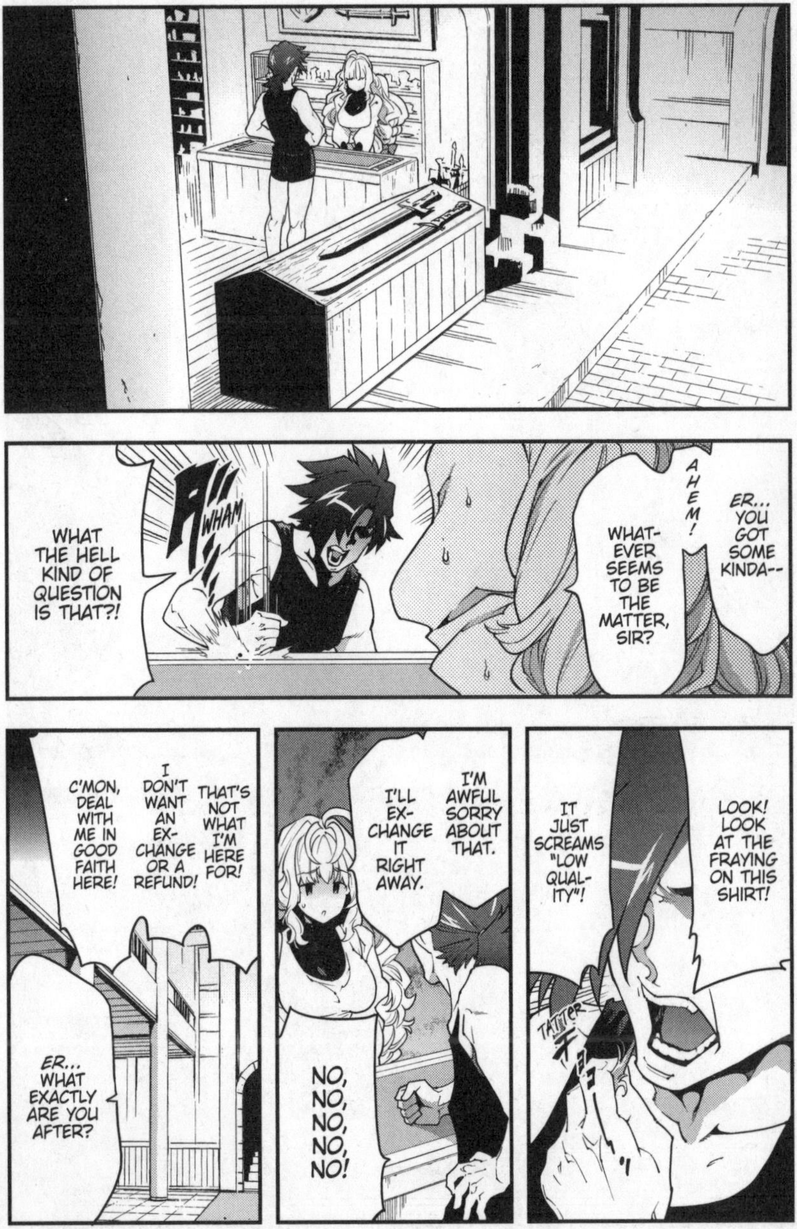
ER... YOU GOT SOME KINDA--
AHEM!
WHAT-EVER SEEMS TO BE THE MATTER, SIR?
WHAM
WHAT THE HELL KIND OF QUESTION IS THAT?!
LOOK! LOOK AT THE FRAYING ON THIS SHIRT!
IT JUST SCREAMS "LOW QUAL-ITY"!
TATTER
I'M AWFUL SORRY ABOUT THAT.
I'LL EX-CHANGE IT RIGHT AWAY.
NO, NO, NO, NO, NO!
THAT'S NOT WHAT I'M HERE FOR!
I DON'T WANT AN EX-CHANGE OR A REFUND!
C'MON, DEAL WITH ME IN GOOD FAITH HERE!
ER... WHAT EXACTLY ARE YOU AFTER?

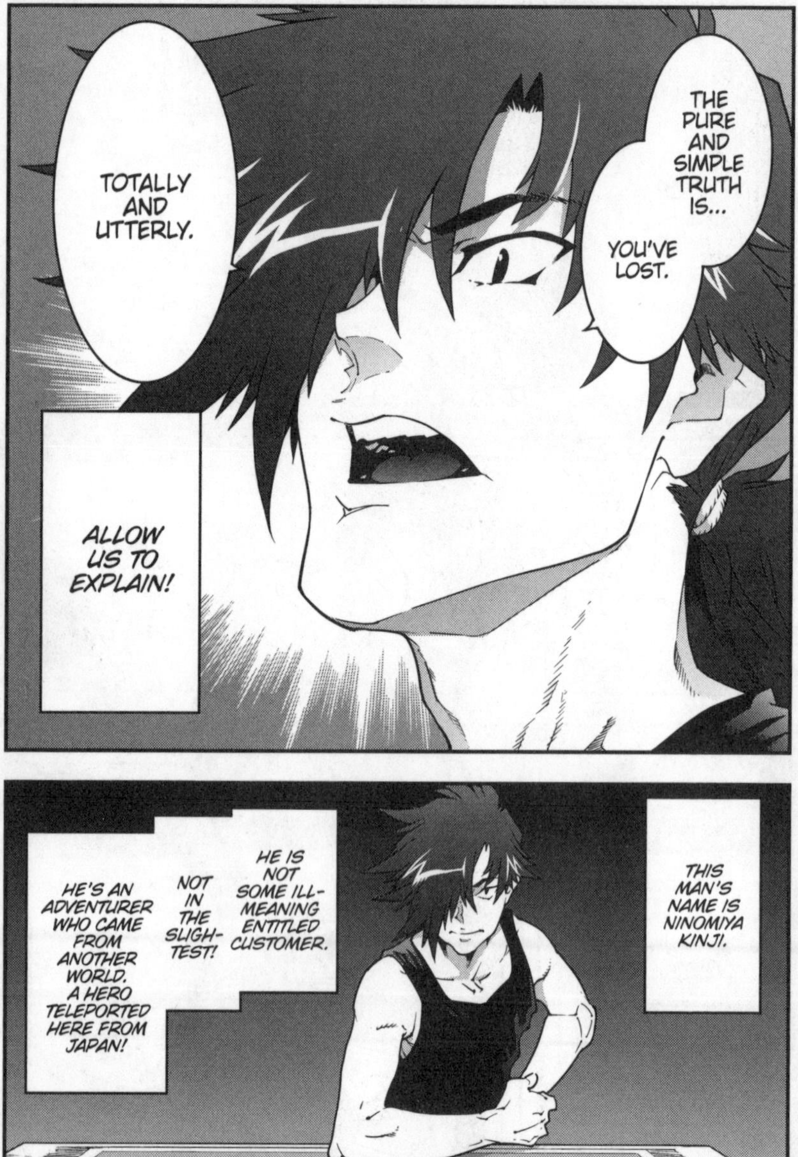
THE PURE AND SIMPLE TRUTH IS...
YOU'VE LOST.
TOTALLY AND UTTERLY.
ALLOW US TO EXPLAIN!
THIS MAN'S NAME IS NINOMIYA KINJI.
HE IS NOT SOME ILL-MEANING ENTITLED CUSTOMER.
NOT IN THE SLIGH-TEST!
HE'S AN ADVENTURER WHO CAME FROM ANOTHER WORLD. A HERO TELEPORTED HERE FROM JAPAN!

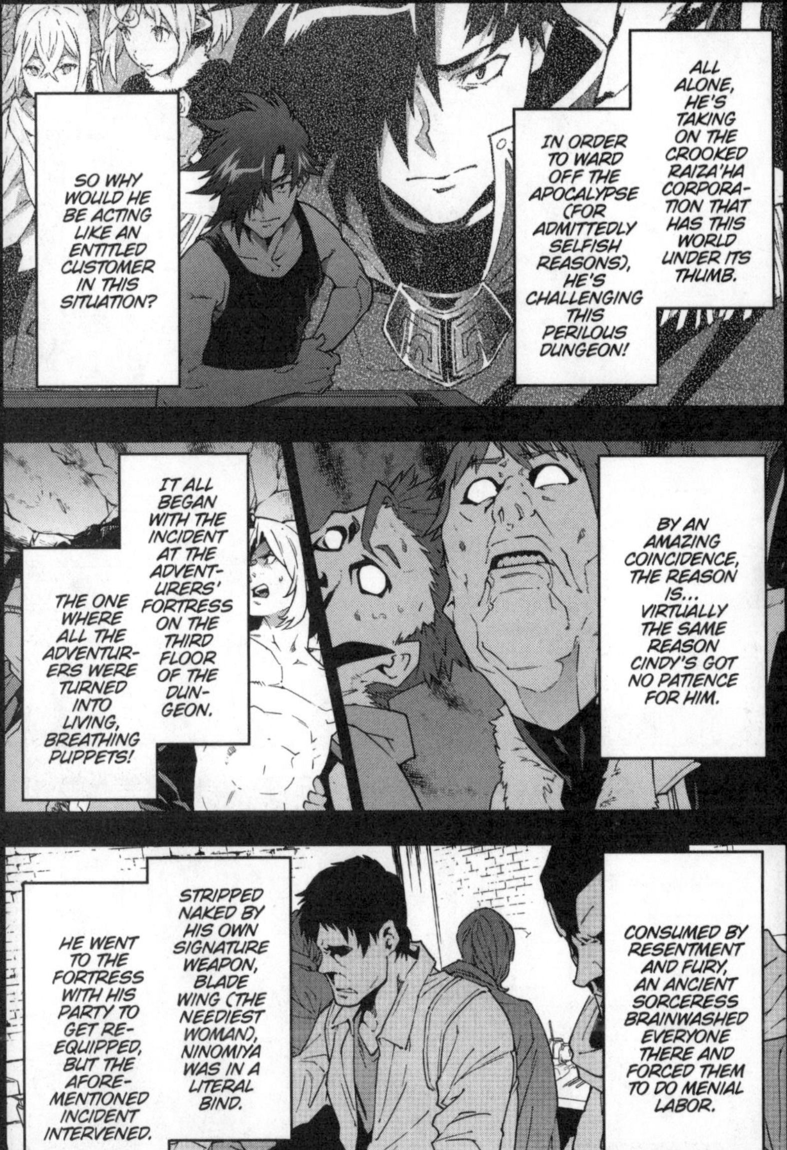
ALL ALONE, HE'S TAKING ON THE CROOKED RAIZA'HA CORPORATION THAT HAS THIS WORLD UNDER ITS THUMB.
IN ORDER TO WARD OFF THE APOCALYPSE (FOR ADMITTEDLY SELFISH REASONS), HE'S CHALLENGING THIS PERILOUS DUNGEON!
SO WHY WOULD HE BE ACTING LIKE AN ENTITLED CUSTOMER IN THIS SITUATION?
BY AN AMAZING COINCIDENCE, THE REASON IS... VIRTUALLY THE SAME REASON CINDY'S GOT NO PATIENCE FOR HIM.
IT ALL BEGAN WITH THE INCIDENT AT THE ADVENTURERS' FORTRESS ON THE THIRD FLOOR OF THE DUNGEON.
THE ONE WHERE ALL THE ADVENTURERS WERE TURNED INTO LIVING, BREATHING PUPPETS!
CONSUMED BY RESENTMENT AND FURY, AN ANCIENT SORCERESS BRAINWASHED EVERYONE THERE AND FORCED THEM TO DO MENIAL LABOR.
STRIPPED NAKED BY HIS OWN SIGNATURE WEAPON, BLADE WING (THE NEEDIEST WOMAN), NINOMIYA WAS IN A LITERAL BIND.
HE WENT TO THE FORTRESS WITH HIS PARTY TO GET RE-EQUIPPED, BUT THE AFORE-MENTIONED INCIDENT INTERVENED.

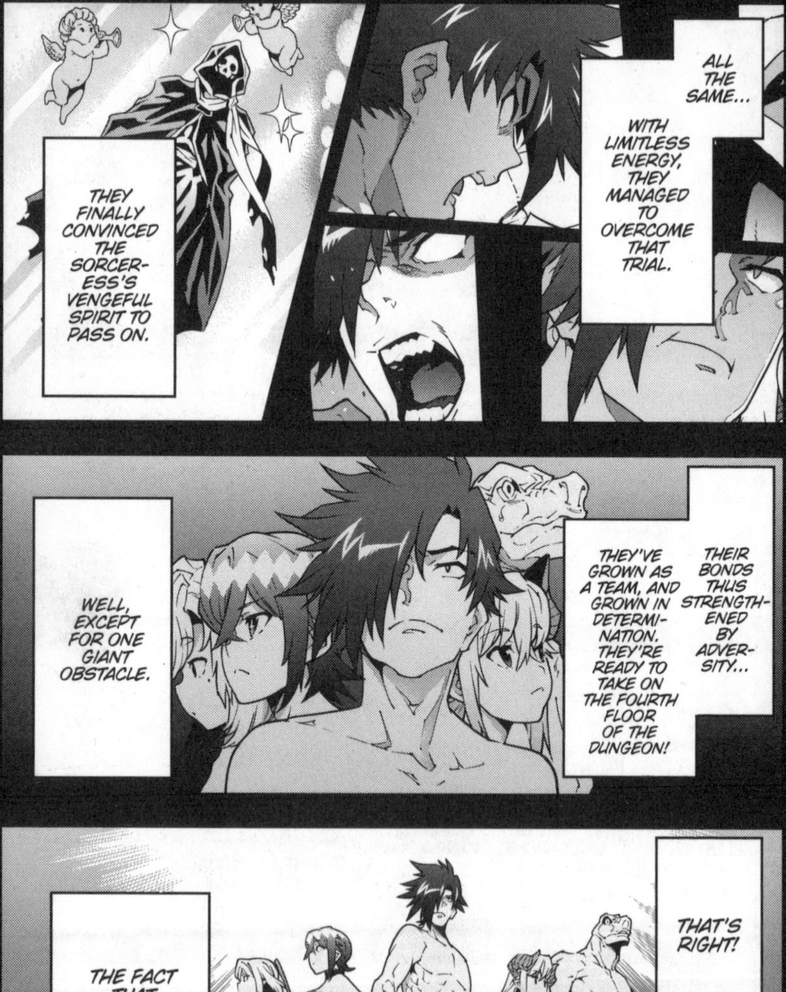
ALL THE SAME...
WITH LIMITLESS ENERGY, THEY MANAGED TO OVERCOME THAT TRIAL.
THEY FINALLY CONVINCED THE SORCERESS'S VENGEFUL SPIRIT TO PASS ON.
THEIR BONDS THUS STRENGTHENED BY ADVERSITY...
THEY'VE GROWN AS A TEAM, AND GROWN IN DETERMINATION. THEY'RE READY TO TAKE ON THE FOURTH FLOOR OF THE DUNGEON!
WELL, EXCEPT FOR ONE GIANT OBSTACLE.
THAT'S RIGHT!
THE FACT THAT THEY WERE PRETTY MUCH NAKED!

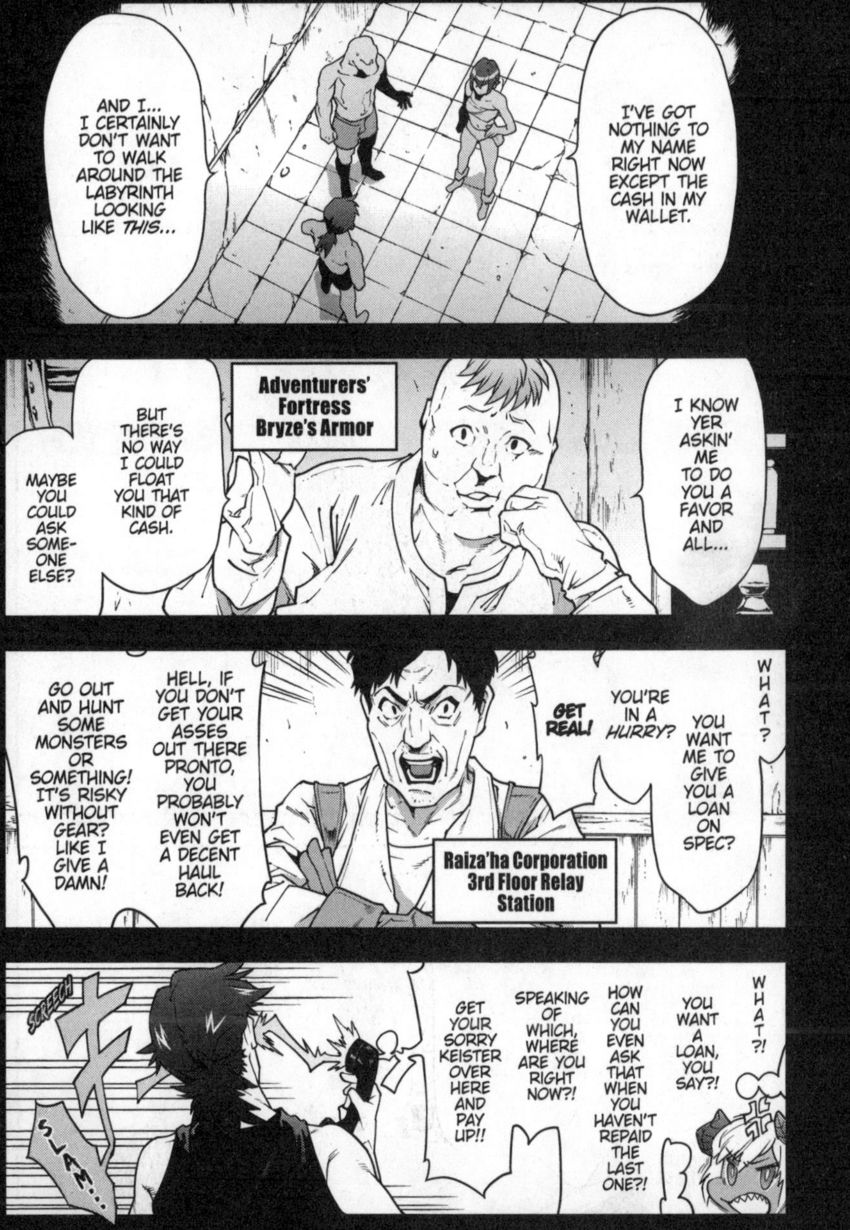
I'VE GOT NOTHING TO MY NAME RIGHT NOW EXCEPT THE CASH IN MY WALLET.
AND I... I CERTAINLY DON'T WANT TO WALK AROUND THE LABYRINTH LOOKING LIKE *THIS*...
Adventurers' Fortress Bryze's Armor
I KNOW YER ASKIN' ME TO DO YOU A FAVOR AND ALL...
BUT THERE'S NO WAY I COULD FLOAT YOU THAT KIND OF CASH.
MAYBE YOU COULD ASK SOME-ONE ELSE?
WHAT?
YOU WANT ME TO GIVE YOU A LOAN ON SPEC?
YOU'RE IN A *HURRY*?
GET REAL!
HELL, IF YOU DON'T GET YOUR ASSES OUT THERE PRONTO, YOU PROBABLY WON'T EVEN GET A DECENT HAUL BACK!
GO OUT AND HUNT SOME MONSTERS OR SOMETHING! IT'S RISKY WITHOUT GEAR? LIKE I GIVE A DAMN!
Raiza'ha Corporation 3rd Floor Relay Station
WHAT?!
YOU WANT A LOAN, YOU SAY?!
HOW CAN YOU EVEN ASK THAT WHEN YOU HAVEN'T REPAID THE LAST ONE?!
SPEAKING OF WHICH, WHERE ARE YOU RIGHT NOW?!
GET YOUR SORRY KEISTER OVER HERE AND PAY UP!!
SCREECH
SLAM...

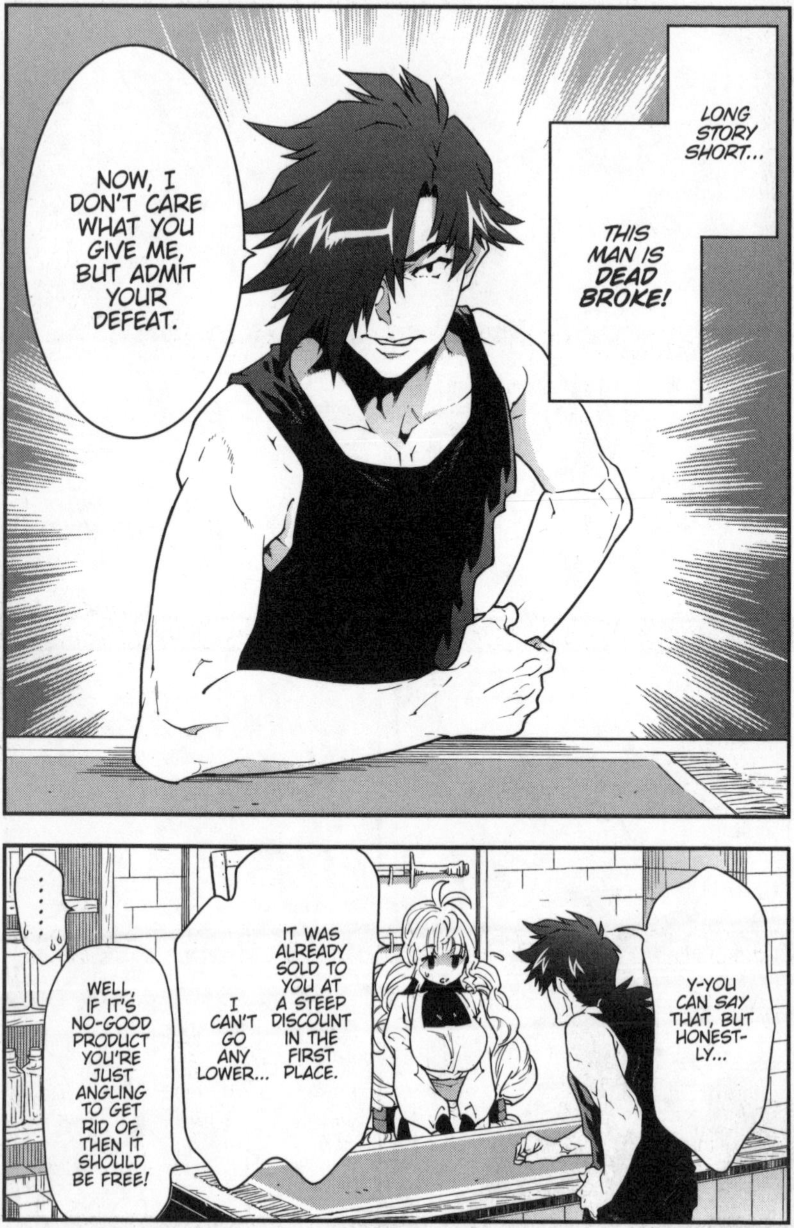
LONG STORY SHORT...
THIS MAN IS DEAD BROKE!
NOW, I DON'T CARE WHAT YOU GIVE ME, BUT ADMIT YOUR DEFEAT.
Y-YOU CAN SAY THAT, BUT HONEST-LY...
IT WAS ALREADY SOLD TO YOU AT A STEEP DISCOUNT IN THE FIRST PLACE.
I CAN'T GO ANY LOWER...
......
WELL, IF IT'S NO-GOOD PRODUCT YOU'RE JUST ANGLING TO GET RID OF, THEN IT SHOULD BE FREE!

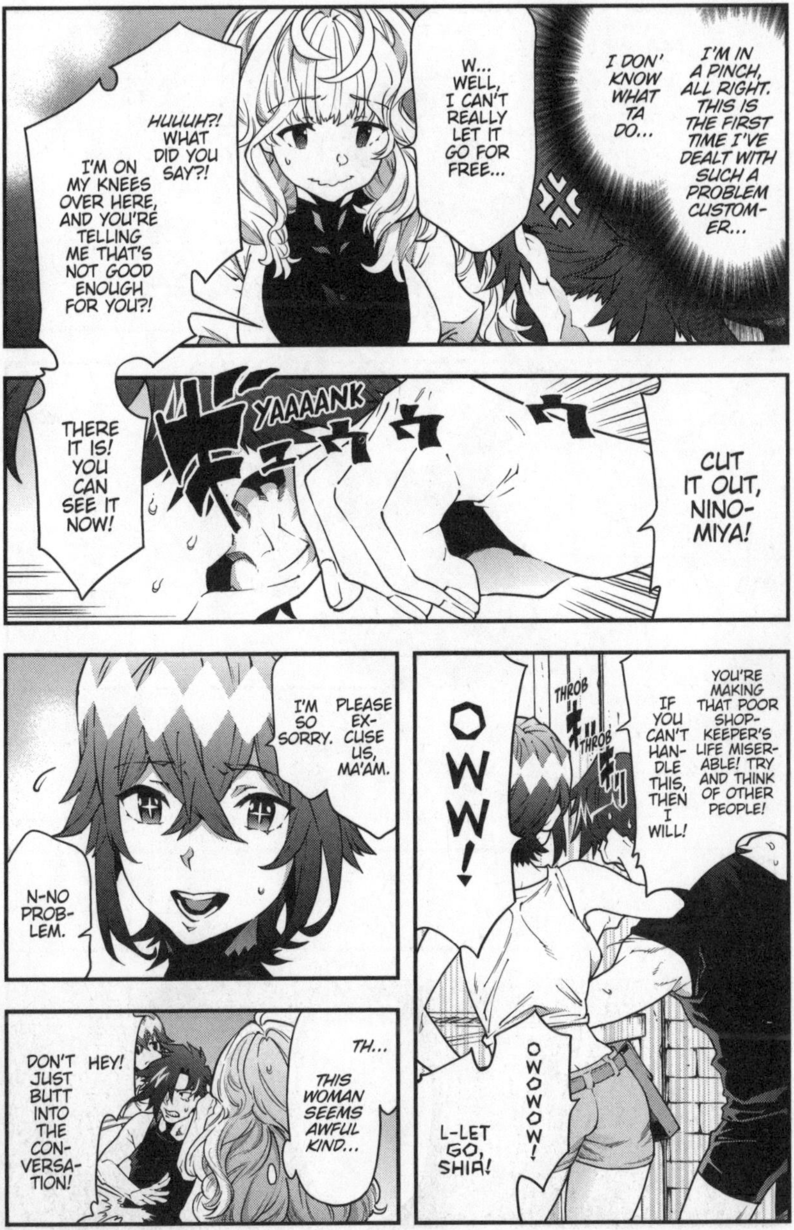
I'M IN A PINCH, ALL RIGHT. THIS IS THE FIRST TIME I'VE DEALT WITH SUCH A PROBLEM CUSTOMER...
I DON' KNOW WHAT TA DO...
W... WELL, I CAN'T REALLY LET IT GO FOR FREE...
HUUUH?! WHAT DID YOU SAY?!
I'M ON MY KNEES OVER HERE, AND YOU'RE TELLING ME THAT'S NOT GOOD ENOUGH FOR YOU?!
CUT IT OUT, NINOMIYA!
YAAAANK
THERE IT IS! YOU CAN SEE IT NOW!
YOU'RE MAKING THAT POOR SHOPKEEPER'S LIFE MISERABLE! TRY AND THINK OF OTHER PEOPLE!
IF YOU CAN'T HANDLE THIS, THEN I WILL!
THROB
THROB
OWW!
OWOWOW!
L-LET GO, SHIA!
PLEASE EXCUSE US, MA'AM.
I'M SO SORRY.
N-NO PROBLEM.
TH...
THIS WOMAN SEEMS AWFUL KIND...
HEY!
DON'T JUST BUTT INTO THE CONVERSATION!

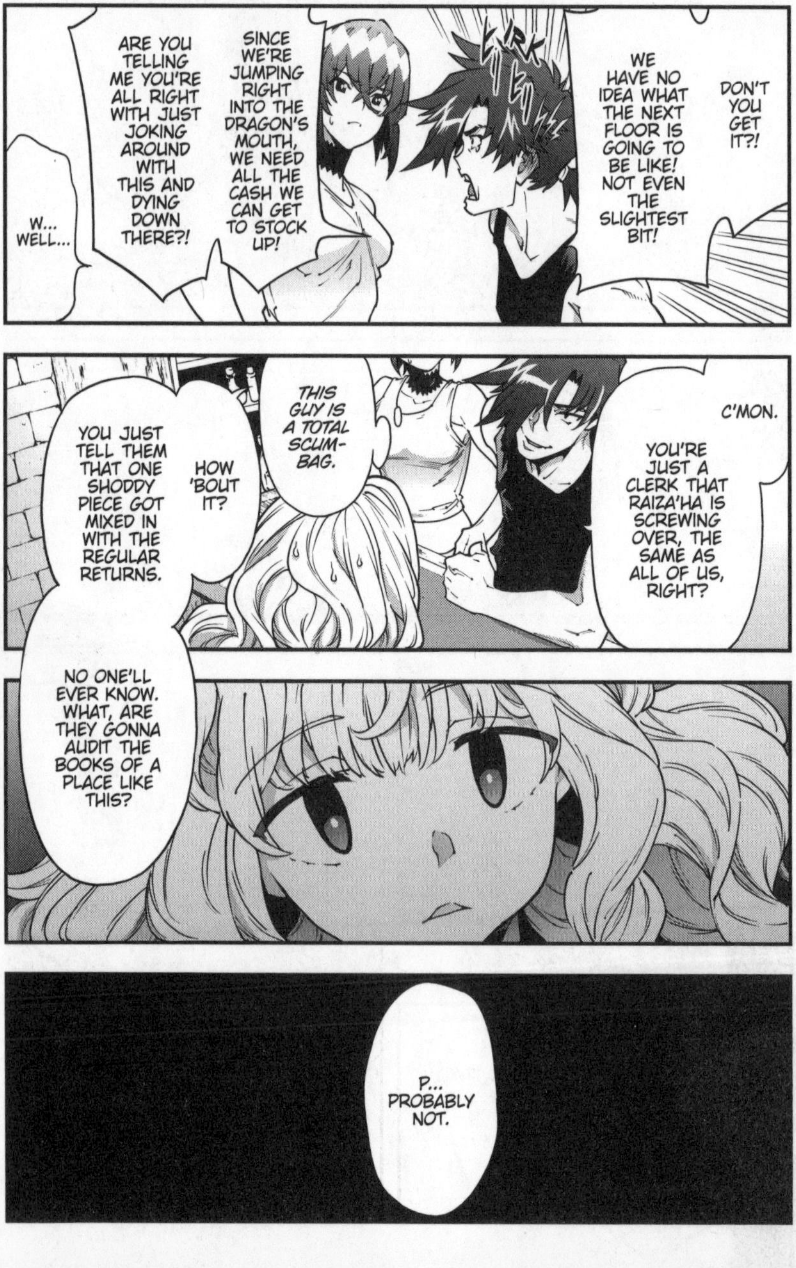
DON'T YOU GET IT?!
WE HAVE NO IDEA WHAT THE NEXT FLOOR IS GOING TO BE LIKE! NOT EVEN THE SLIGHTEST BIT!
SINCE WE'RE JUMPING RIGHT INTO THE DRAGON'S MOUTH, WE NEED ALL THE CASH WE CAN GET TO STOCK UP!
ARE YOU TELLING ME YOU'RE ALL RIGHT WITH JUST JOKING AROUND WITH THIS AND DYING DOWN THERE?!
W... WELL...
C'MON.
YOU'RE JUST A CLERK THAT RAIZA'HA IS SCREWING OVER, THE SAME AS ALL OF US, RIGHT?
THIS GUY IS A TOTAL SCUM-BAG.
HOW 'BOUT IT?
YOU JUST TELL THEM THAT ONE SHODDY PIECE GOT MIXED IN WITH THE REGULAR RETURNS.
NO ONE'LL EVER KNOW. WHAT, ARE THEY GONNA AUDIT THE BOOKS OF A PLACE LIKE THIS?
P... PROBABLY NOT.

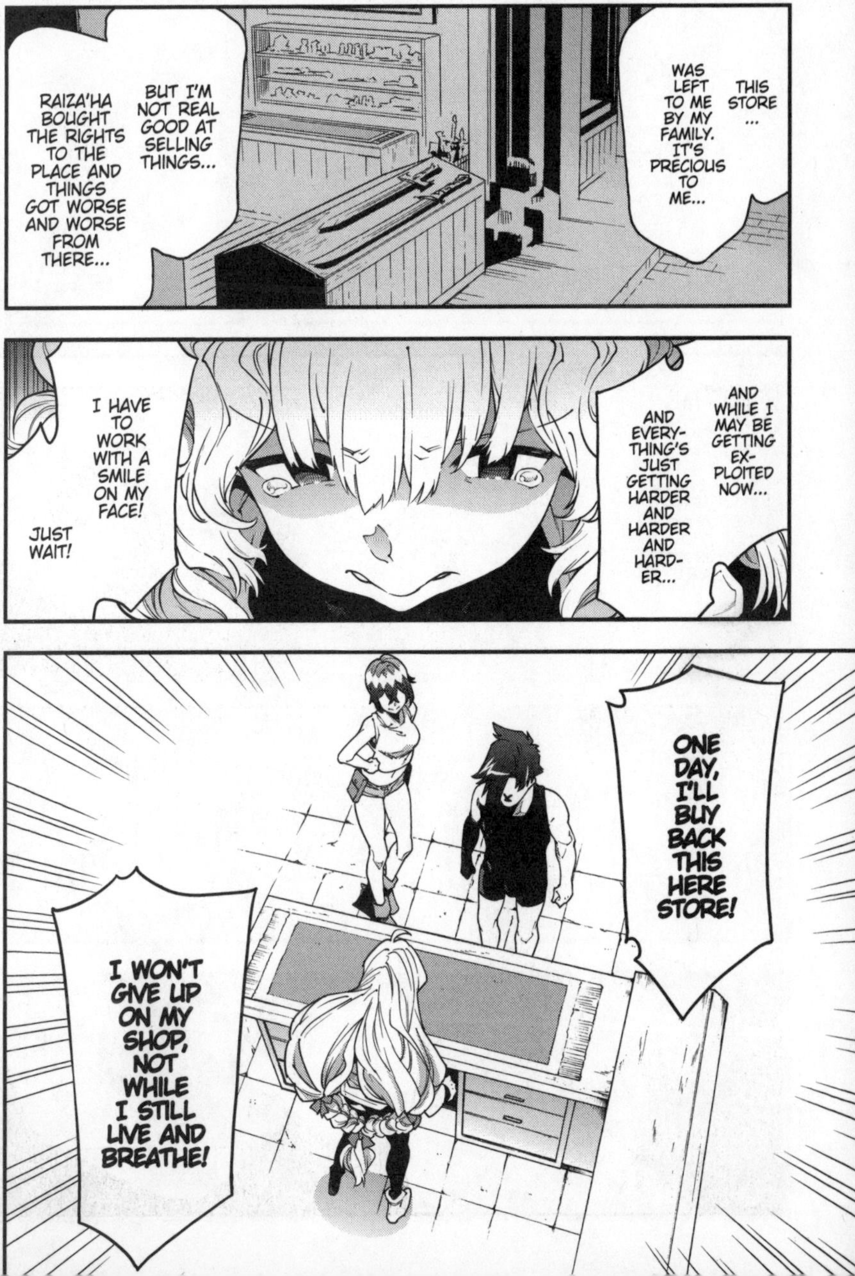
THIS STORE ...
WAS LEFT TO ME BY MY FAMILY. IT'S PRECIOUS TO ME...
BUT I'M NOT REAL GOOD AT SELLING THINGS...
RAIZA'HA BOUGHT THE RIGHTS TO THE PLACE AND THINGS GOT WORSE AND WORSE FROM THERE...
AND WHILE I MAY BE GETTING EXPLOITED NOW...
AND EVERYTHING'S JUST GETTING HARDER AND HARDER AND HARDER...
I HAVE TO WORK WITH A SMILE ON MY FACE!
JUST WAIT!
ONE DAY, I'LL BUY BACK THIS HERE STORE!
I WON'T GIVE UP ON MY SHOP, NOT WHILE I STILL LIVE AND BREATHE!

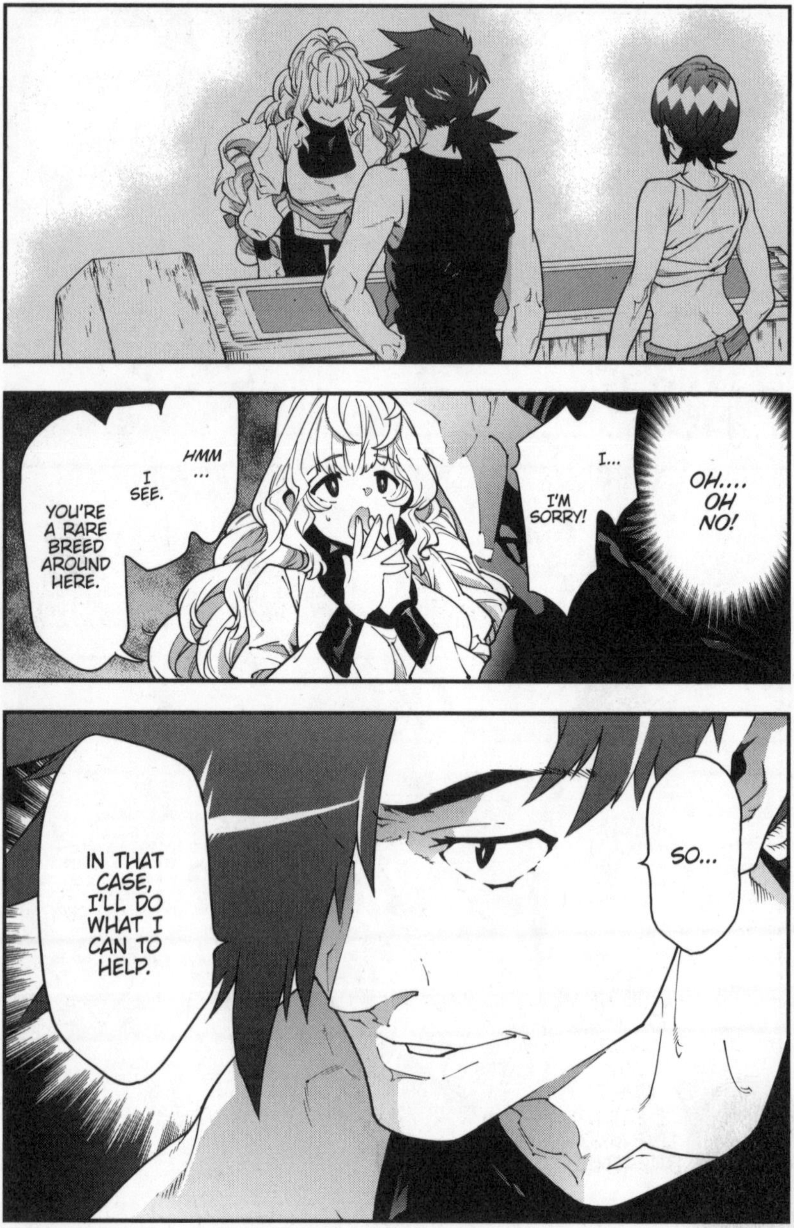
OH.... OH NO!
I... I'M SORRY!
HMM ... I SEE. YOU'RE A RARE BREED AROUND HERE.
SO...
IN THAT CASE, I'LL DO WHAT I CAN TO HELP.

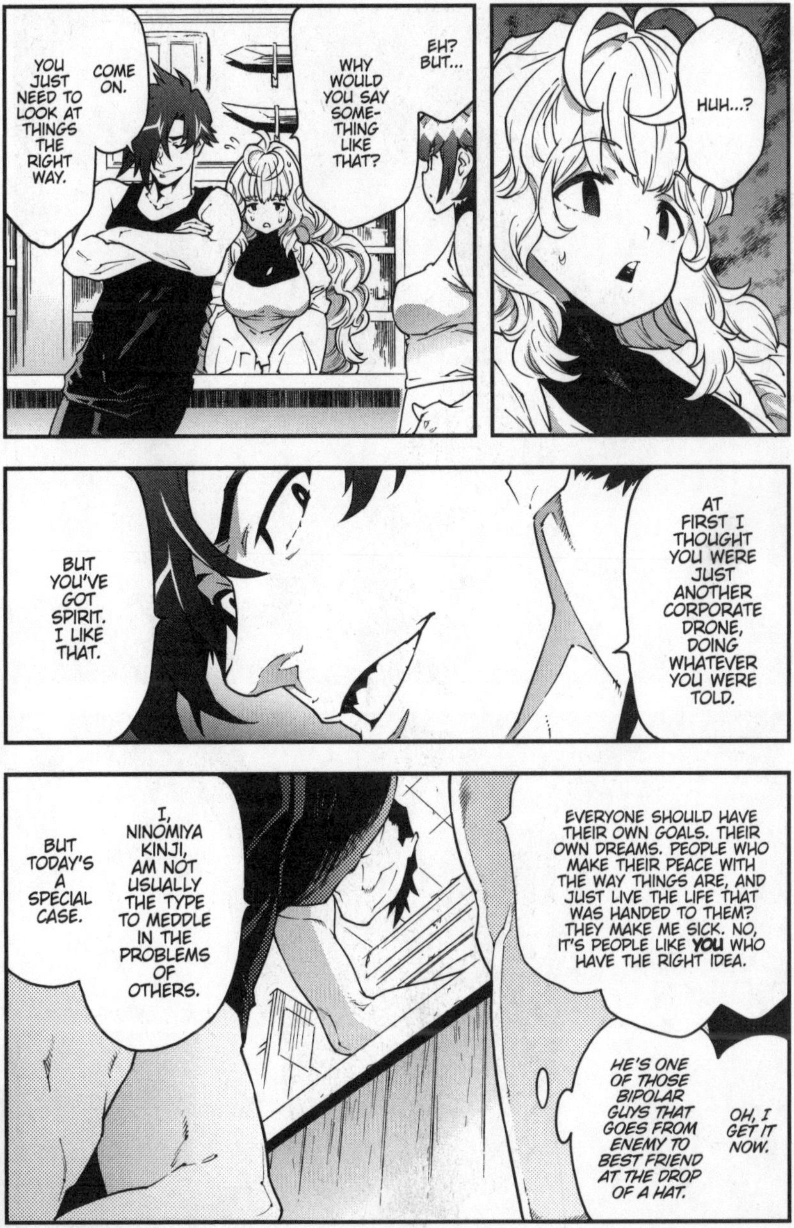
HUH...?
EH? BUT...
WHY WOULD YOU SAY SOME-THING LIKE THAT?
COME ON.
YOU JUST NEED TO LOOK AT THINGS THE RIGHT WAY.
AT FIRST I THOUGHT YOU WERE JUST ANOTHER CORPORATE DRONE, DOING WHATEVER YOU WERE TOLD.
BUT YOU'VE GOT SPIRIT. I LIKE THAT.
EVERYONE SHOULD HAVE THEIR OWN GOALS. THEIR OWN DREAMS. PEOPLE WHO MAKE THEIR PEACE WITH THE WAY THINGS ARE, AND JUST LIVE THE LIFE THAT WAS HANDED TO THEM? THEY MAKE ME SICK. NO, IT'S PEOPLE LIKE **YOU** WHO HAVE THE RIGHT IDEA.
I, NINOMIYA KINJI, AM NOT USUALLY THE TYPE TO MEDDLE IN THE PROBLEMS OF OTHERS.
BUT TODAY'S A SPECIAL CASE.
OH, I GET IT NOW.
HE'S ONE OF THOSE BIPOLAR GUYS THAT GOES FROM ENEMY TO BEST FRIEND AT THE DROP OF A HAT.

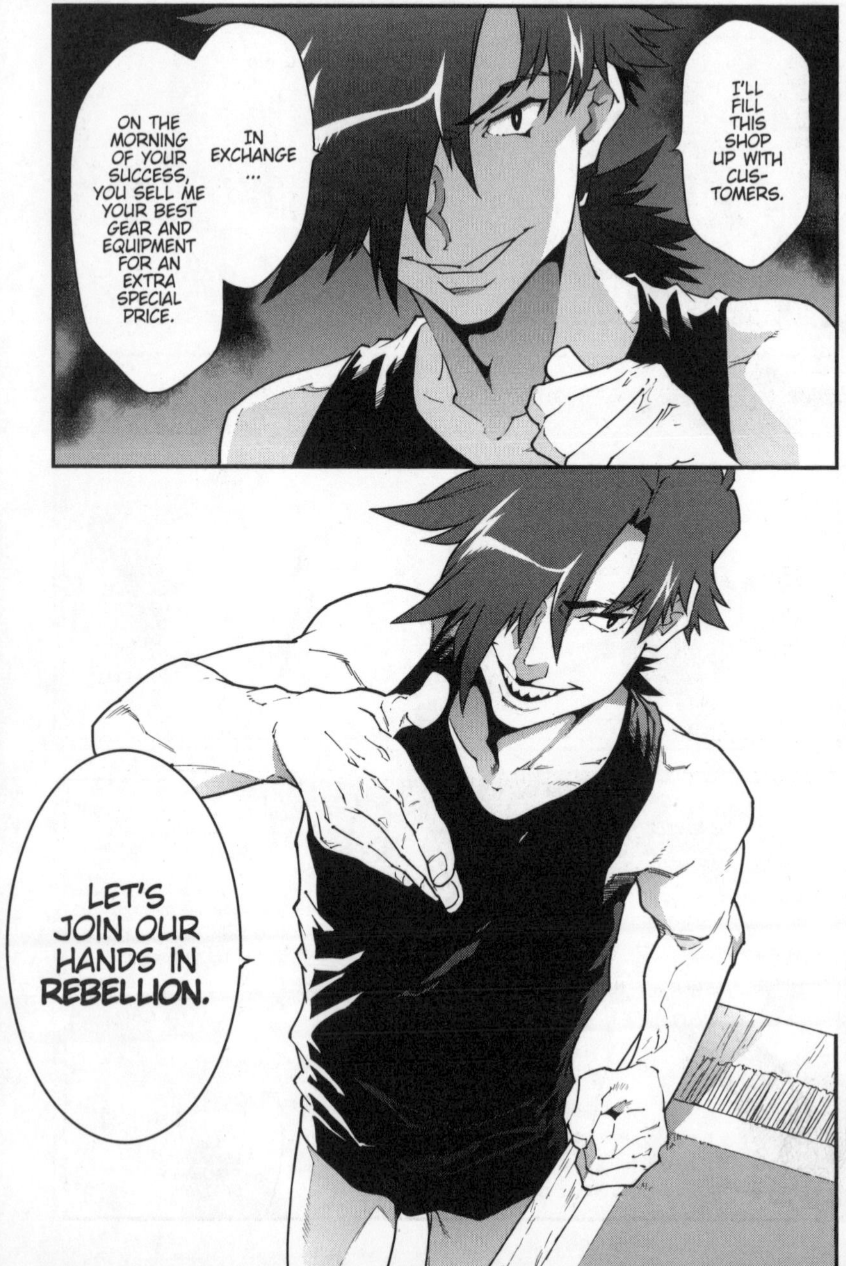
I'LL FILL THIS SHOP UP WITH CUS-TOMERS.
IN EXCHANGE ...
ON THE MORNING OF YOUR SUCCESS, YOU SELL ME YOUR BEST GEAR AND EQUIPMENT FOR AN EXTRA SPECIAL PRICE.
LET'S JOIN OUR HANDS IN REBELLION.

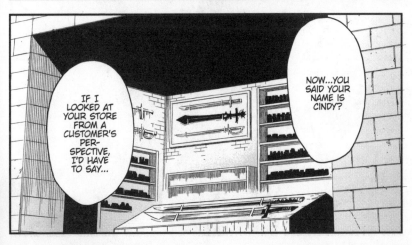

NOW...YOU SAID YOUR NAME IS CINDY?

IF I LOOKED AT YOUR STORE FROM A CUSTOMER'S PER-SPECTIVE, I'D HAVE TO SAY...

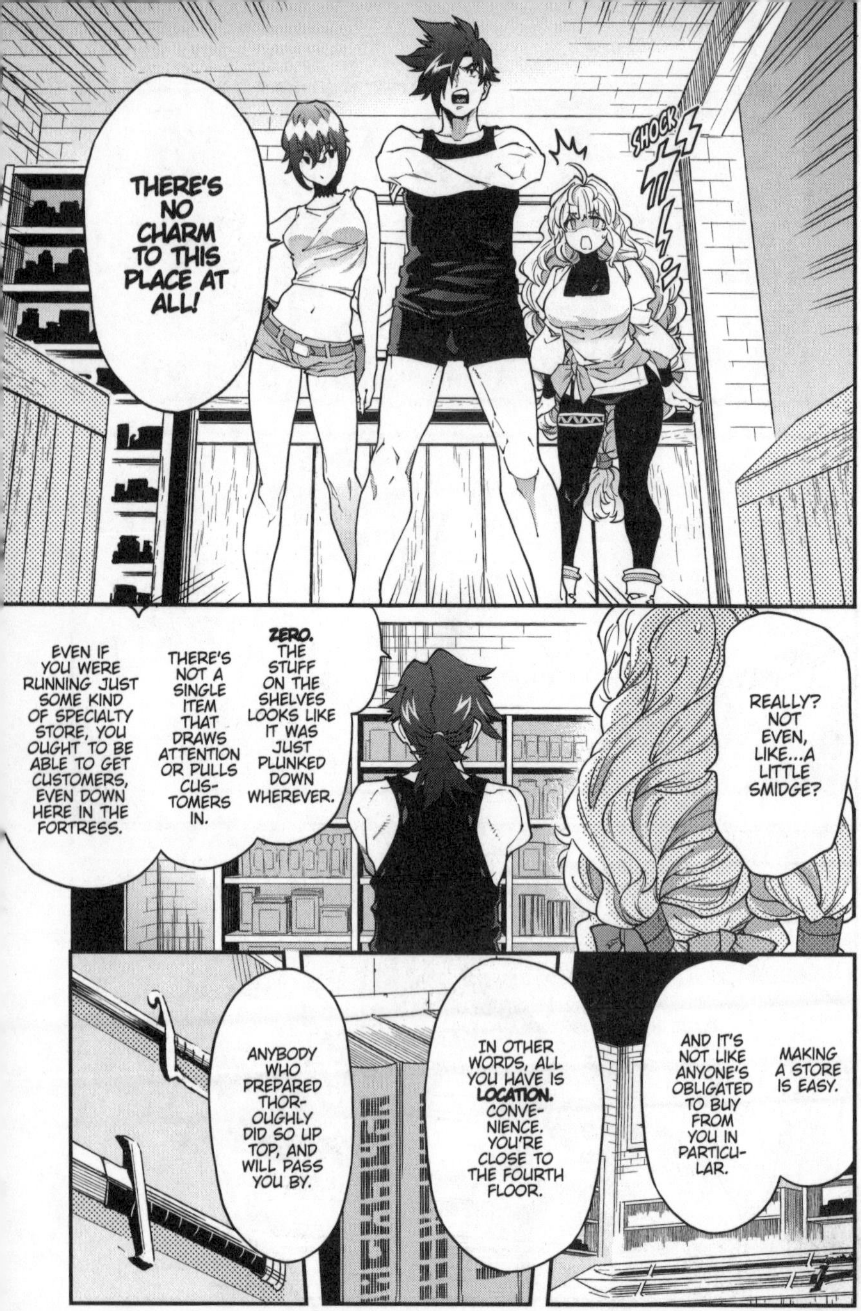
SHOCK
THERE'S NO CHARM TO THIS PLACE AT ALL!
REALLY? NOT EVEN, LIKE...A LITTLE SMIDGE?
ZERO. THE STUFF ON THE SHELVES LOOKS LIKE IT WAS JUST PLUNKED DOWN WHEREVER.
THERE'S NOT A SINGLE ITEM THAT DRAWS ATTENTION OR PULLS CUSTOMERS IN.
EVEN IF YOU WERE RUNNING JUST SOME KIND OF SPECIALTY STORE, YOU OUGHT TO BE ABLE TO GET CUSTOMERS, EVEN DOWN HERE IN THE FORTRESS.
MAKING A STORE IS EASY.
AND IT'S NOT LIKE ANYONE'S OBLIGATED TO BUY FROM YOU IN PARTICULAR.
IN OTHER WORDS, ALL YOU HAVE IS LOCATION. CONVENIENCE. YOU'RE CLOSE TO THE FOURTH FLOOR.
ANYBODY WHO PREPARED THOROUGHLY DID SO UP TOP, AND WILL PASS YOU BY.

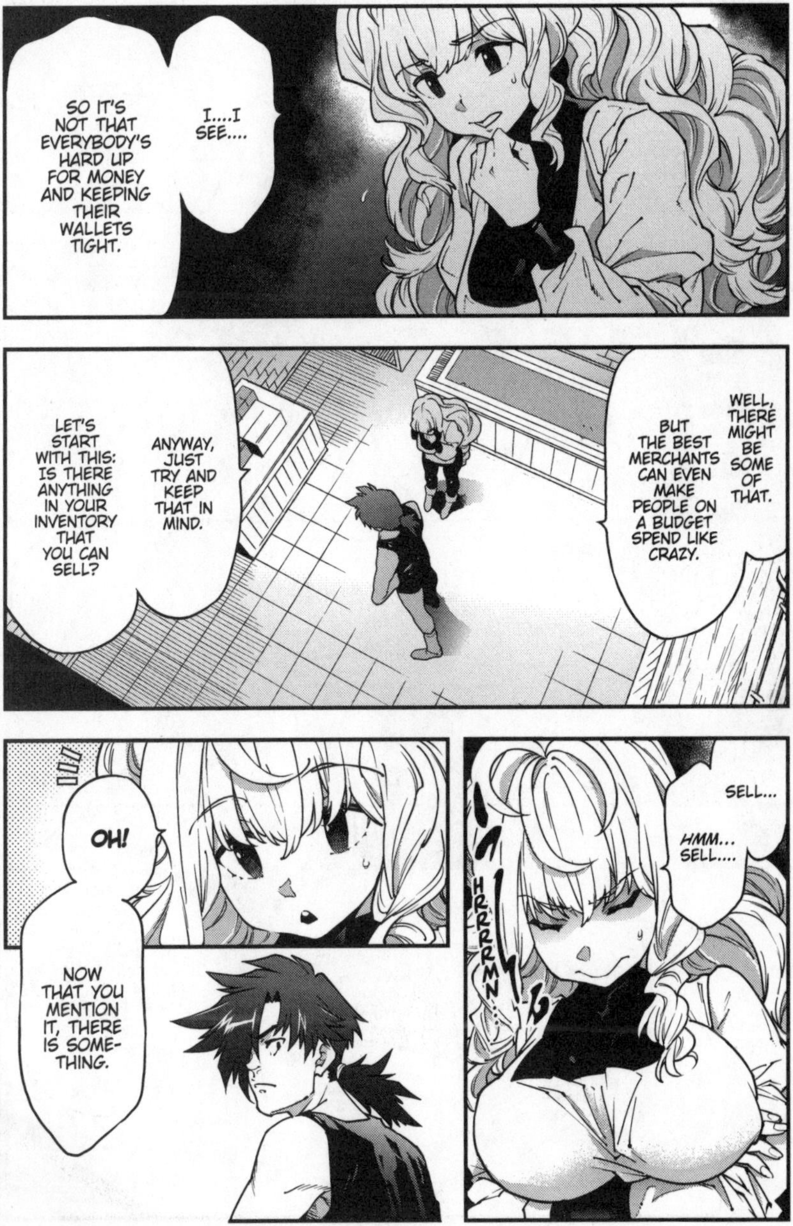
I....I SEE....
SO IT'S NOT THAT EVERYBODY'S HARD UP FOR MONEY AND KEEPING THEIR WALLETS TIGHT.
WELL, THERE MIGHT BE SOME OF THAT.
BUT THE BEST MERCHANTS CAN EVEN MAKE PEOPLE ON A BUDGET SPEND LIKE CRAZY.
ANYWAY, JUST TRY AND KEEP THAT IN MIND.
LET'S START WITH THIS: IS THERE ANYTHING IN YOUR INVENTORY THAT YOU CAN SELL?
SELL...
HMM... SELL....
HRRRRMN...
OH!
NOW THAT YOU MENTION IT, THERE IS SOMETHING.

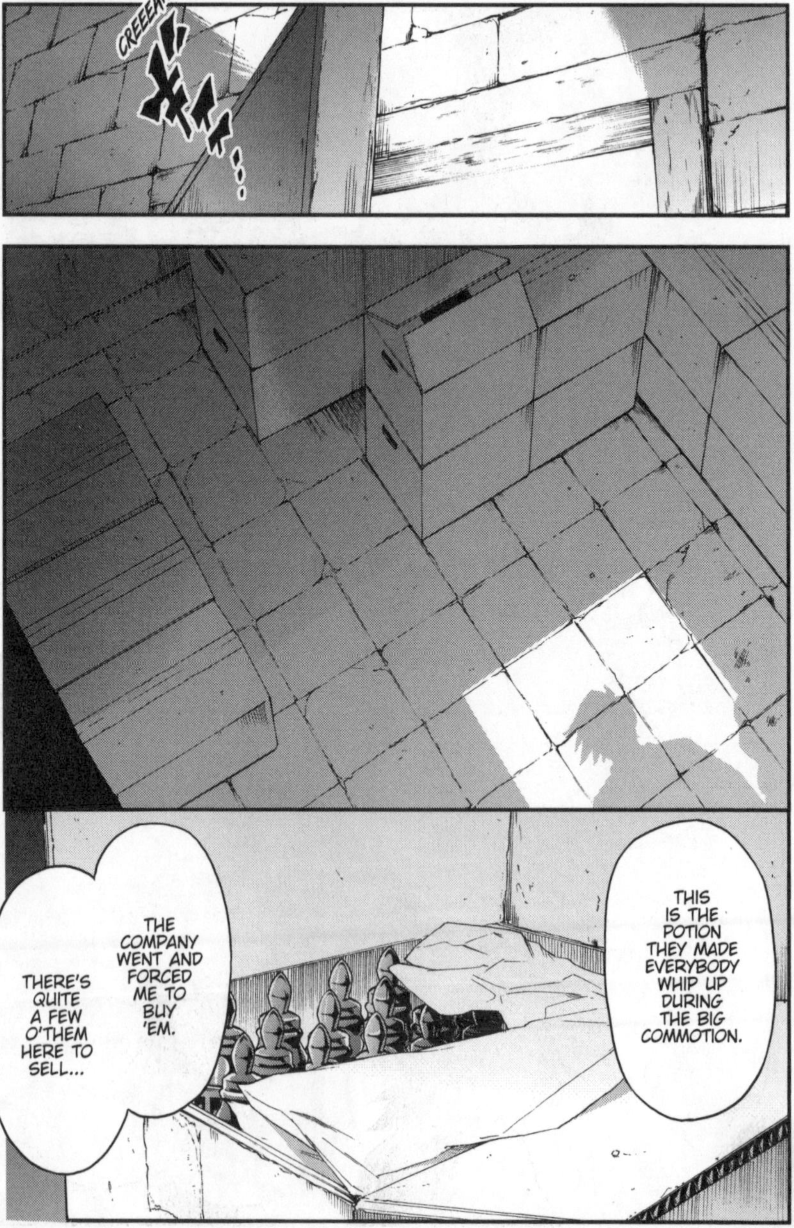
CREEEAK
THIS IS THE POTION THEY MADE EVERYBODY WHIP UP DURING THE BIG COMMOTION.
THE COMPANY WENT AND FORCED ME TO BUY 'EM.
THERE'S QUITE A FEW O'THEM HERE TO SELL...

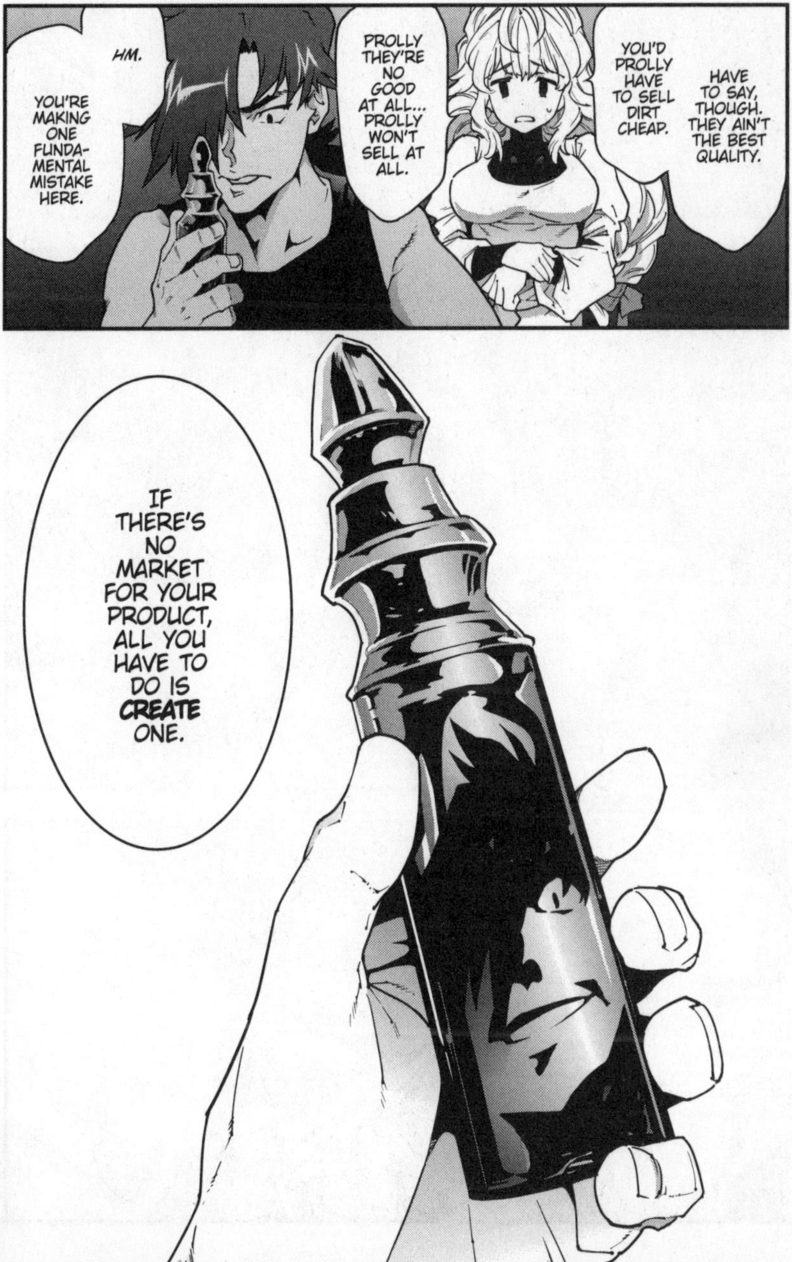
HAVE TO SAY, THOUGH. THEY AIN'T THE BEST QUALITY.
YOU'D PROLLY HAVE TO SELL DIRT CHEAP.
PROLLY THEY'RE NO GOOD AT ALL... PROLLY WON'T SELL AT ALL.
HM.
YOU'RE MAKING ONE FUNDA-MENTAL MISTAKE HERE.
IF THERE'S NO MARKET FOR YOUR PRODUCT, ALL YOU HAVE TO DO IS **CREATE** ONE.

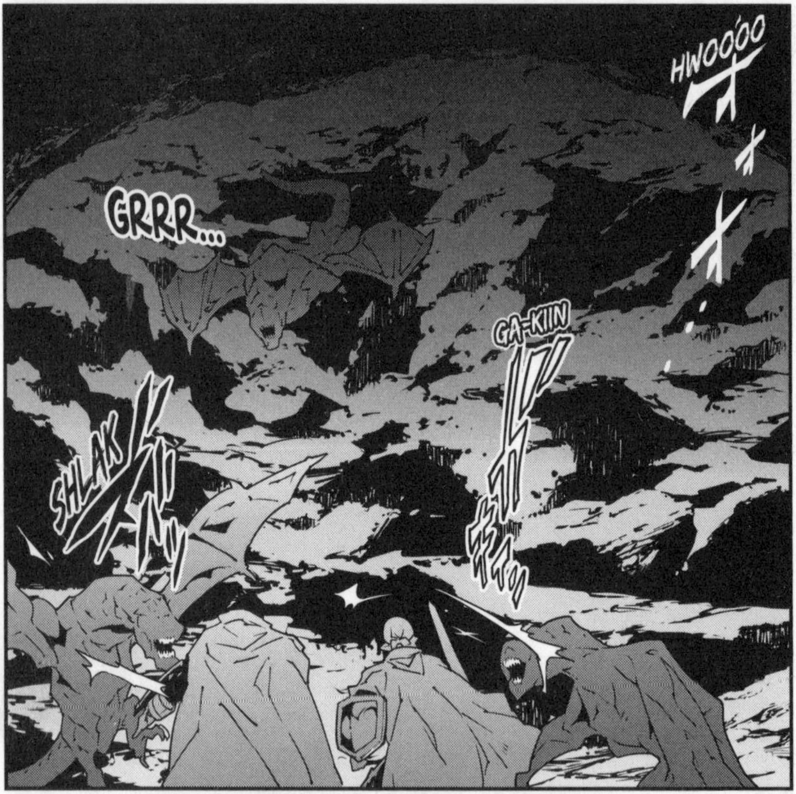
HWOOOO
GA-KIIN
GRRR...
SHLAK

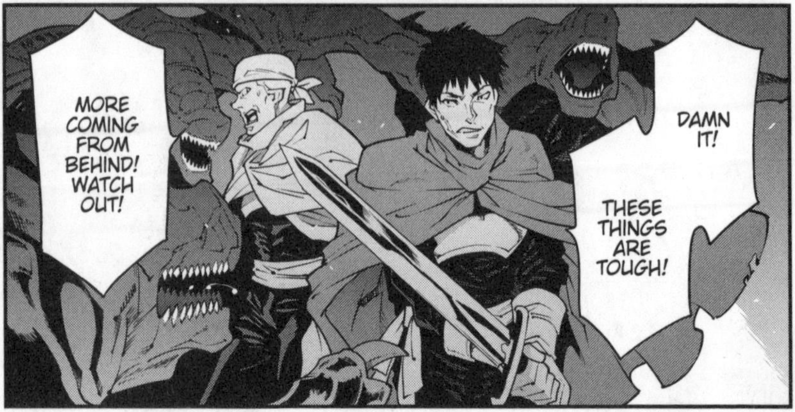
DAMN IT!
THESE THINGS ARE TOUGH!
MORE COMING FROM BEHIND! WATCH OUT!

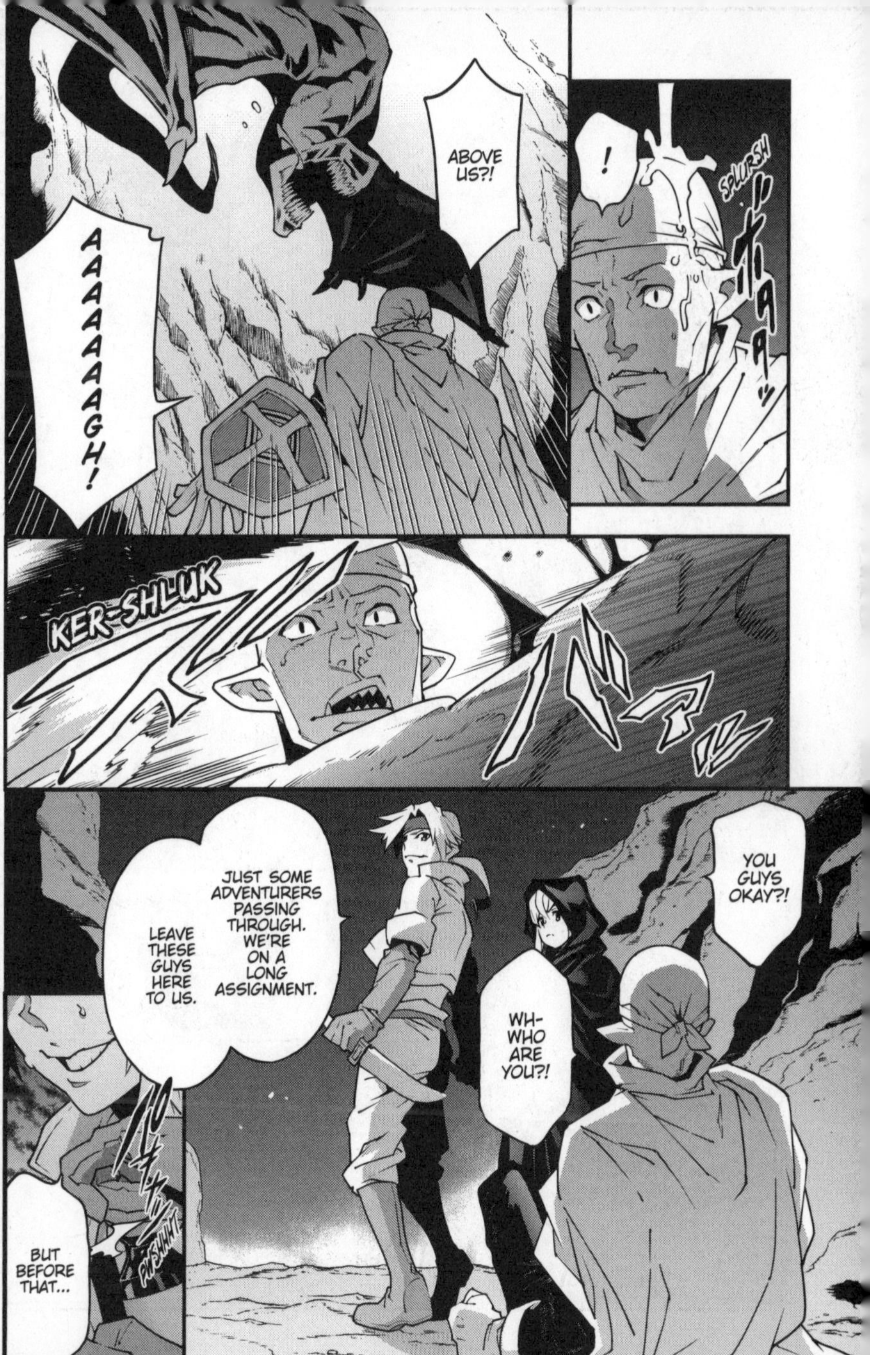
!
SPLURSH
ABOVE US?!
AAAAAAAAAGH!
KER-SHLUK
YOU GUYS OKAY?!
WH-WHO ARE YOU?!
JUST SOME ADVENTURERS PASSING THROUGH. WE'RE ON A LONG ASSIGNMENT.
LEAVE THESE GUYS HERE TO US.
PWSHHH
BUT BEFORE THAT...

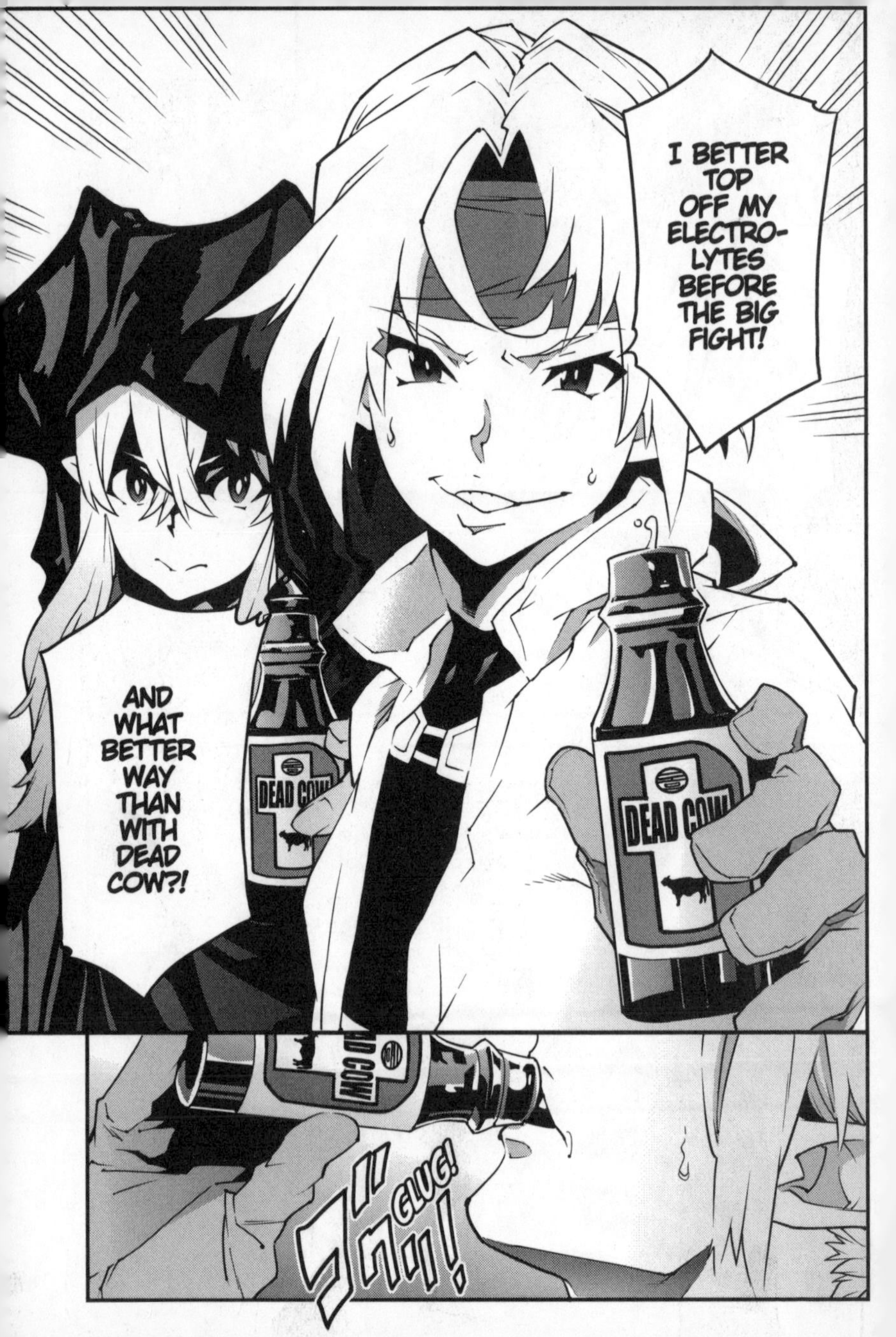
I BETTER TOP OFF MY ELECTRO-LYTES BEFORE THE BIG FIGHT!
AND WHAT BETTER WAY THAN WITH DEAD COW?!
DEAD COW
DEAD COW
DEAD COW
GLUG!

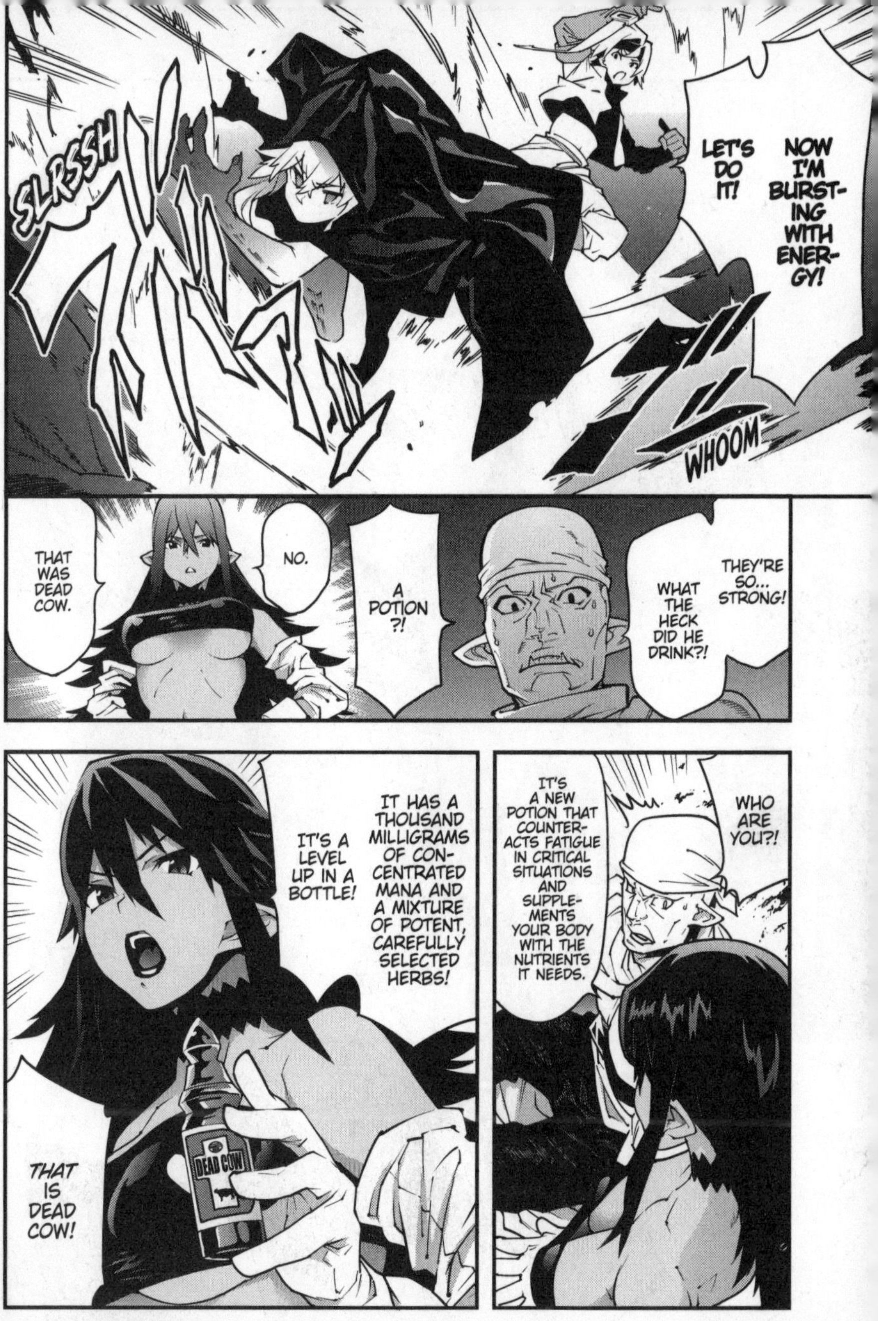
NOW I'M BURST-ING WITH ENER-GY!
LET'S DO IT!
SLRSSH
WHOOM
THEY'RE SO... STRONG!
WHAT THE HECK DID HE DRINK?!
A POTION?!
NO.
THAT WAS DEAD COW.
WHO ARE YOU?!
IT'S A NEW POTION THAT COUNTER-ACTS FATIGUE IN CRITICAL SITUATIONS AND SUPPLE-MENTS YOUR BODY WITH THE NUTRIENTS IT NEEDS.
IT HAS A THOUSAND MILLIGRAMS OF CON-CENTRATED MANA AND A MIXTURE OF POTENT, CAREFULLY SELECTED HERBS!
IT'S A LEVEL UP IN A BOTTLE!
DEAD COW
THAT IS DEAD COW!

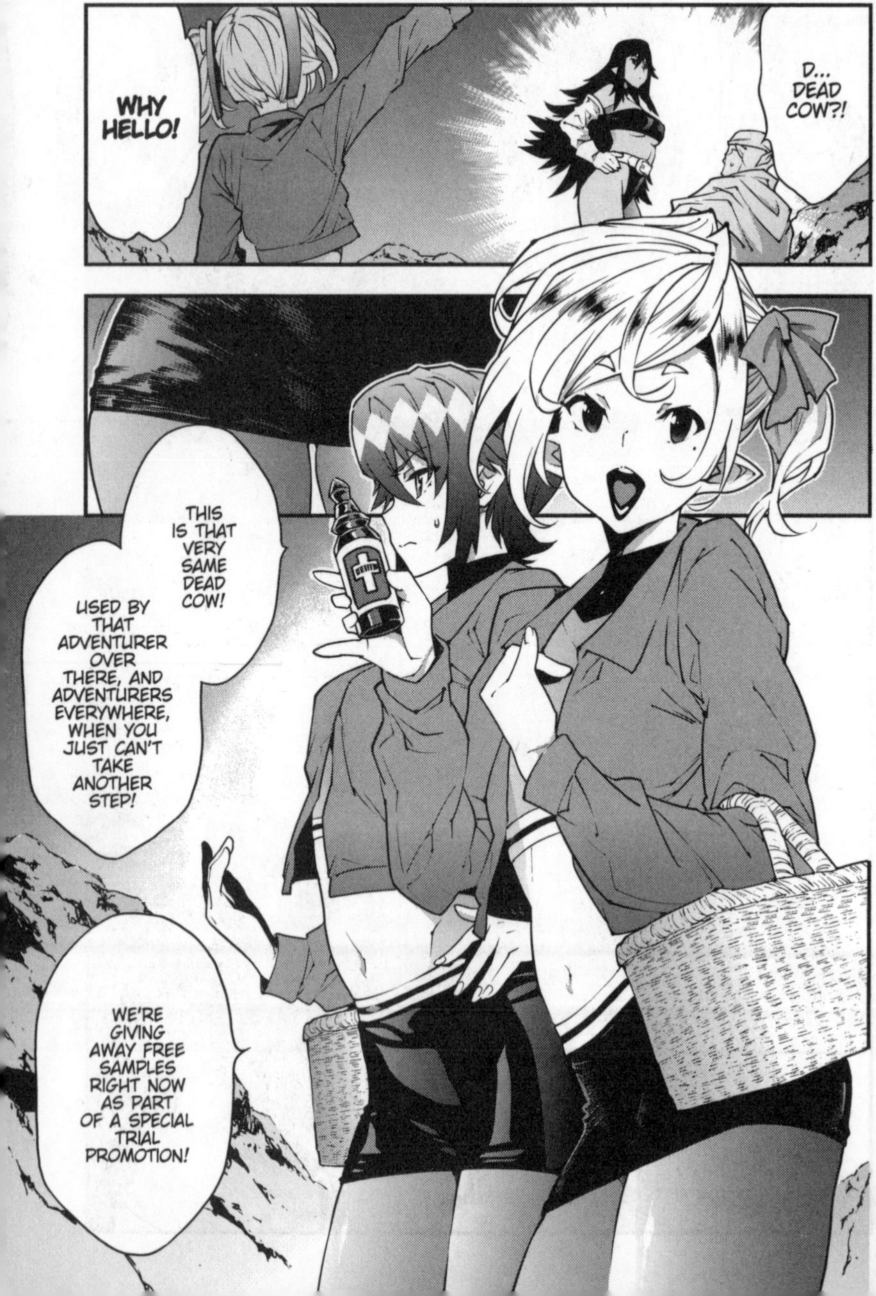
D... DEAD COW?!
WHY HELLO!
THIS IS THAT VERY SAME DEAD COW!
USED BY THAT ADVENTURER OVER THERE, AND ADVENTURERS EVERYWHERE, WHEN YOU JUST CAN'T TAKE ANOTHER STEP!
WE'RE GIVING AWAY FREE SAMPLES RIGHT NOW AS PART OF A SPECIAL TRIAL PROMOTION!

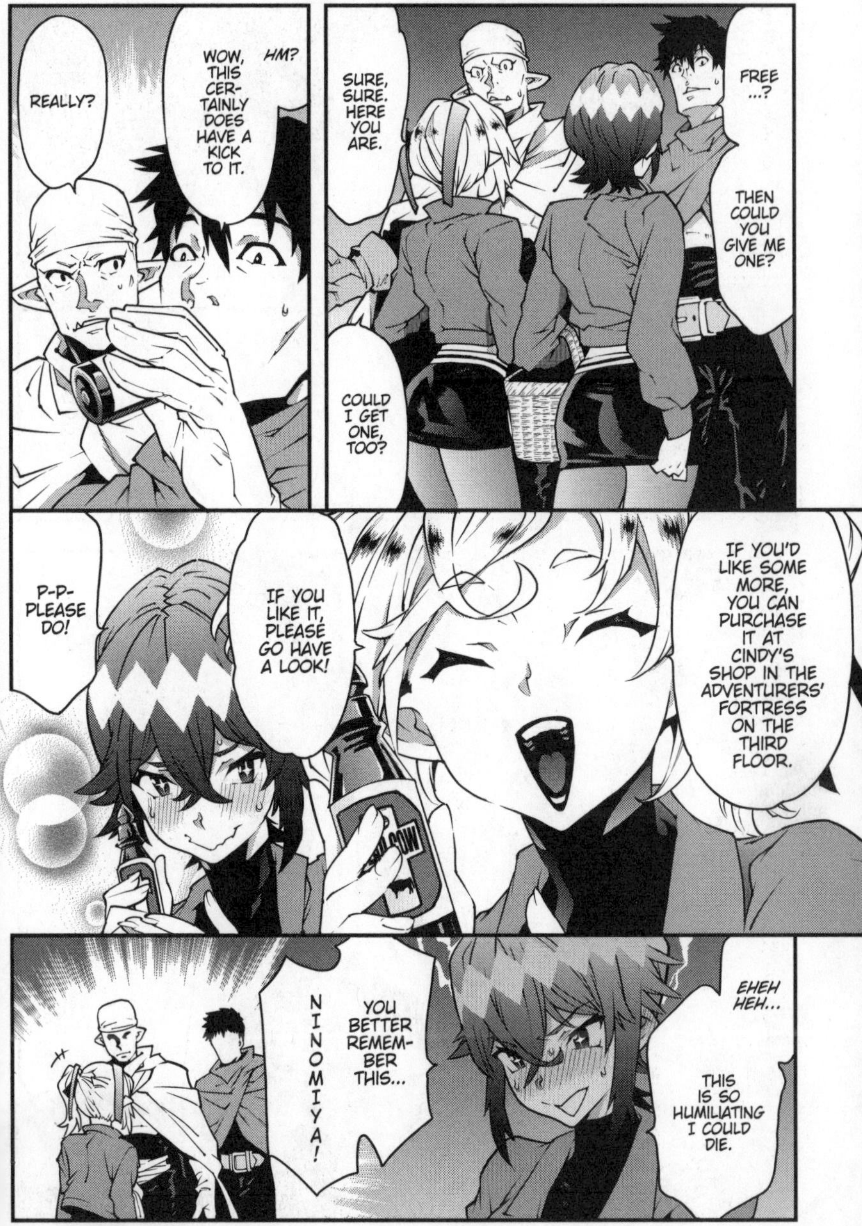
FREE ...?
THEN COULD YOU GIVE ME ONE?
SURE, SURE. HERE YOU ARE.
COULD I GET ONE, TOO?
HM?
WOW, THIS CER-TAINLY DOES HAVE A KICK TO IT.
REALLY?
IF YOU'D LIKE SOME MORE, YOU CAN PURCHASE IT AT CINDY'S SHOP IN THE ADVENTURERS' FORTRESS ON THE THIRD FLOOR.
IF YOU LIKE IT, PLEASE GO HAVE A LOOK!
P-P-PLEASE DO!
EHEH HEH...
THIS IS SO HUMILIATING I COULD DIE.
YOU BETTER REMEMBER-BER THIS...
NINOMIYA!

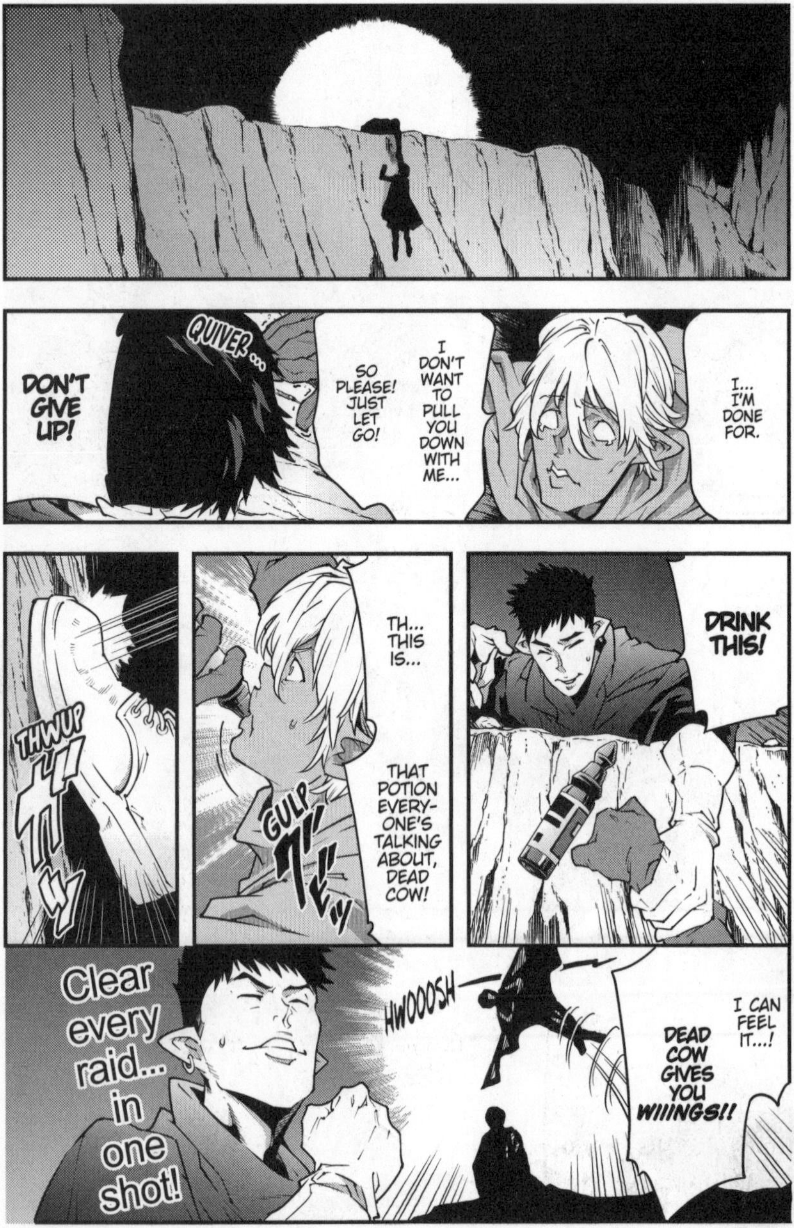
I... I'M DONE FOR.
I DON'T WANT TO PULL YOU DOWN WITH ME...
SO PLEASE! JUST LET GO!
QUIVER...
DON'T GIVE UP!
DRINK THIS!
TH... THIS IS...
THAT POTION EVERYONE'S TALKING ABOUT, DEAD COW!
GULP
THWUP
I CAN FEEL IT...!
DEAD COW GIVES YOU WIIINGS!!
HWOOOSH
Clear every raid... in one shot!

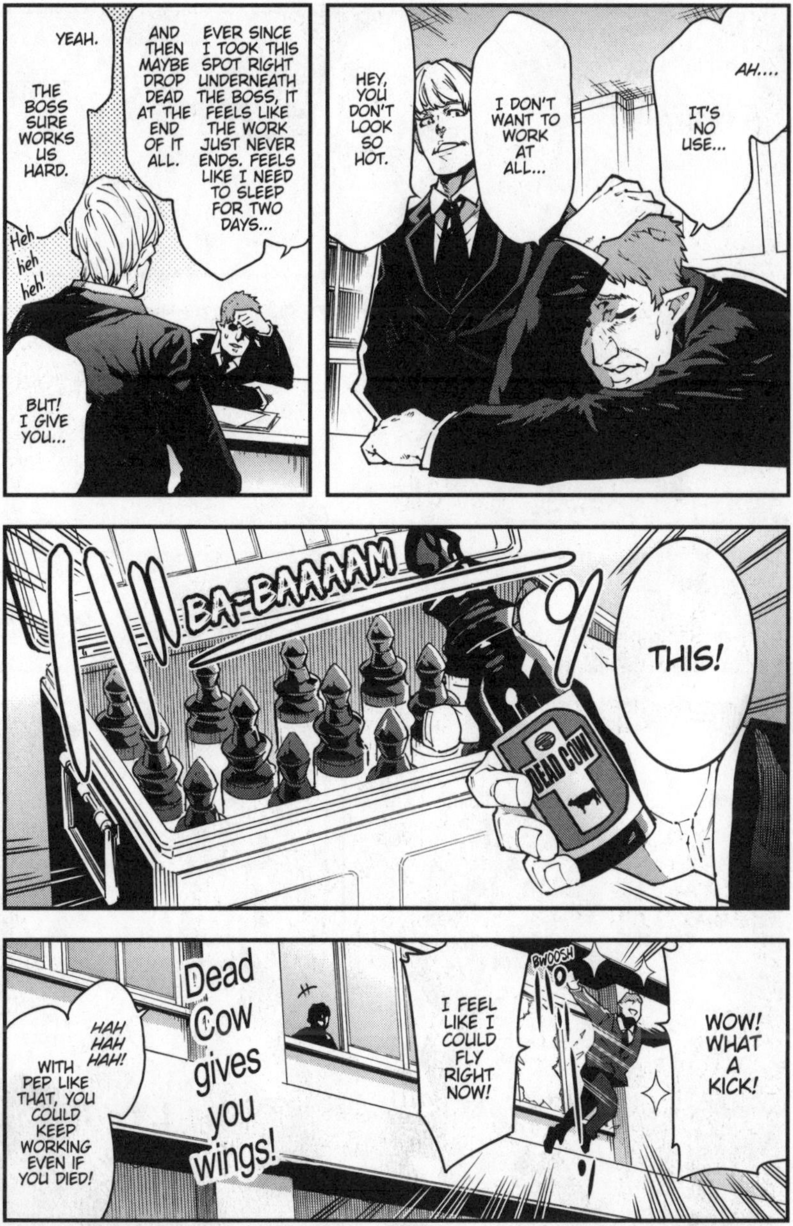
AH....
IT'S NO USE...
I DON'T WANT TO WORK AT ALL...
HEY, YOU DON'T LOOK SO HOT.
EVER SINCE I TOOK THIS SPOT RIGHT UNDERNEATH THE BOSS, IT FEELS LIKE THE WORK JUST NEVER ENDS. FEELS LIKE I NEED TO SLEEP FOR TWO DAYS...
AND THEN MAYBE DROP DEAD AT THE END OF IT ALL.
YEAH.
THE BOSS SURE WORKS US HARD.
Heh hieh heh!
BUT! I GIVE YOU...
BA-BAAAAAM
THIS!
DEAD COW
WOW! WHAT A KICK!
BWOOSH
I FEEL LIKE I COULD FLY RIGHT NOW!
Dead Cow gives you wings!
HAH HAH HAH!
WITH PEP LIKE THAT, YOU COULD KEEP WORKING EVEN IF YOU DIED!

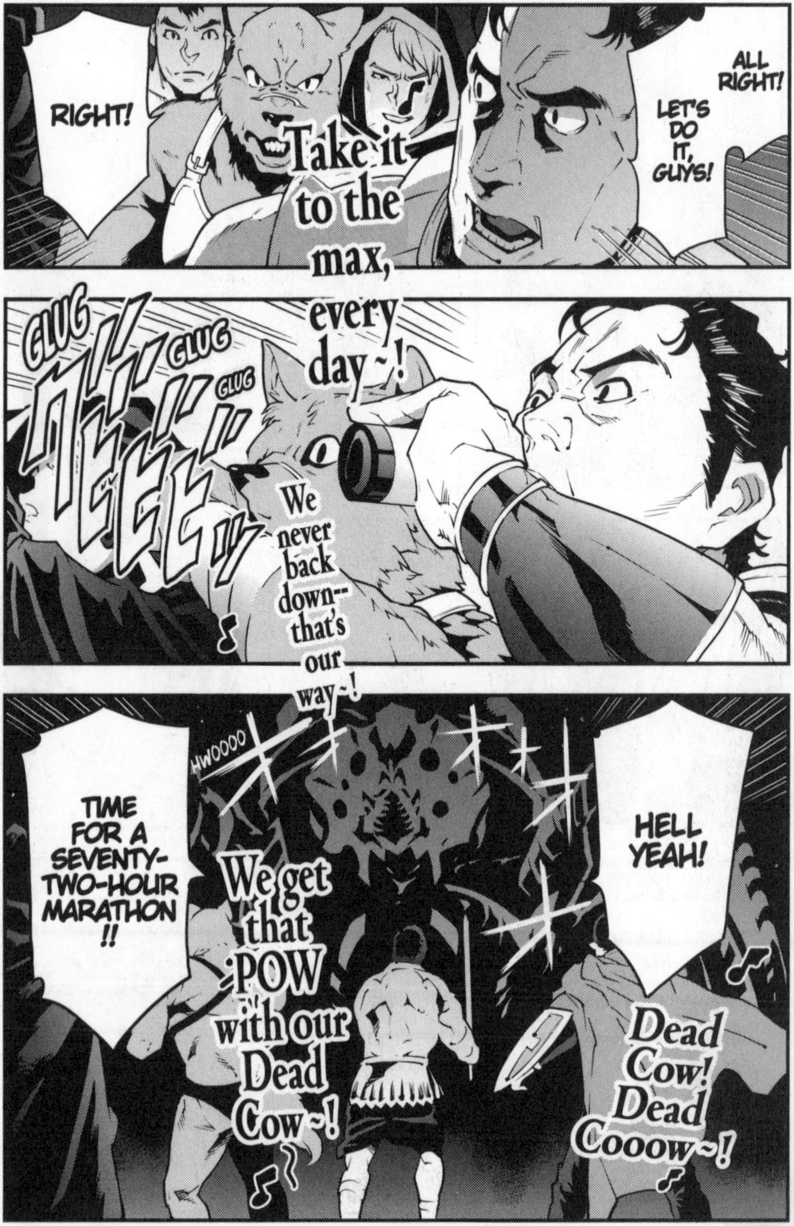
ALL RIGHT!
LET'S DO IT, GUYS!
Take it to the max, every day~!
RIGHT!
We never back down--that's our way~!
GLUG
GLUG
GLUG
HELL YEAH!
Dead Cow! Dead Cooow~!
We get that POW with our Dead Cow~!
HWOOOO
TIME FOR A SEVENTY-TWO-HOUR MARATHON!!

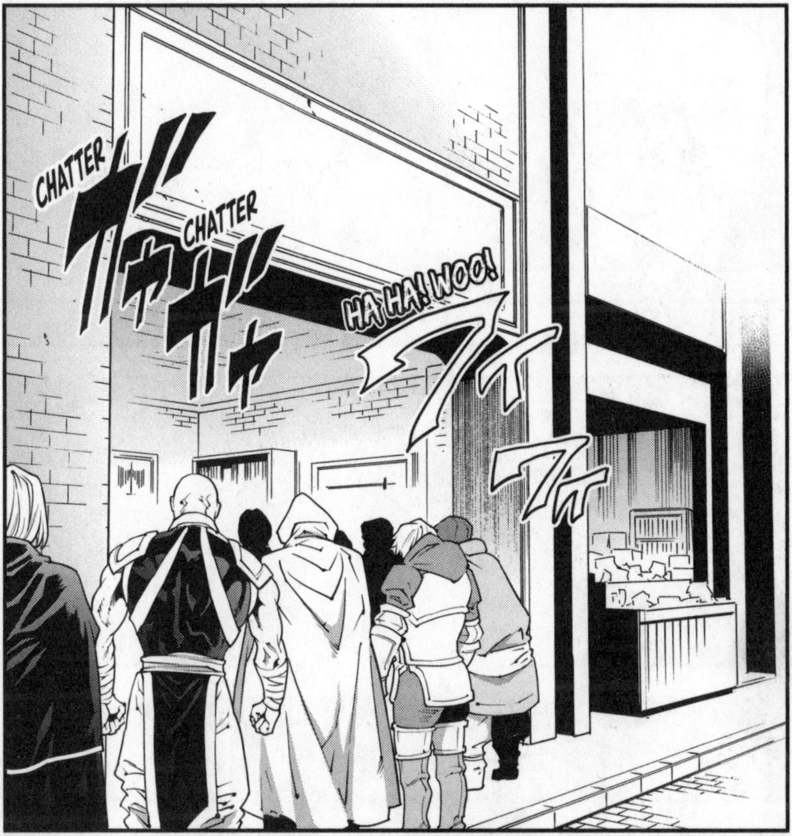
CHATTER
CHATTER
HA HA! WOO!

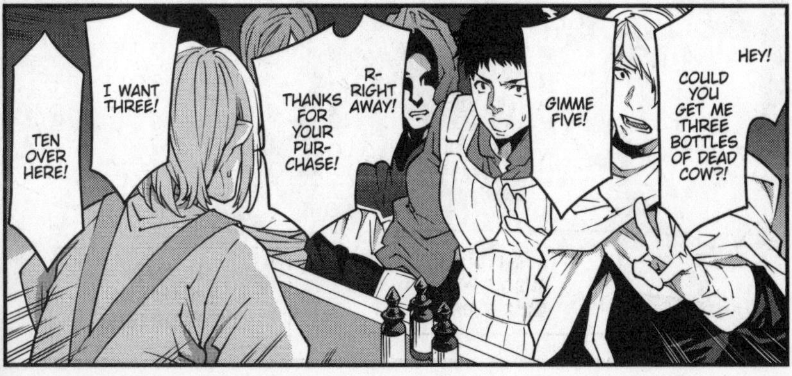
HEY! COULD YOU GET ME THREE BOTTLES OF DEAD COW?!
GIMME FIVE!
R-RIGHT AWAY!
THANKS FOR YOUR PURCHASE!
I WANT THREE!
TEN OVER HERE!

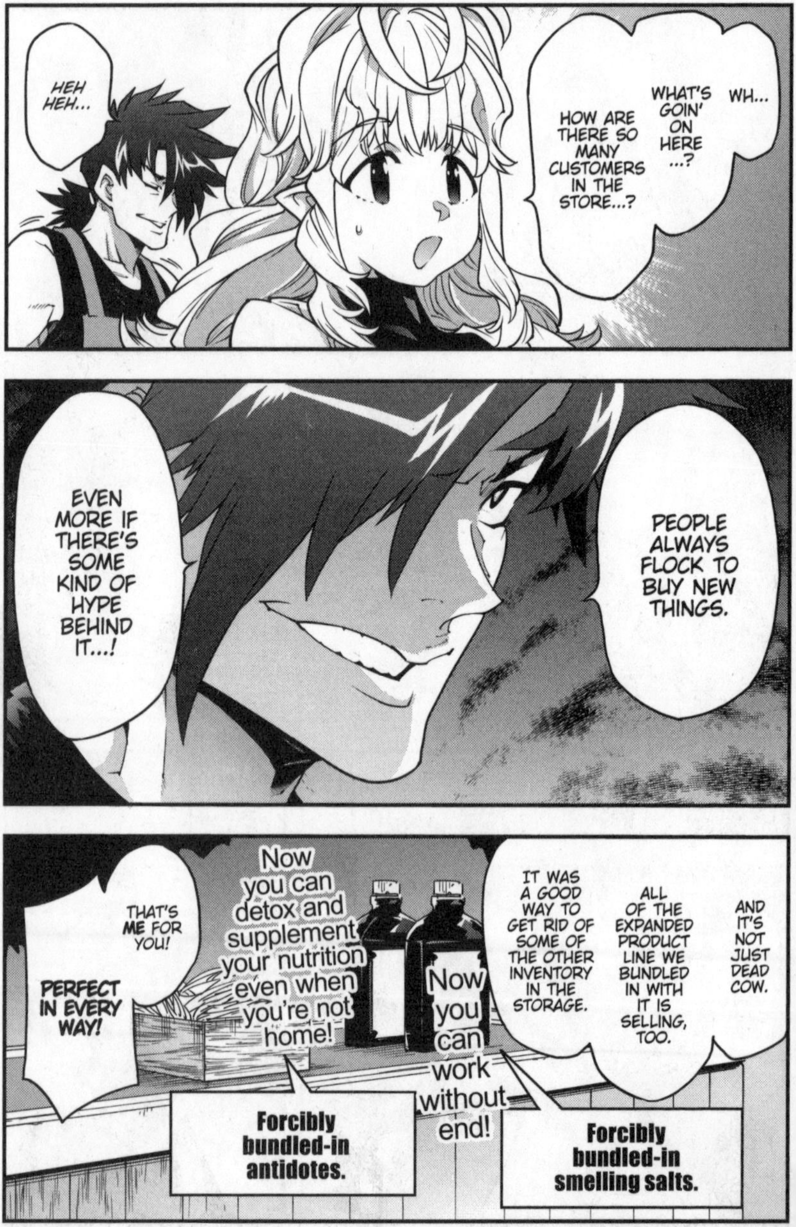
WH...
WHAT'S GOIN' ON HERE ...?
HOW ARE THERE SO MANY CUSTOMERS IN THE STORE...?
HEH HEH...
PEOPLE ALWAYS FLOCK TO BUY NEW THINGS.
EVEN MORE IF THERE'S SOME KIND OF HYPE BEHIND IT...!
AND IT'S NOT JUST DEAD COW.
ALL OF THE EXPANDED PRODUCT LINE WE BUNDLED IN WITH IT IS SELLING, TOO.
IT WAS A GOOD WAY TO GET RID OF SOME OF THE OTHER INVENTORY IN THE STORAGE.
Now you can work without end!
Forcibly bundled-in smelling salts.
Now you can detox and supplement your nutrition even when you're not home!
Forcibly bundled-in antidotes.
THAT'S ME FOR YOU!
PERFECT IN EVERY WAY!

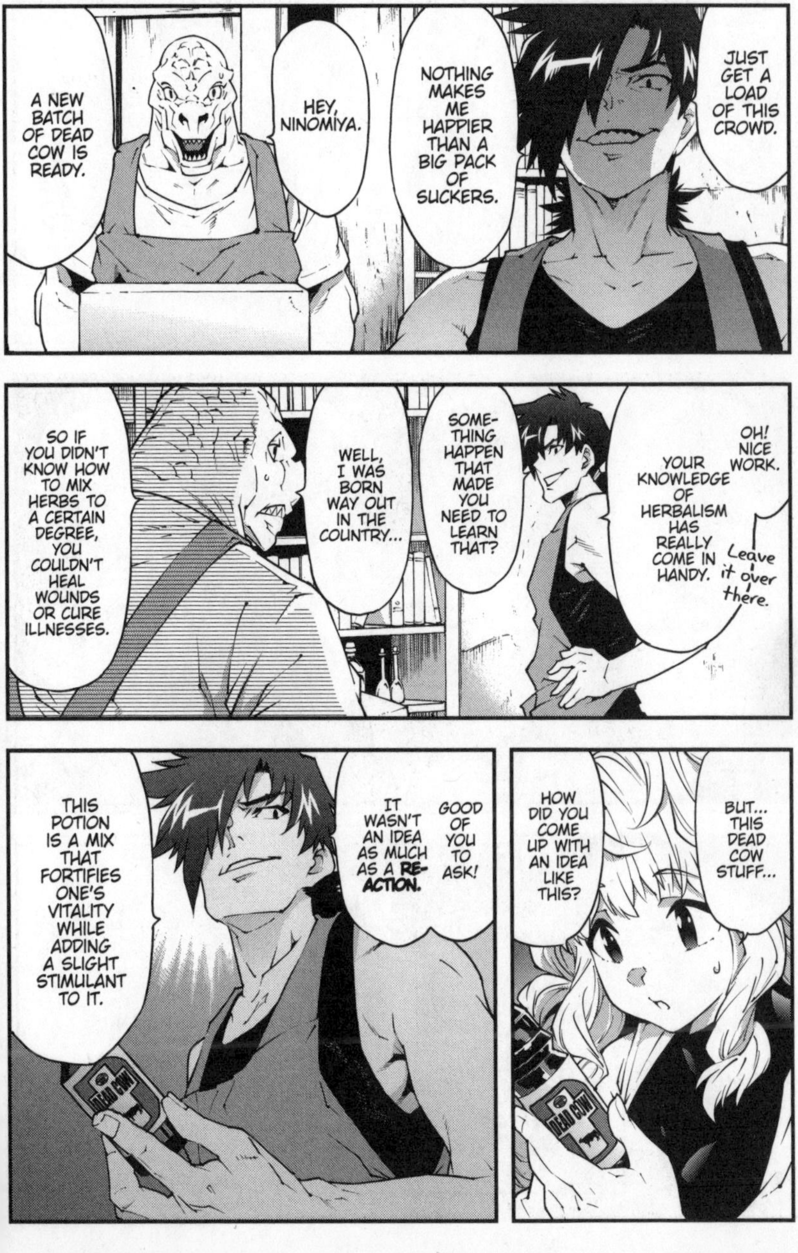
JUST GET A LOAD OF THIS CROWD.
NOTHING MAKES ME HAPPIER THAN A BIG PACK OF SUCKERS.
HEY, NINOMIYA.
A NEW BATCH OF DEAD COW IS READY.
OH! NICE WORK.
YOUR KNOWLEDGE OF HERBALISM HAS REALLY COME IN HANDY.
Leave it over there.
SOME-THING HAPPEN THAT MADE YOU NEED TO LEARN THAT?
WELL, I WAS BORN WAY OUT IN THE COUNTRY...
SO IF YOU DIDN'T KNOW HOW TO MIX HERBS TO A CERTAIN DEGREE, YOU COULDN'T HEAL WOUNDS OR CURE ILLNESSES.
BUT... THIS DEAD COW STUFF...
HOW DID YOU COME UP WITH AN IDEA LIKE THIS?
DEAD COW
GOOD OF YOU TO ASK!
IT WASN'T AN IDEA AS MUCH AS A **RE-ACTION.**
THIS POTION IS A MIX THAT FORTIFIES ONE'S VITALITY WHILE ADDING A SLIGHT STIMULANT TO IT.
DEAD COW

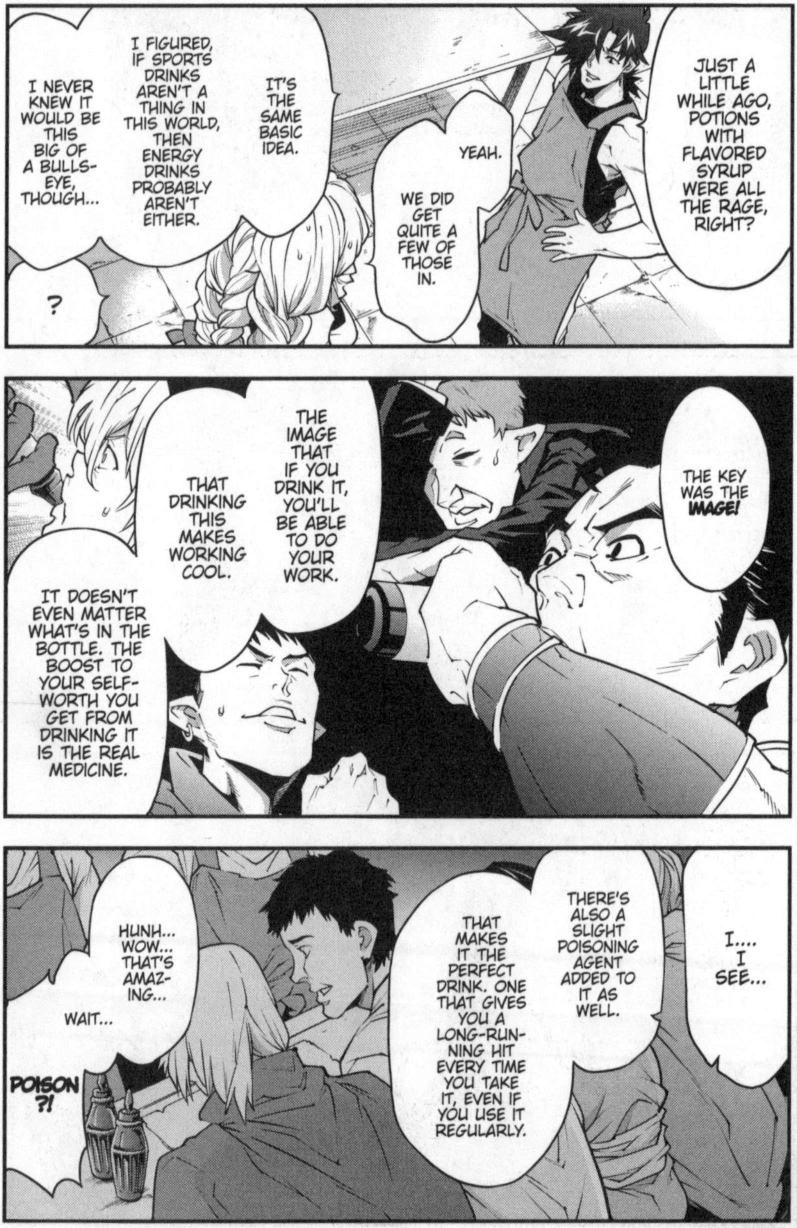

JUST A LITTLE WHILE AGO, POTIONS WITH FLAVORED SYRUP WERE ALL THE RAGE, RIGHT?
YEAH.
WE DID GET QUITE A FEW OF THOSE IN.
IT'S THE SAME BASIC IDEA.
I FIGURED, IF SPORTS DRINKS AREN'T A THING IN THIS WORLD, THEN ENERGY DRINKS PROBABLY AREN'T EITHER.
I NEVER KNEW IT WOULD BE THIS BIG OF A BULLS-EYE, THOUGH...
?
THE KEY WAS THE **IMAGE!**
THE IMAGE THAT IF YOU DRINK IT, YOU'LL BE ABLE TO DO YOUR WORK.
THAT DRINKING THIS MAKES WORKING COOL.
IT DOESN'T EVEN MATTER WHAT'S IN THE BOTTLE. THE BOOST TO YOUR SELF-WORTH YOU GET FROM DRINKING IT IS THE REAL MEDICINE.
I.... I SEE...
THERE'S ALSO A SLIGHT POISONING AGENT ADDED TO IT AS WELL.
THAT MAKES IT THE PERFECT DRINK. ONE THAT GIVES YOU A LONG-RUNNING HIT EVERY TIME YOU TAKE IT, EVEN IF YOU USE IT REGULARLY.
HUNH... WOW... THAT'S AMAZ-ING...
WAIT...
POISON ?!

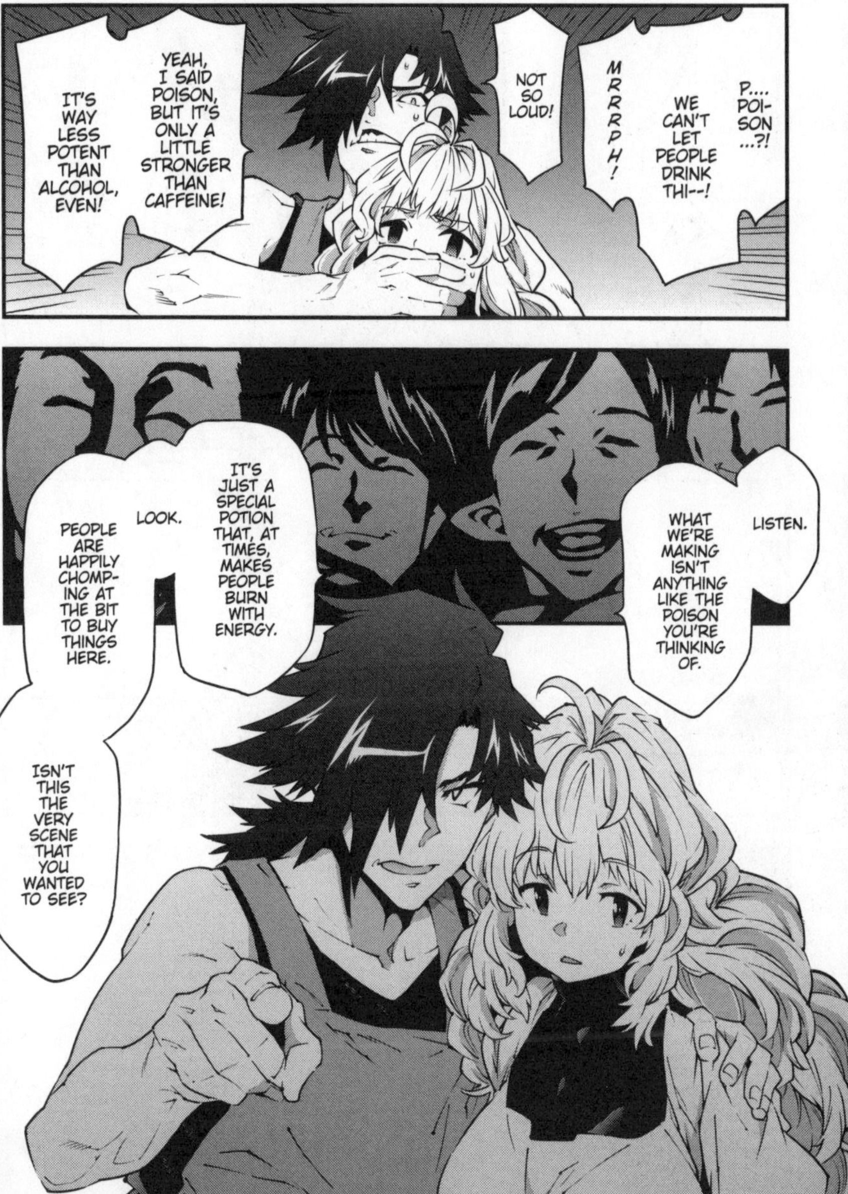
P.... POI-SON ...?!
MRRRPH!
WE CAN'T LET PEOPLE DRINK THI--!
NOT SO LOUD!
YEAH, I SAID POISON, BUT IT'S ONLY A LITTLE STRONGER THAN CAFFEINE!
IT'S WAY LESS POTENT THAN ALCOHOL, EVEN!
LISTEN.
WHAT WE'RE MAKING ISN'T ANYTHING LIKE THE POISON YOU'RE THINKING OF.
IT'S JUST A SPECIAL POTION THAT, AT TIMES, MAKES PEOPLE BURN WITH ENERGY.
LOOK.
PEOPLE ARE HAPPILY CHOMPING AT THE BIT TO BUY THINGS HERE.
ISN'T THIS THE VERY SCENE THAT YOU WANTED TO SEE?

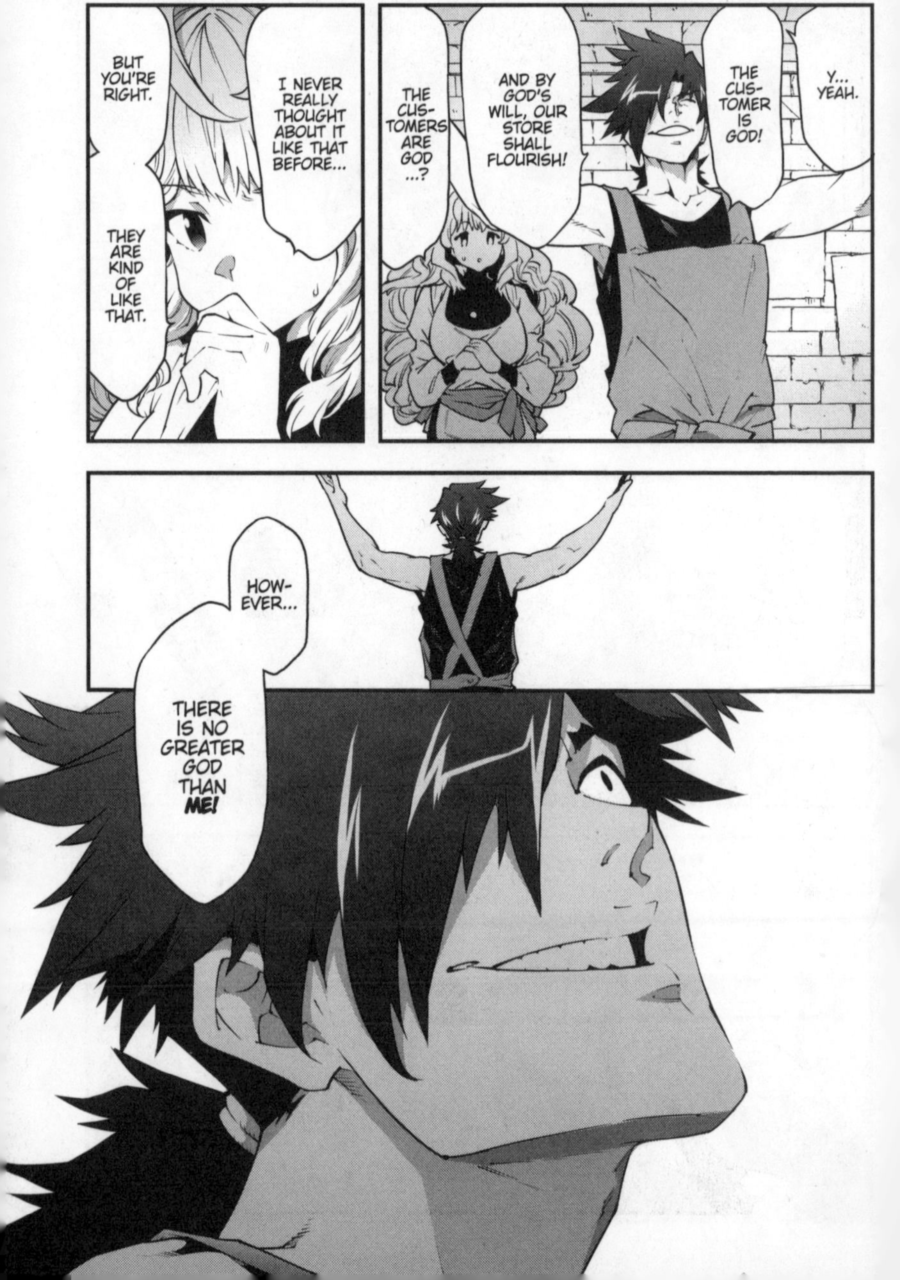
Y... YEAH.
THE CUS- TOMER IS GOD!
AND BY GOD'S WILL, OUR STORE SHALL FLOURISH!
THE CUS- TOMERS ARE GOD ...?
I NEVER REALLY THOUGHT ABOUT IT LIKE THAT BEFORE...
BUT YOU'RE RIGHT.
THEY ARE KIND OF LIKE THAT.
HOW- EVER...
THERE IS NO GREATER GOD THAN **ME!**

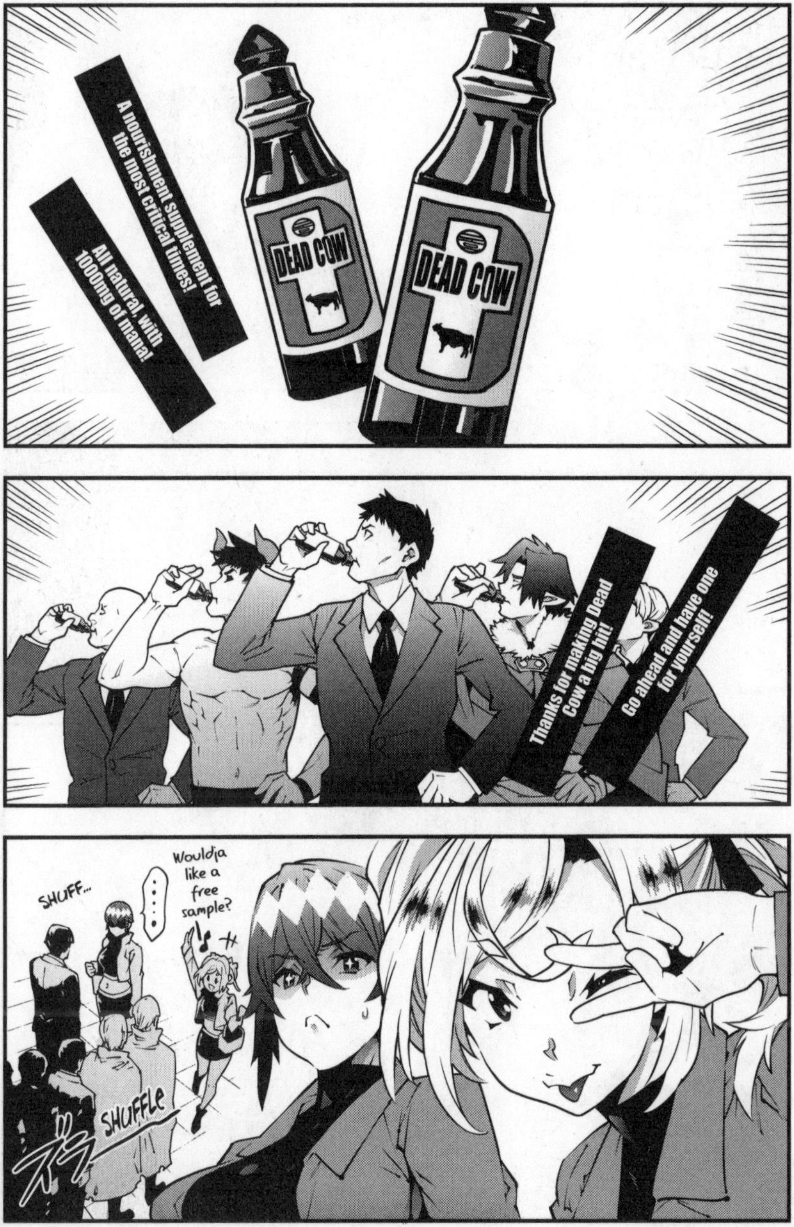
A nourishment supplement for the most critical times!
All natural, with 1000mg of mana!
DEAD COW
DEAD COW
Thanks for making Dead Cow a big hit!
Go ahead and have one for yourself!
Wouldja like a free sample?
. . . .
SHUFF...
SHUFFLE

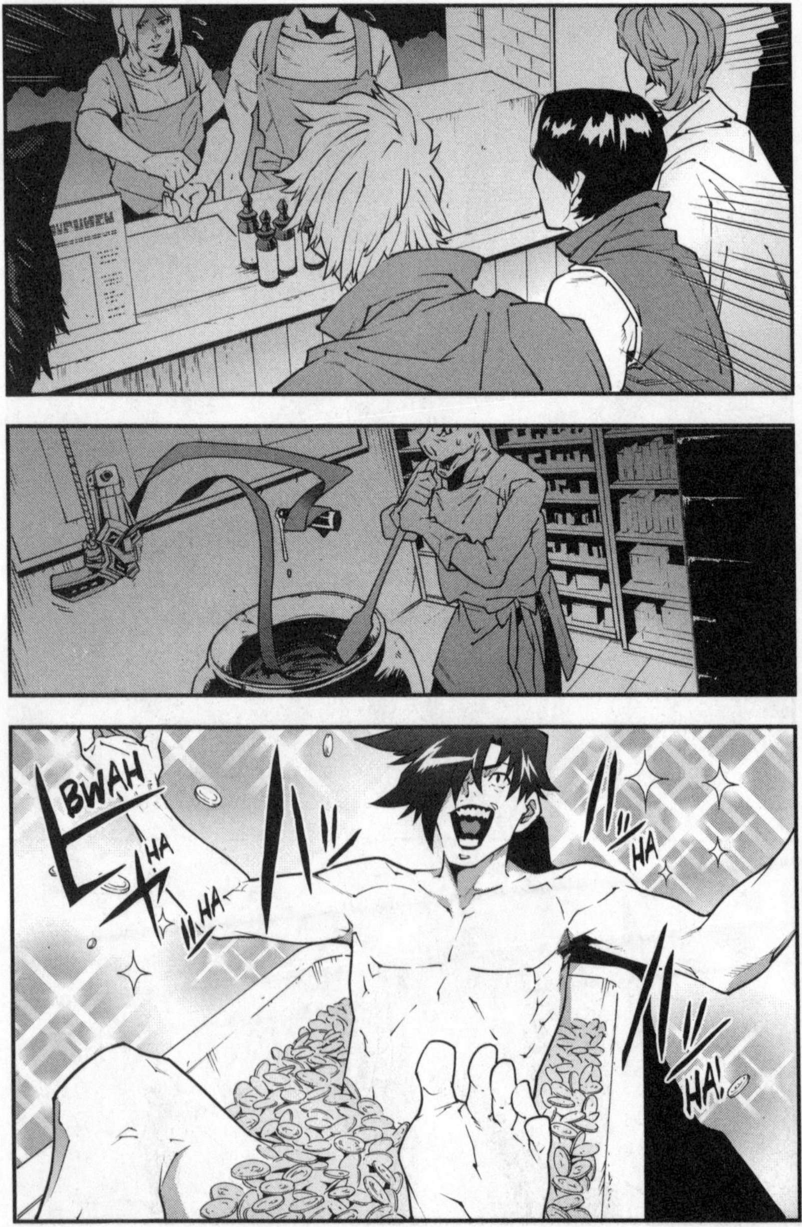
BWAH
HA
HA
HA
HA!

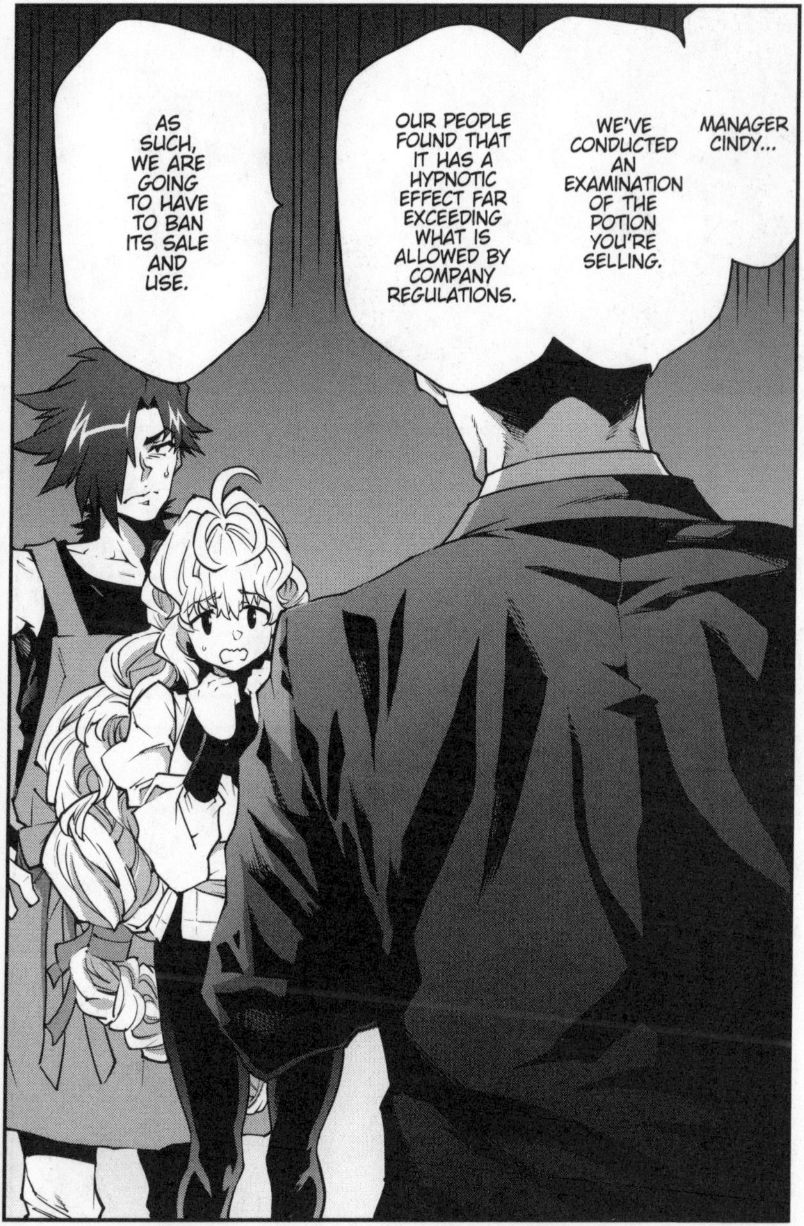
MANAGER CINDY...
WE'VE CONDUCTED AN EXAMINATION OF THE POTION YOU'RE SELLING.
OUR PEOPLE FOUND THAT IT HAS A HYPNOTIC EFFECT FAR EXCEEDING WHAT IS ALLOWED BY COMPANY REGULATIONS.
AS SUCH, WE ARE GOING TO HAVE TO BAN ITS SALE AND USE.

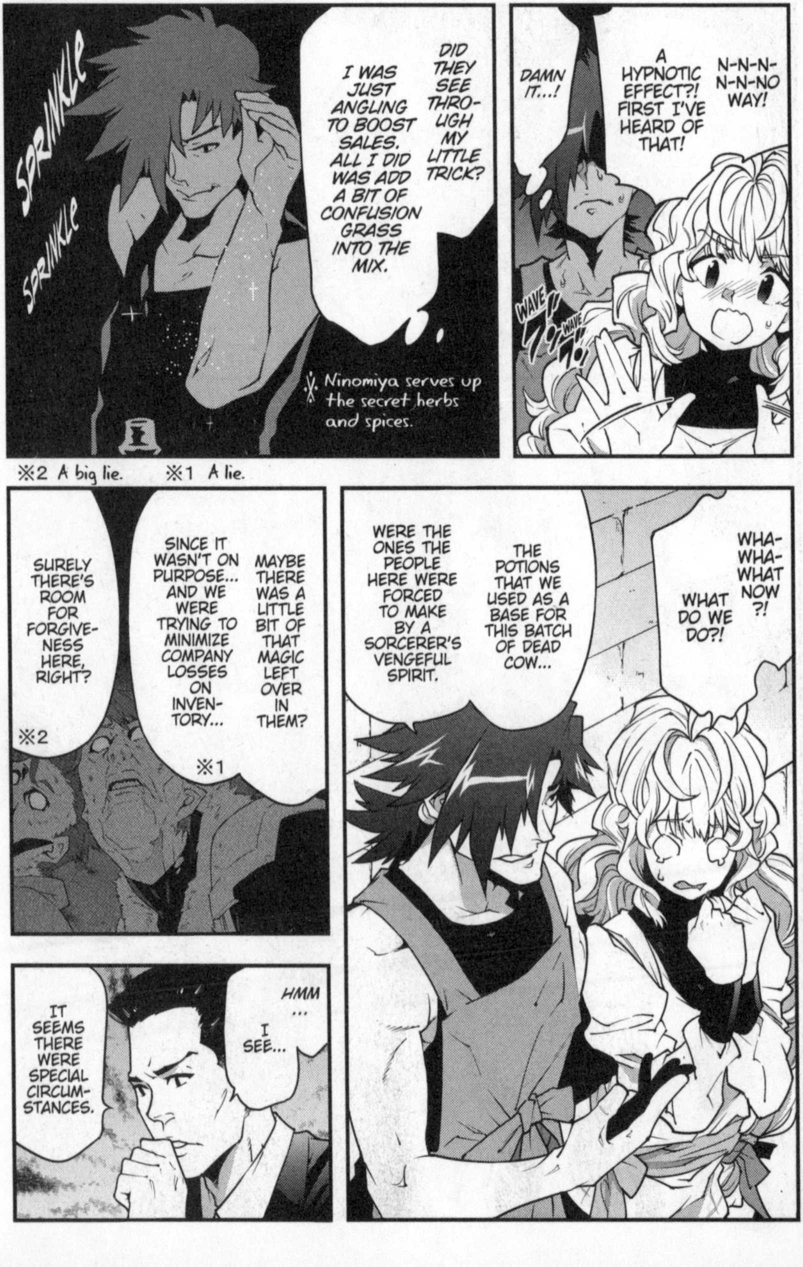
N-N-N-N-N-NO WAY!
A HYPNOTIC EFFECT?! FIRST I'VE HEARD OF THAT!
DAMN IT...!
WAVE WAVE
DID THEY SEE THROUGH MY LITTLE TRICK?
I WAS JUST ANGLING TO BOOST SALES. ALL I DID WAS ADD A BIT OF CONFUSION GRASS INTO THE MIX.
SPRINKLE SPRINKLE
※ Ninomiya serves up the secret herbs and spices.
※2 A big lie. ※1 A lie.
WHA-WHA-WHAT NOW?!
WHAT DO WE DO?!
THE POTIONS THAT WE USED AS A BASE FOR THIS BATCH OF DEAD COW...
WERE THE ONES THE PEOPLE HERE WERE FORCED TO MAKE BY A SORCERER'S VENGEFUL SPIRIT.
MAYBE THERE WAS A LITTLE BIT OF THAT MAGIC LEFT OVER IN THEM?
SINCE IT WASN'T ON PURPOSE... AND WE WERE TRYING TO MINIMIZE COMPANY LOSSES ON INVENTORY... ※1
SURELY THERE'S ROOM FOR FORGIVENESS HERE, RIGHT? ※2
HMM... I SEE...
IT SEEMS THERE WERE SPECIAL CIRCUMSTANCES.

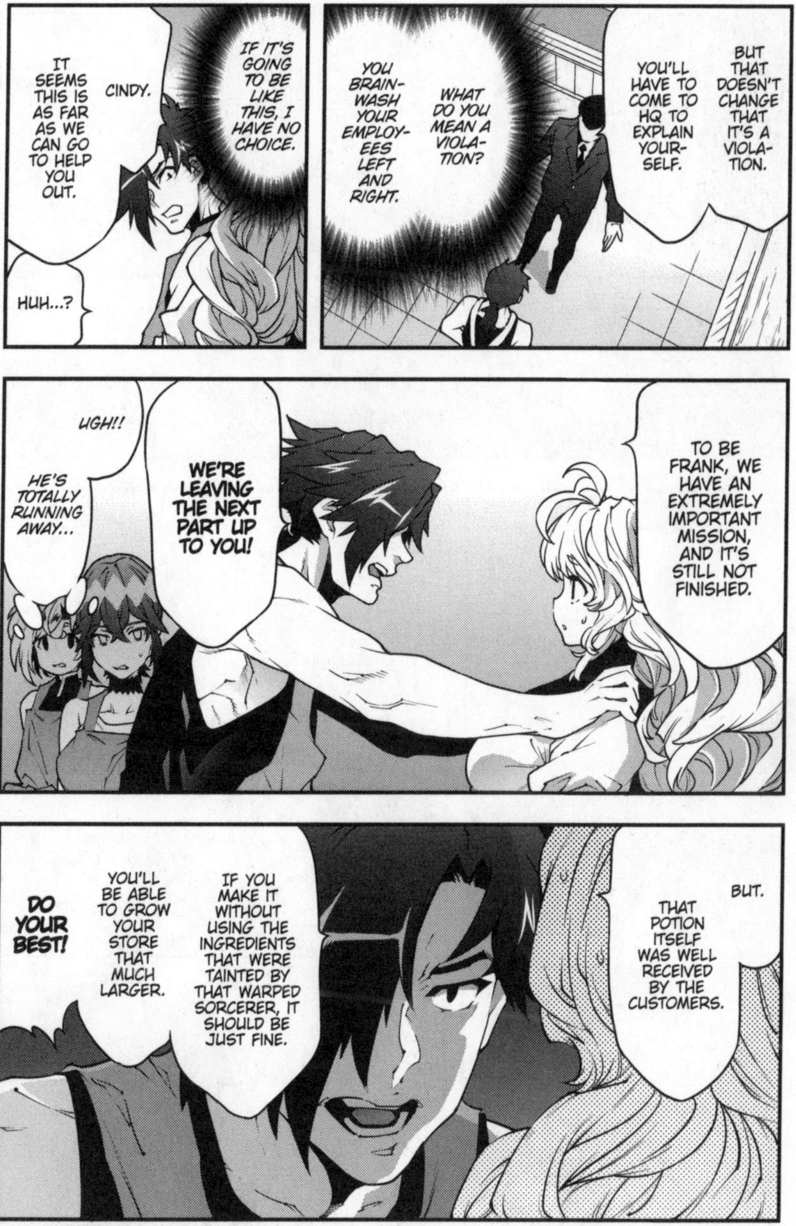
BUT THAT DOESN'T CHANGE THAT IT'S A VIOLATION.
YOU'LL HAVE TO COME TO HQ TO EXPLAIN YOURSELF.
WHAT DO YOU MEAN A VIOLATION?
YOU BRAINWASH YOUR EMPLOYEES LEFT AND RIGHT.
IF IT'S GOING TO BE LIKE THIS, I HAVE NO CHOICE.
CINDY.
IT SEEMS THIS IS AS FAR AS WE CAN GO TO HELP YOU OUT.
HUH...?
TO BE FRANK, WE HAVE AN EXTREMELY IMPORTANT MISSION, AND IT'S STILL NOT FINISHED.
WE'RE LEAVING THE NEXT PART UP TO YOU!
UGH!!
HE'S TOTALLY RUNNING AWAY...
BUT.
THAT POTION ITSELF WAS WELL RECEIVED BY THE CUSTOMERS.
IF YOU MAKE IT WITHOUT USING THE INGREDIENTS THAT WERE TAINTED BY THAT WARPED SORCERER, IT SHOULD BE JUST FINE.
YOU'LL BE ABLE TO GROW YOUR STORE THAT MUCH LARGER.
DO YOUR BEST!

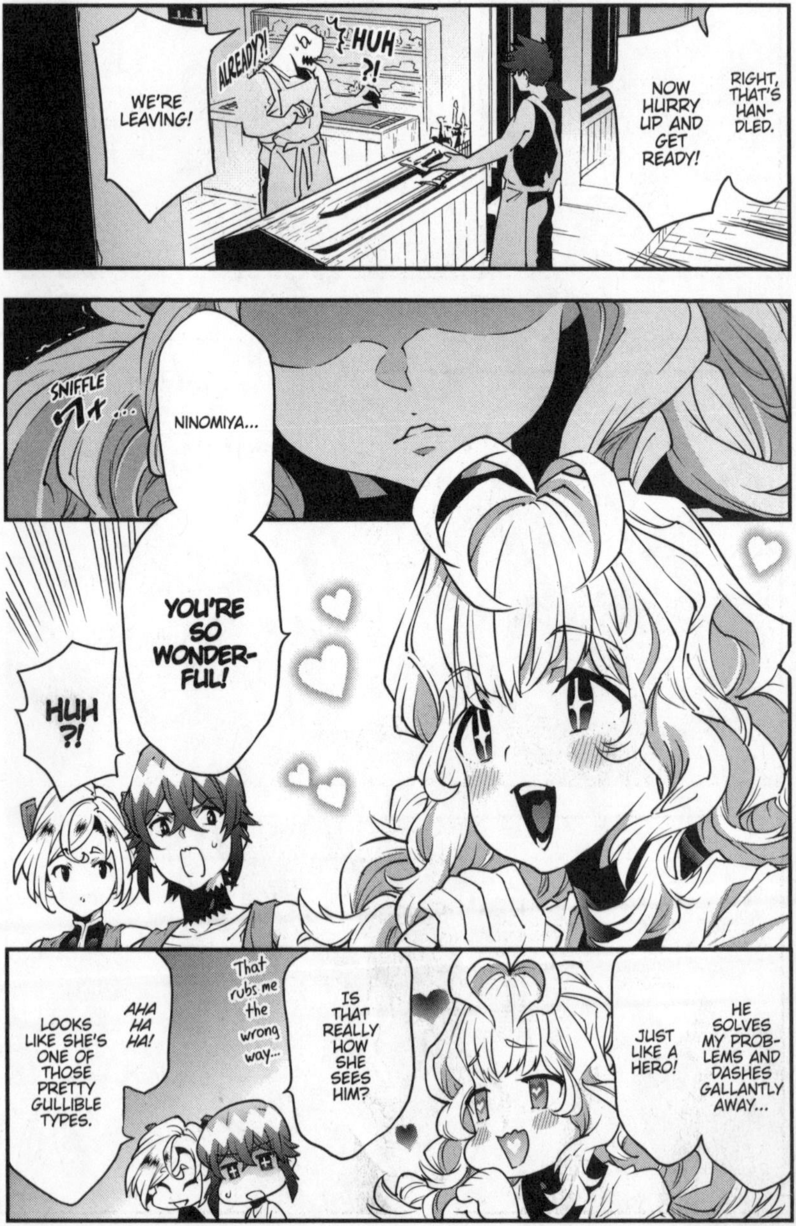

RIGHT, THAT'S HANDLED.
NOW HURRY UP AND GET READY!
HUH ?!
ALREADY?!
WE'RE LEAVING!
SNIFFLE
NINOMIYA...
YOU'RE SO WONDERFUL!
HUH ?!
HE SOLVES MY PROBLEMS AND DASHES GALLANTLY AWAY...
JUST LIKE A HERO!
IS THAT REALLY HOW SHE SEES HIM?
That rubs me the wrong way...
AHA HA HA!
LOOKS LIKE SHE'S ONE OF THOSE PRETTY GULLIBLE TYPES.

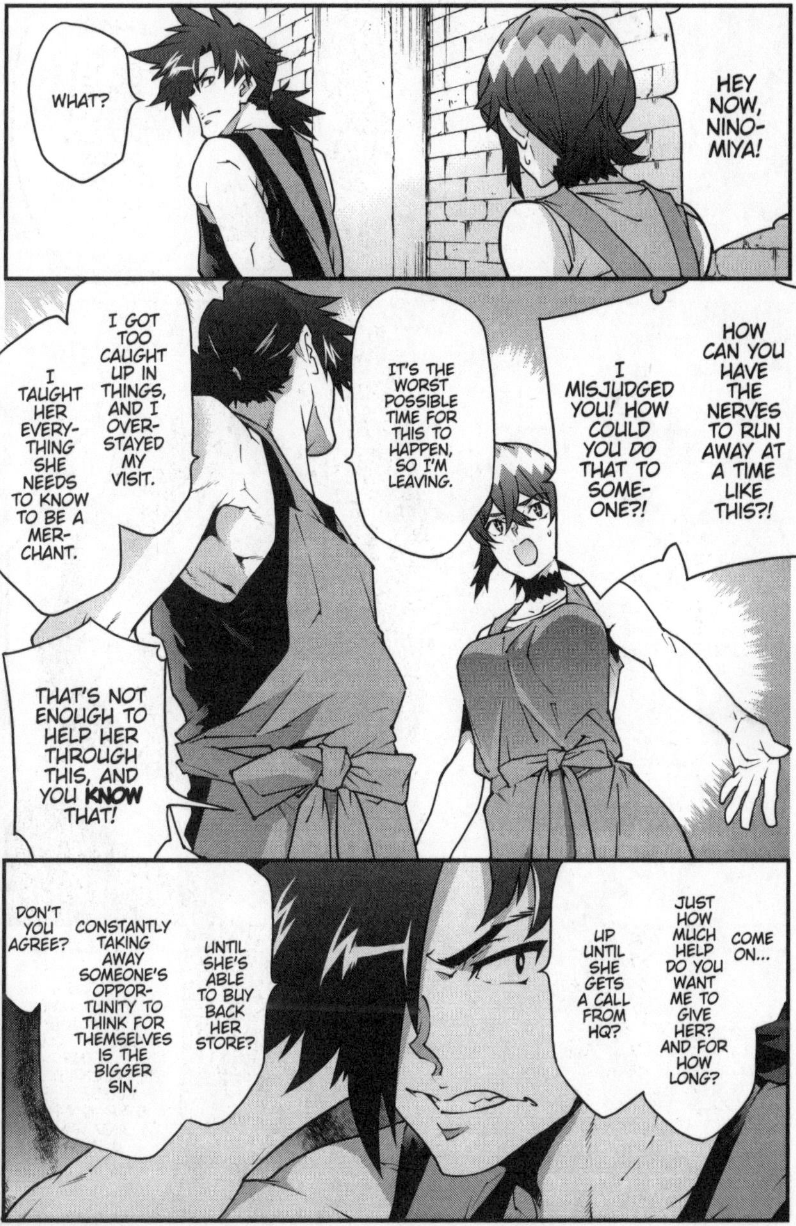
HEY NOW, NINOMIYA!
WHAT?
HOW CAN YOU HAVE THE NERVES TO RUN AWAY AT A TIME LIKE THIS?!
I MISJUDGED YOU! HOW COULD YOU DO THAT TO SOMEONE?!
IT'S THE WORST POSSIBLE TIME FOR THIS TO HAPPEN, SO I'M LEAVING.
I GOT TOO CAUGHT UP IN THINGS, AND I OVERSTAYED MY VISIT.
I TAUGHT HER EVERYTHING SHE NEEDS TO KNOW TO BE A MERCHANT.
THAT'S NOT ENOUGH TO HELP HER THROUGH THIS, AND YOU **KNOW** THAT!
COME ON...
JUST HOW MUCH HELP DO YOU WANT ME TO GIVE HER? AND FOR HOW LONG?
UP UNTIL SHE GETS A CALL FROM HQ?
UNTIL SHE'S ABLE TO BUY BACK HER STORE?
CONSTANTLY TAKING AWAY SOMEONE'S OPPORTUNITY TO THINK FOR THEMSELVES IS THE BIGGER SIN.
DON'T YOU AGREE?

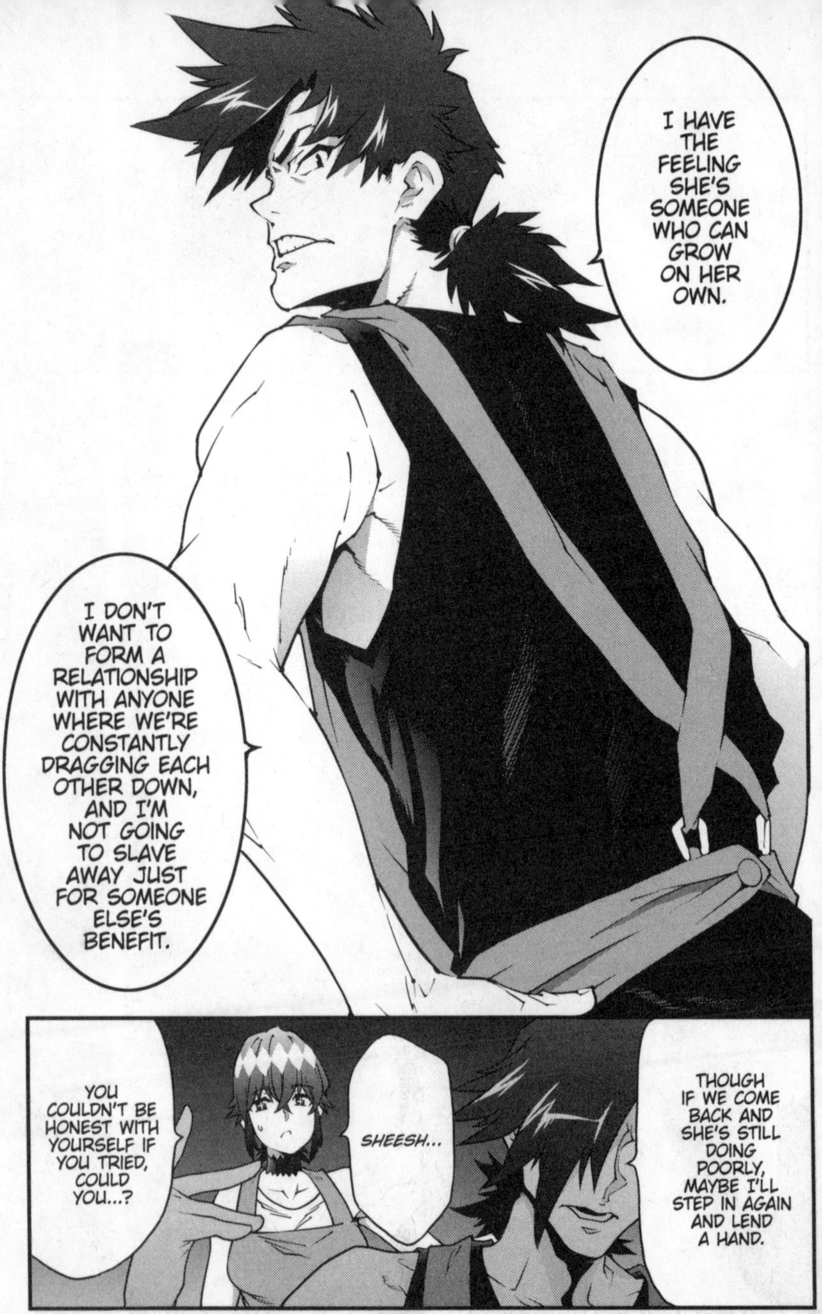
I HAVE THE FEELING SHE'S SOMEONE WHO CAN GROW ON HER OWN.
I DON'T WANT TO FORM A RELATIONSHIP WITH ANYONE WHERE WE'RE CONSTANTLY DRAGGING EACH OTHER DOWN, AND I'M NOT GOING TO SLAVE AWAY JUST FOR SOMEONE ELSE'S BENEFIT.
THOUGH IF WE COME BACK AND SHE'S STILL DOING POORLY, MAYBE I'LL STEP IN AGAIN AND LEND A HAND.
SHEESH...
YOU COULDN'T BE HONEST WITH YOURSELF IF YOU TRIED, COULD YOU...?

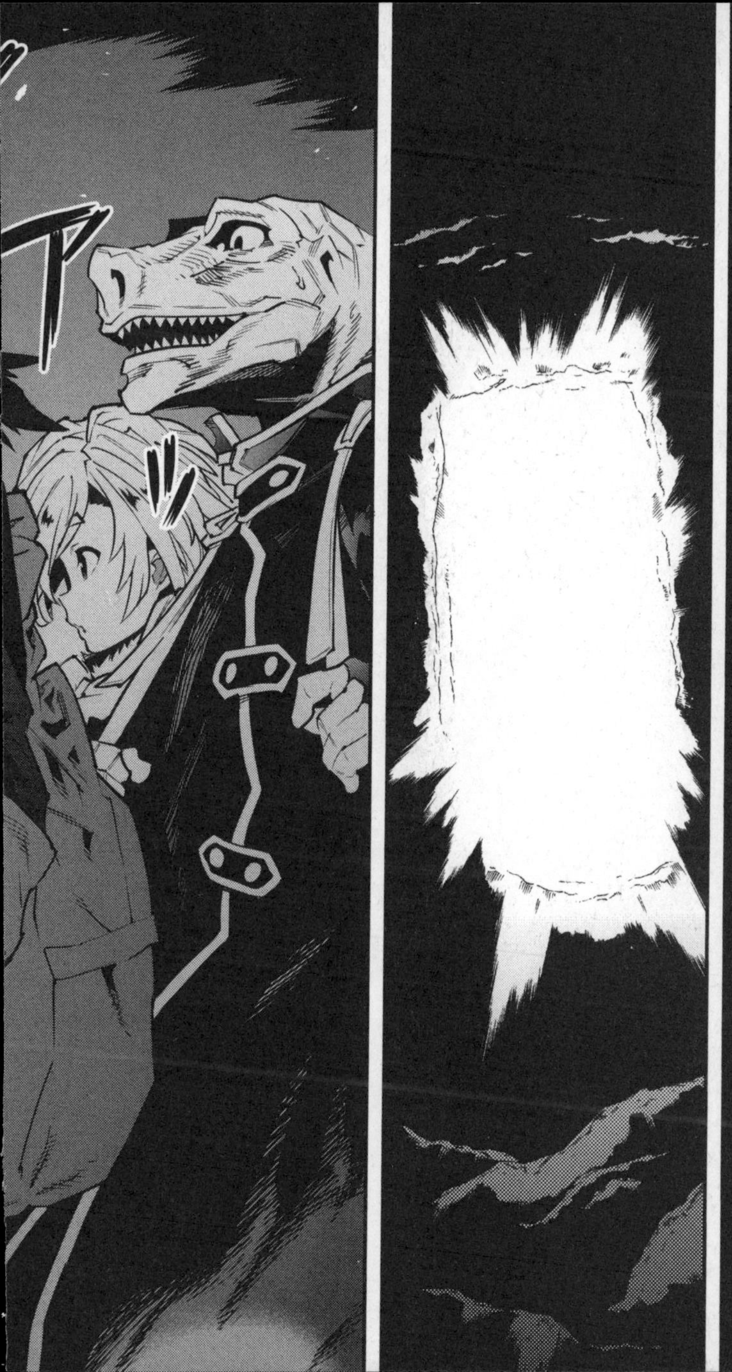

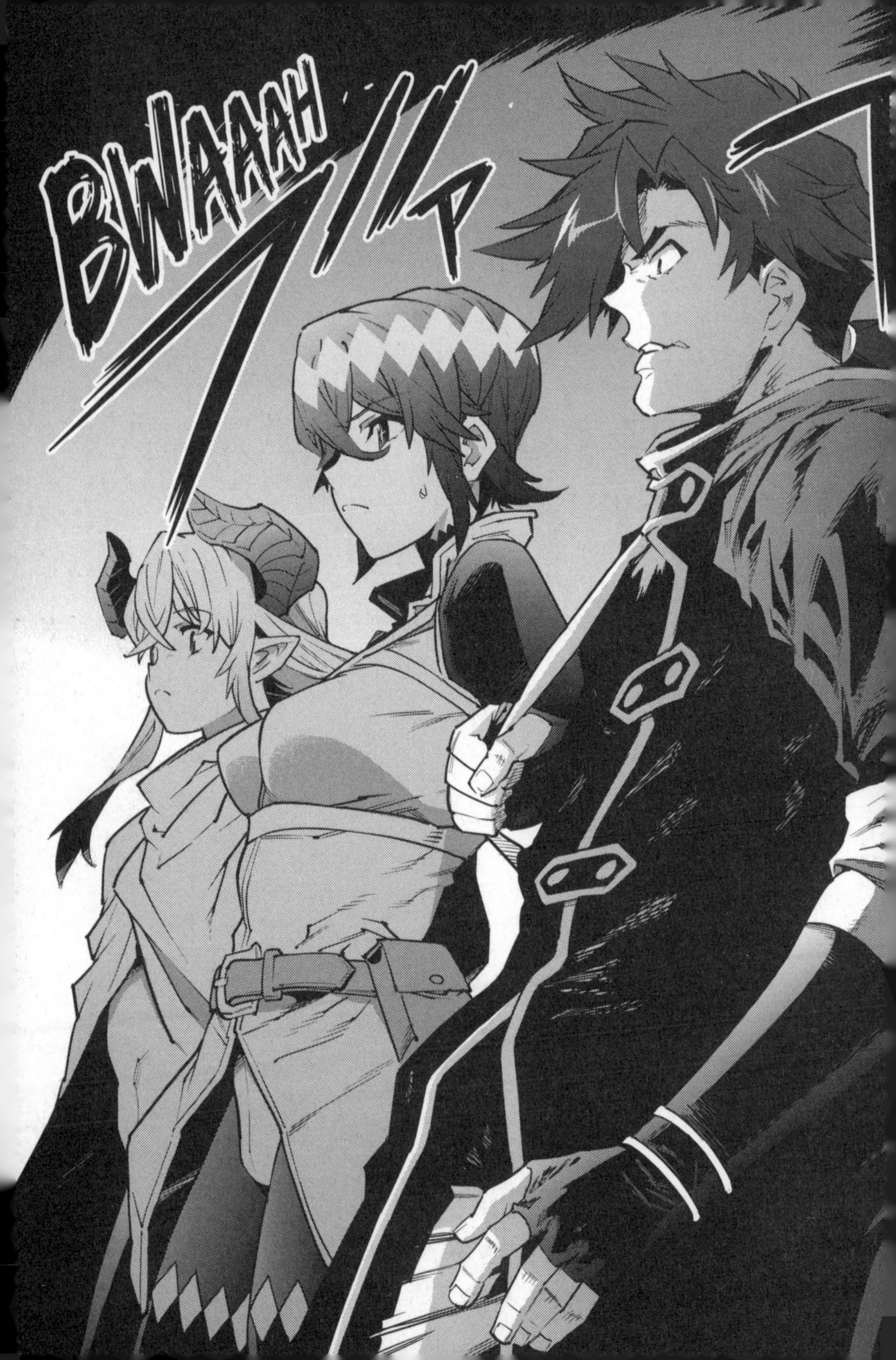
BWAAAH

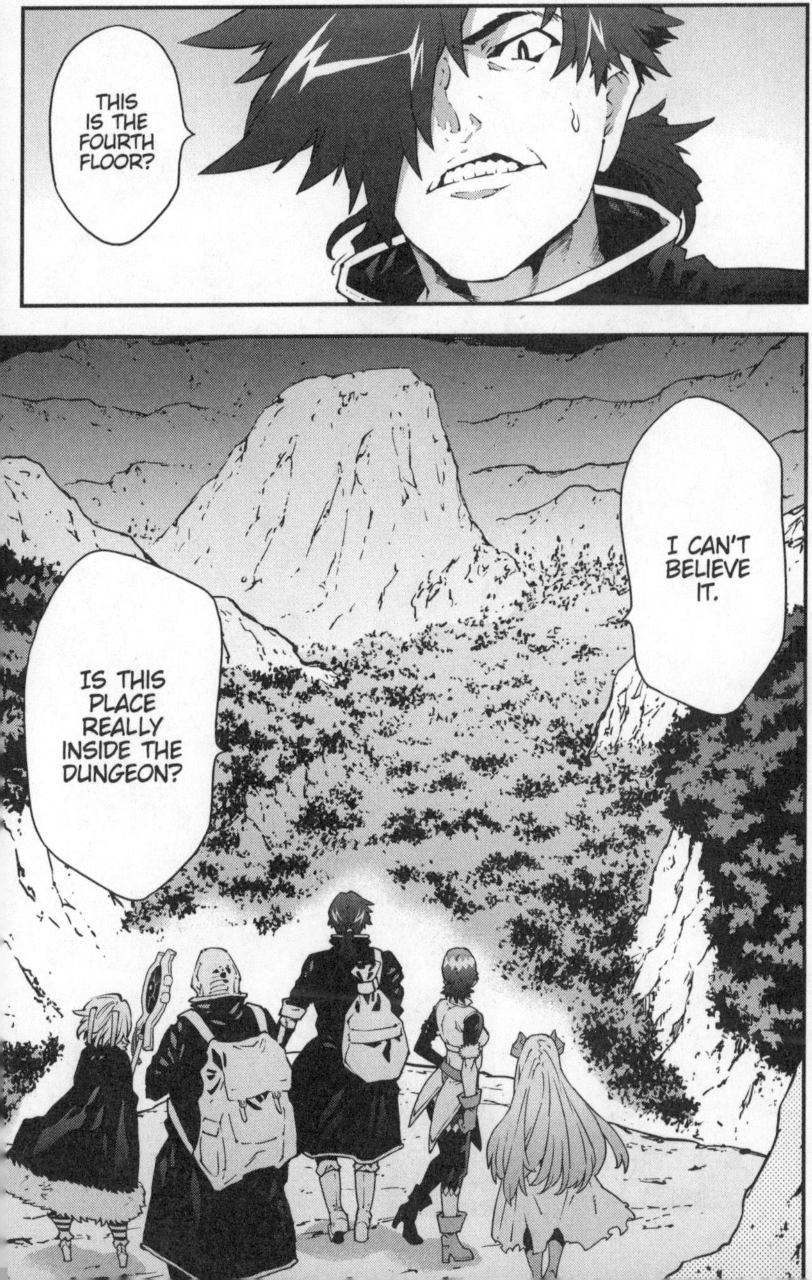
THIS IS THE FOURTH FLOOR?
I CAN'T BELIEVE IT.
IS THIS PLACE REALLY INSIDE THE DUNGEON?

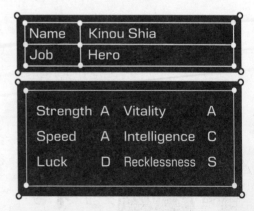

Name	Kinou Shia
Job	Hero

Strength	A	Vitality	A
Speed	A	Intelligence	C
Luck	D	Recklessness	S

THE DUNGEON OF BLACK COMPANY

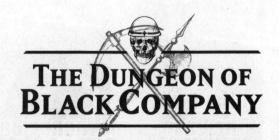

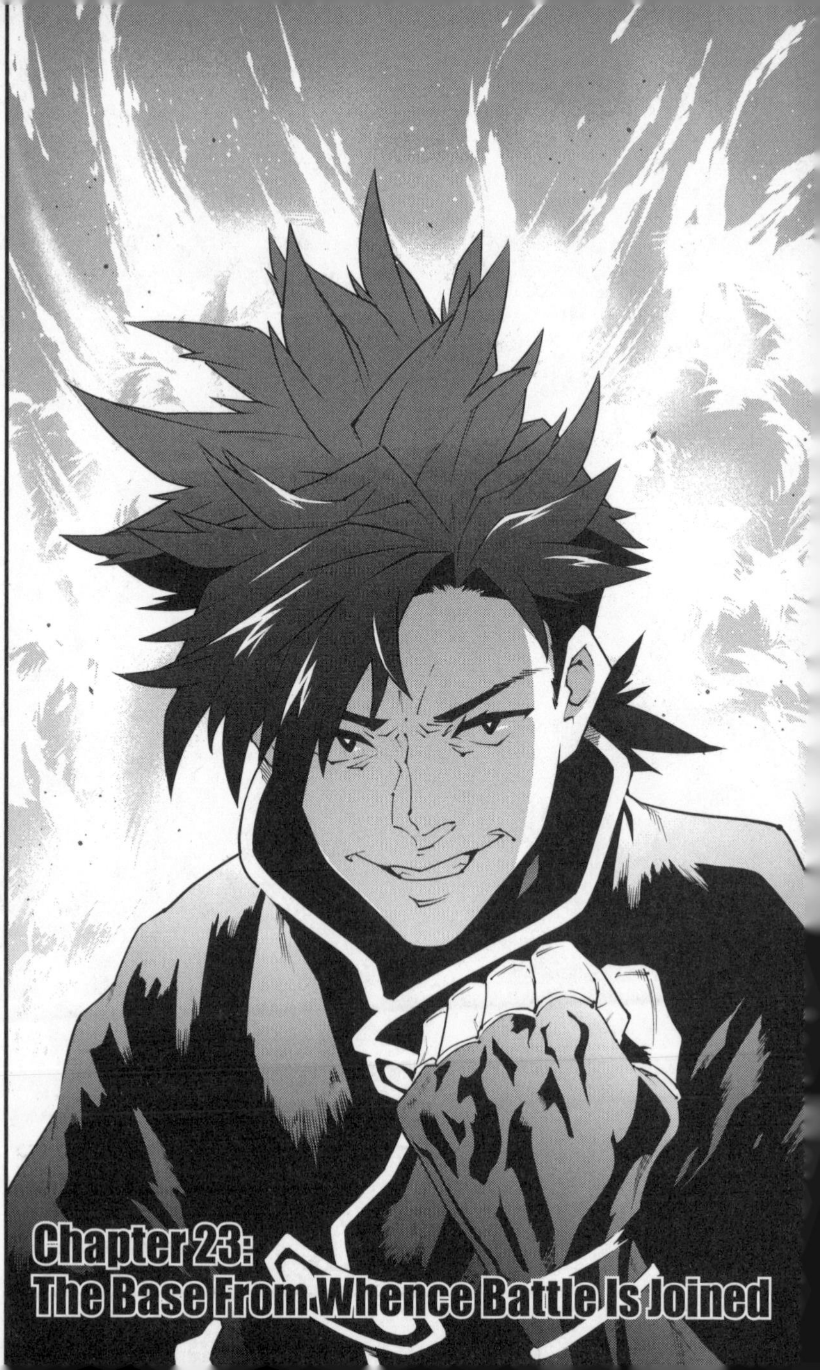
Chapter 23:
The Base From Whence Battle Is Joined

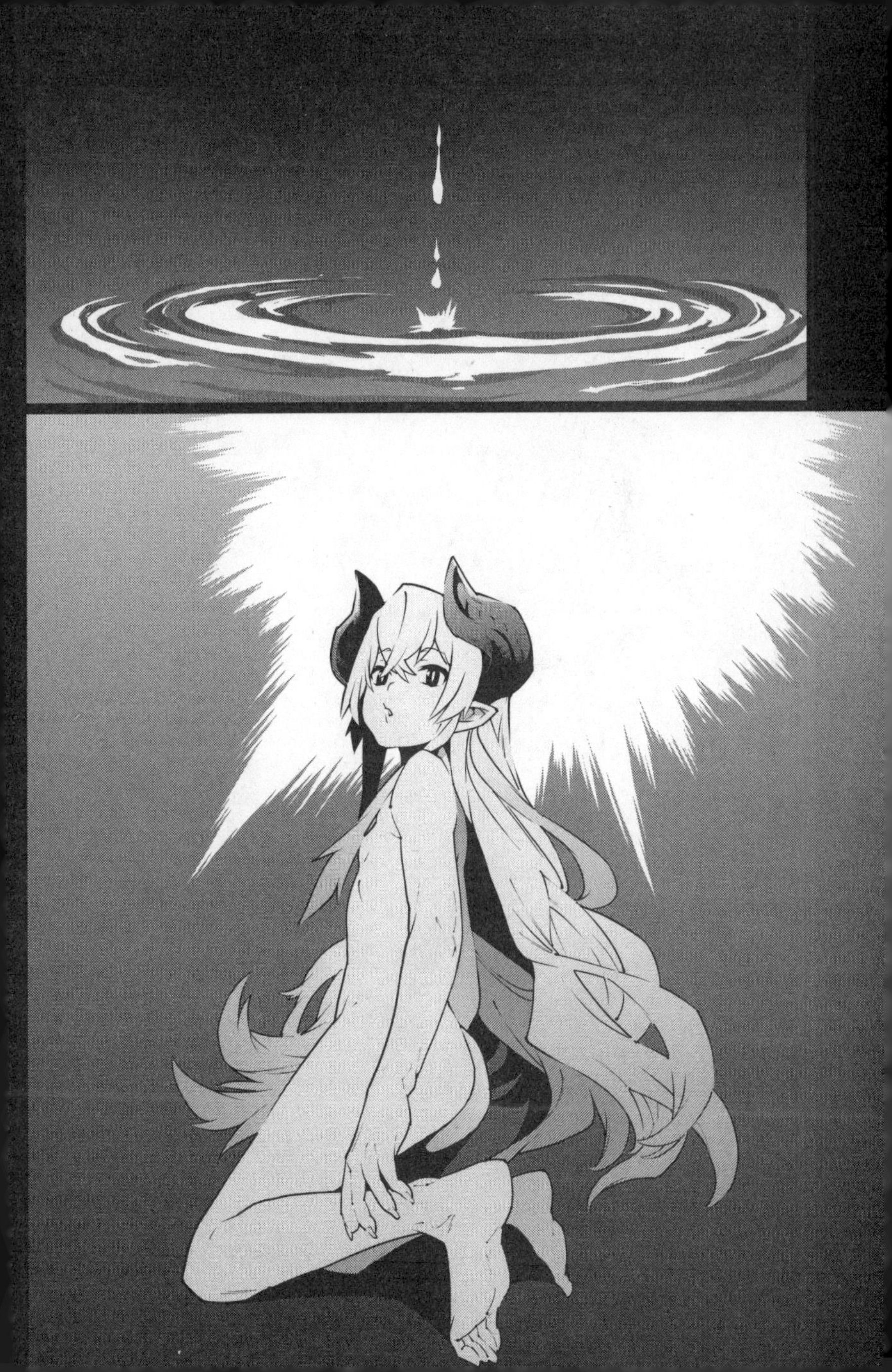

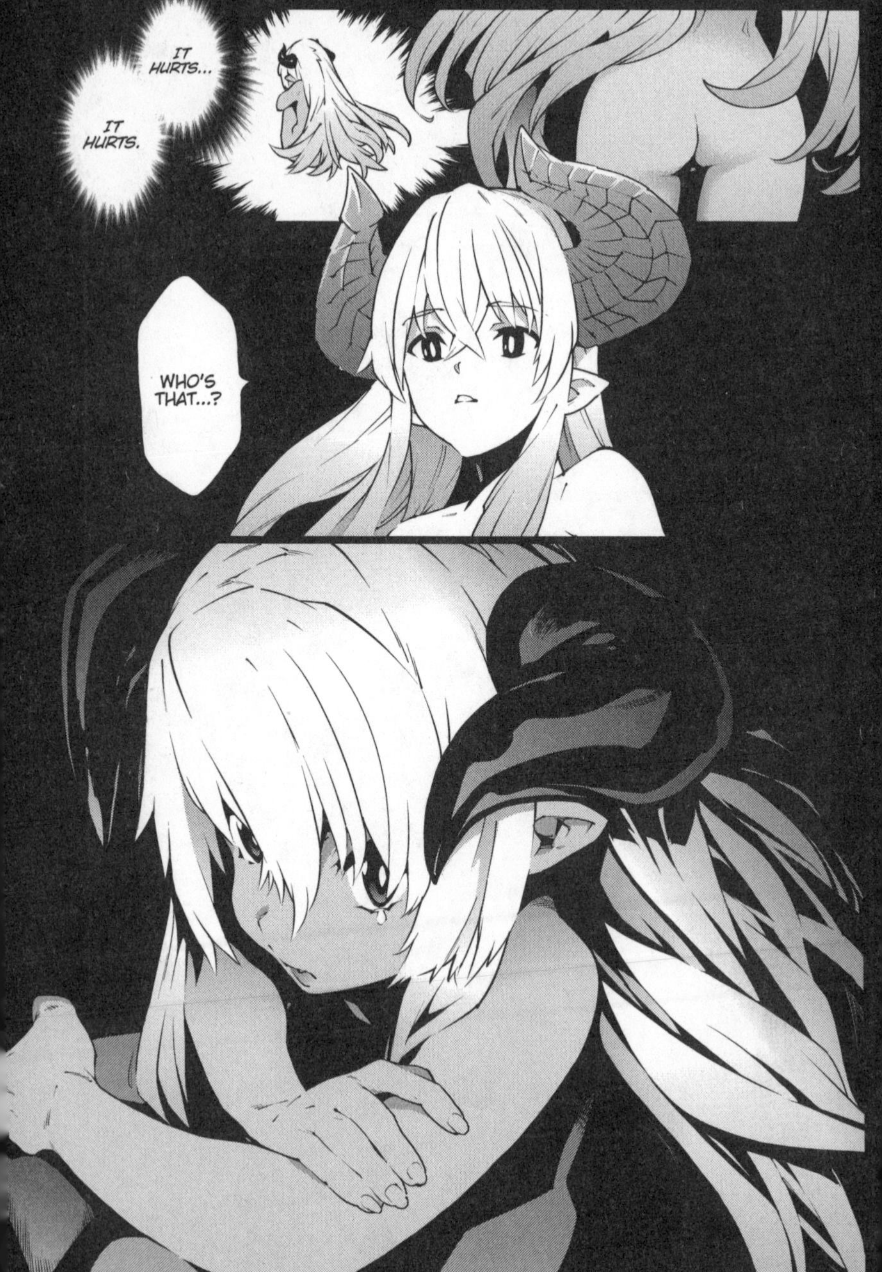
IT HURTS...
IT HURTS.
WHO'S THAT...?

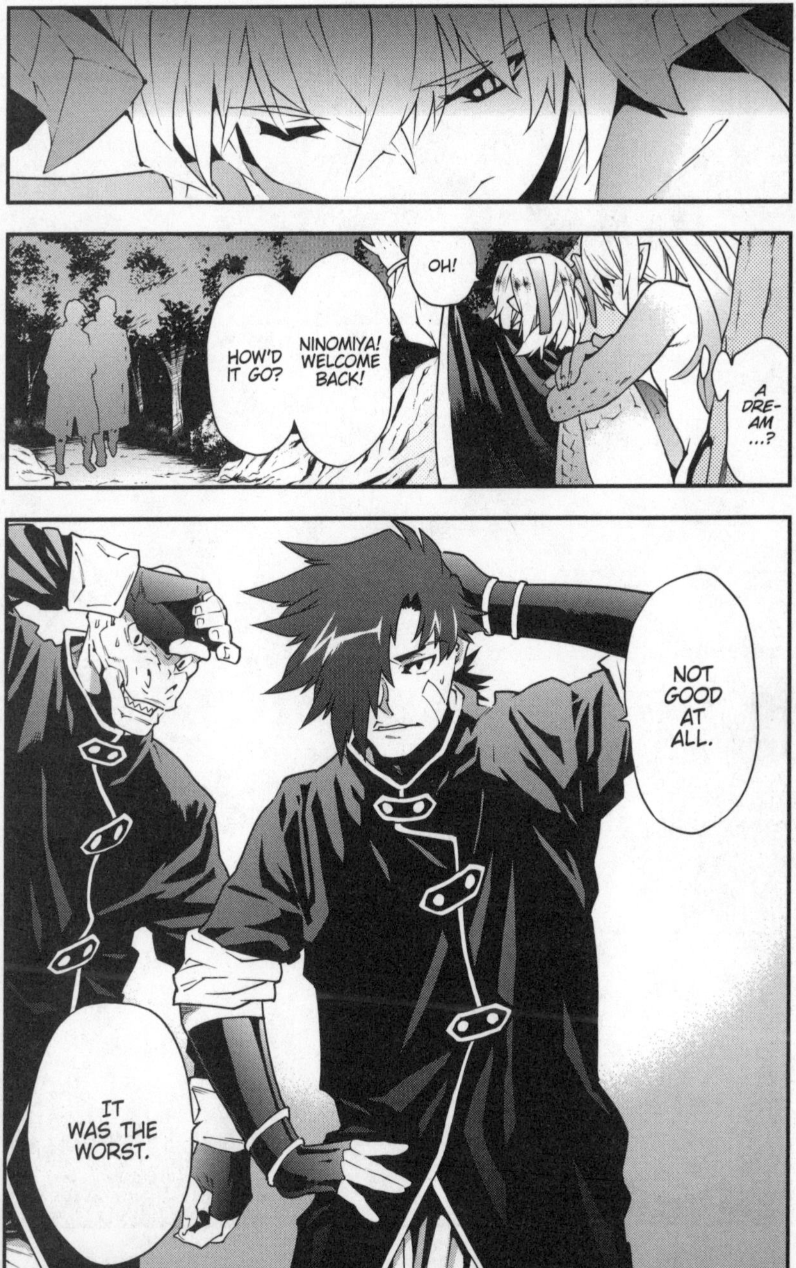
A DRE-AM ...?
OH!
NINOMIYA! WELCOME BACK!
HOW'D IT GO?
NOT GOOD AT ALL.
IT WAS THE WORST.

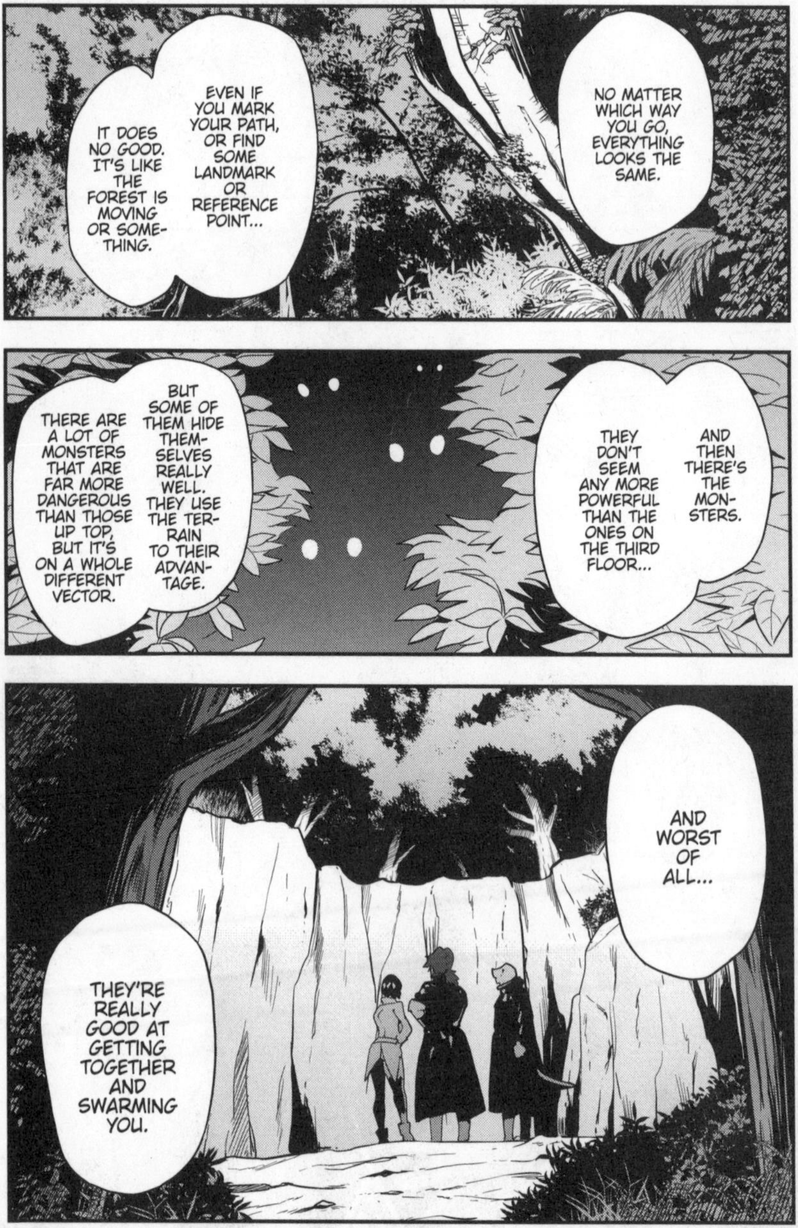
NO MATTER WHICH WAY YOU GO, EVERYTHING LOOKS THE SAME.
EVEN IF YOU MARK YOUR PATH, OR FIND SOME LANDMARK OR REFERENCE POINT...
IT DOES NO GOOD. IT'S LIKE THE FOREST IS MOVING OR SOME-THING.
AND THEN THERE'S THE MON-STERS.
THEY DON'T SEEM ANY MORE POWERFUL THAN THE ONES ON THE THIRD FLOOR...
THERE ARE A LOT OF MONSTERS THAT ARE FAR MORE DANGEROUS THAN THOSE UP TOP, BUT IT'S ON A WHOLE DIFFERENT VECTOR.
BUT SOME OF THEM HIDE THEM-SELVES REALLY WELL. THEY USE THE TER-RAIN TO THEIR ADVAN-TAGE.
AND WORST OF ALL...
THEY'RE REALLY GOOD AT GETTING TOGETHER AND SWARMING YOU.

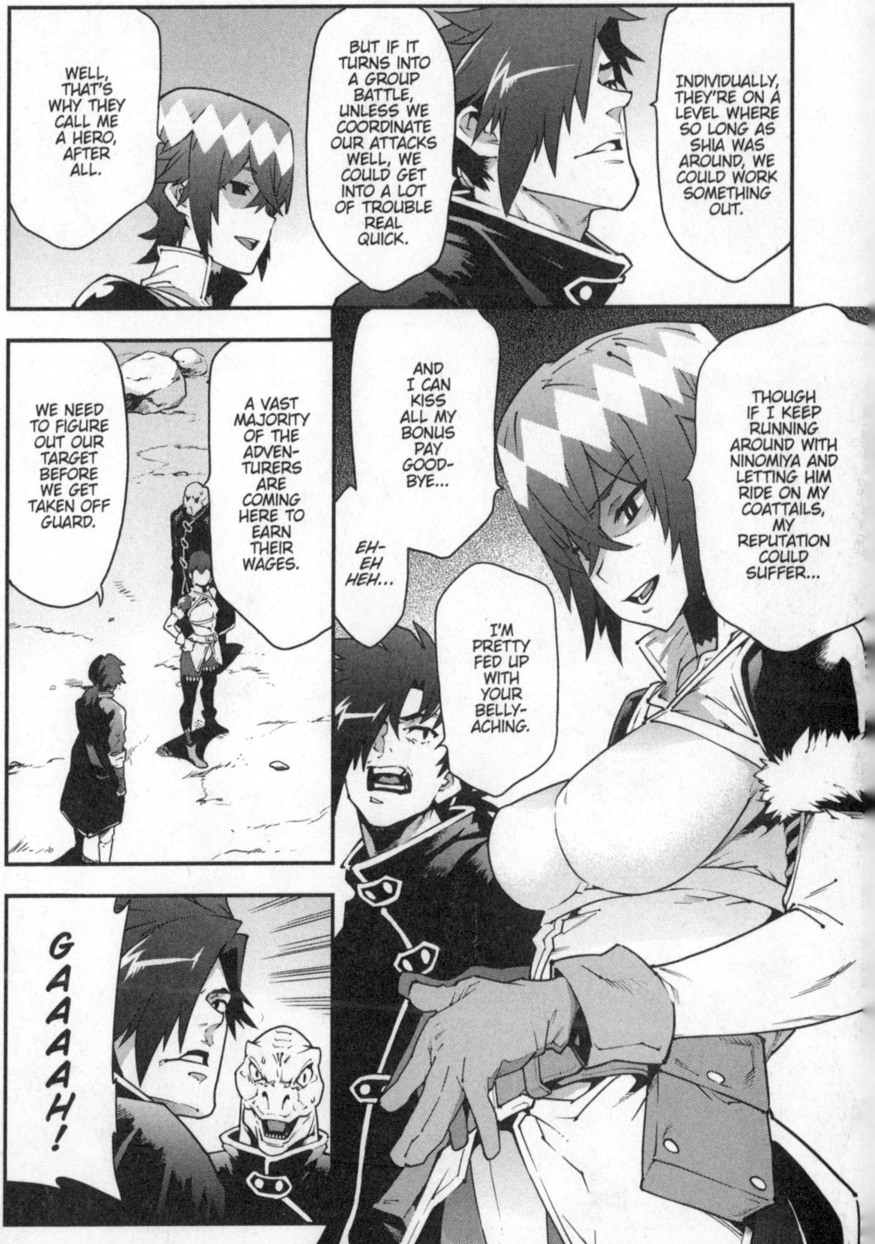
INDIVIDUALLY, THEY'RE ON A LEVEL WHERE SO LONG AS SHIA WAS AROUND, WE COULD WORK SOMETHING OUT.
BUT IF IT TURNS INTO A GROUP BATTLE, UNLESS WE COORDINATE OUR ATTACKS WELL, WE COULD GET INTO A LOT OF TROUBLE REAL QUICK.
WELL, THAT'S WHY THEY CALL ME A HERO, AFTER ALL.
THOUGH IF I KEEP RUNNING AROUND WITH NINOMIYA AND LETTING HIM RIDE ON MY COATTAILS, MY REPUTATION COULD SUFFER...
AND I CAN KISS ALL MY BONUS PAY GOOD-BYE...
EH-EH HEH...
I'M PRETTY FED UP WITH YOUR BELLY-ACHING.
A VAST MAJORITY OF THE ADVEN-TURERS ARE COMING HERE TO EARN THEIR WAGES.
WE NEED TO FIGURE OUT OUR TARGET BEFORE WE GET TAKEN OFF GUARD.
GAAAAAH!

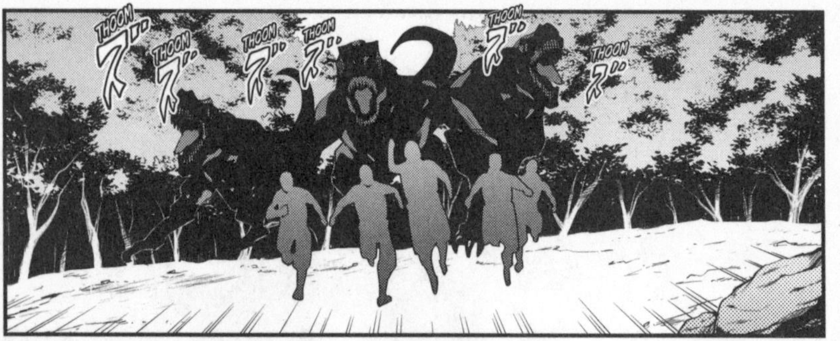
THOOM
THOOM
THOOM
THOOM
THOOM
THOOM
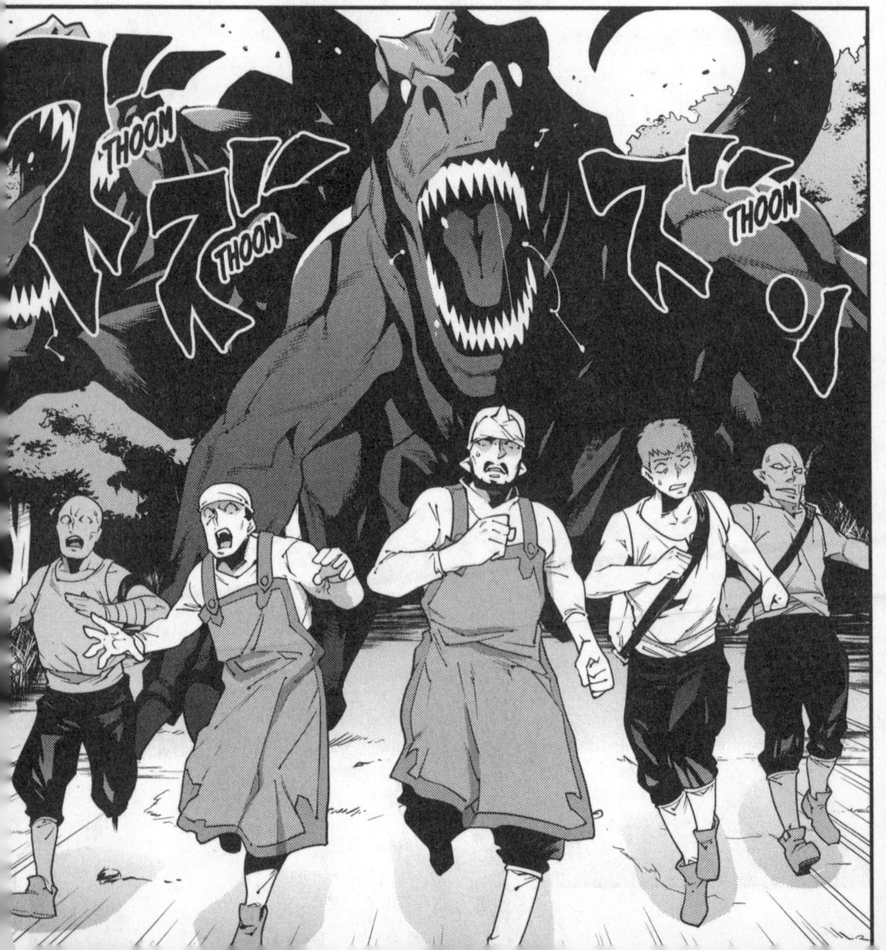
THOOM
THOOM
THOOM

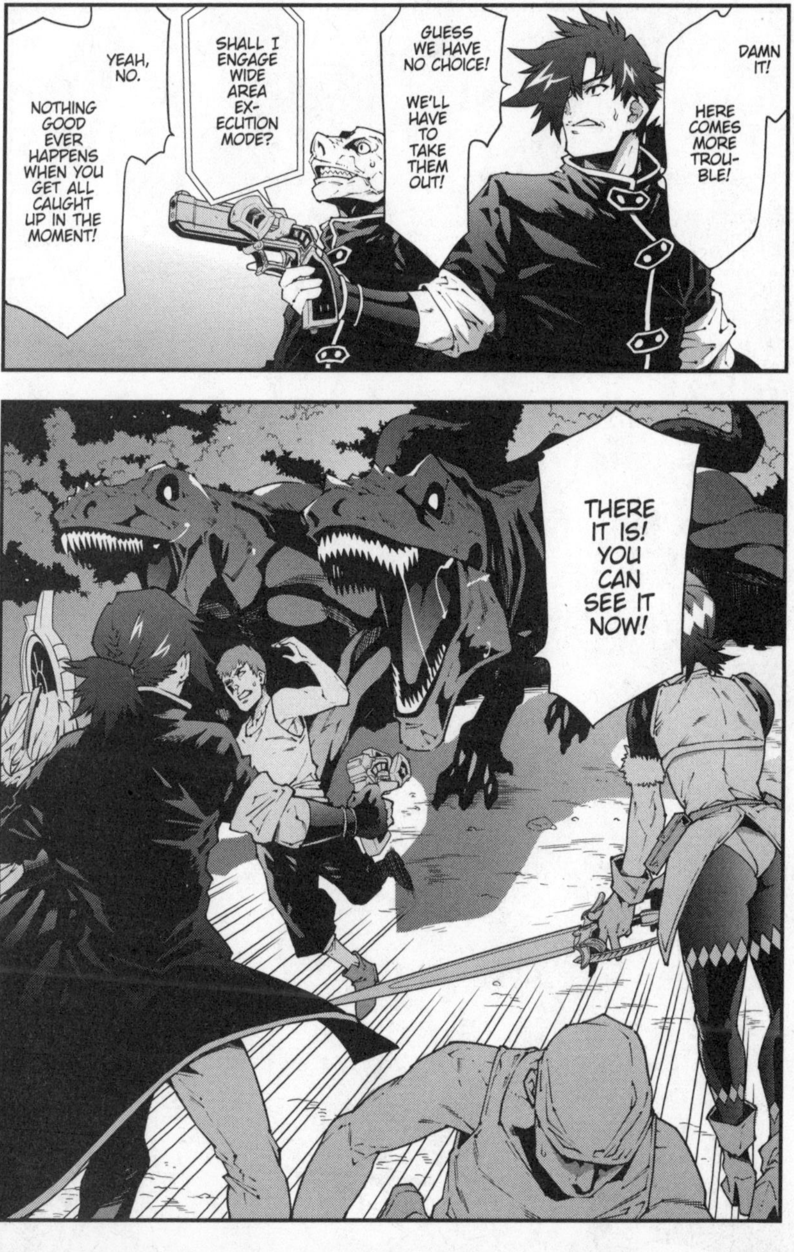
DAMN IT!
HERE COMES MORE TROUBLE!
GUESS WE HAVE NO CHOICE!
WE'LL HAVE TO TAKE THEM OUT!
SHALL I ENGAGE WIDE AREA EXECUTION MODE?
YEAH, NO.
NOTHING GOOD EVER HAPPENS WHEN YOU GET ALL CAUGHT UP IN THE MOMENT!
THERE IT IS! YOU CAN SEE IT NOW!

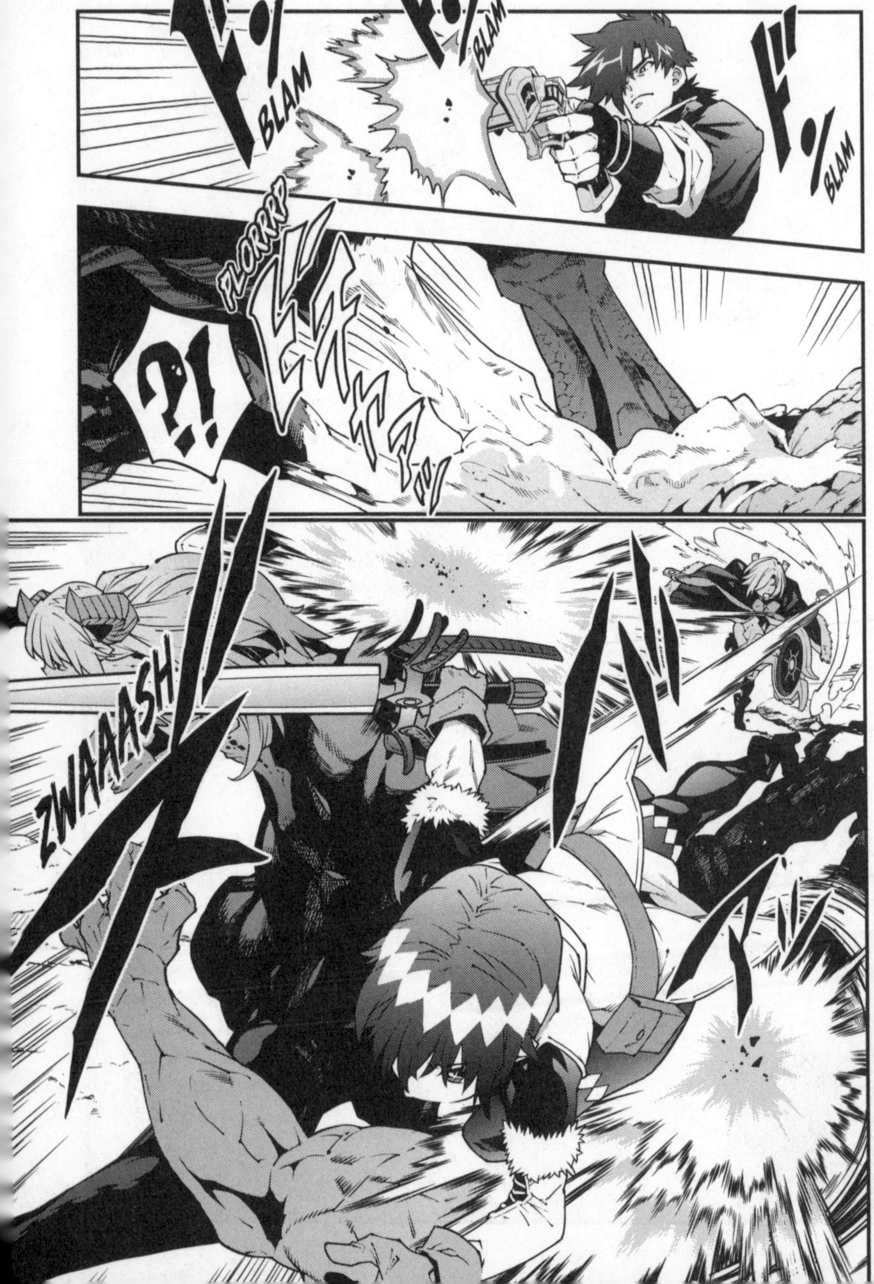
BLAM
BLAM
BLAM
PLORRRP
?!
ZWAAASH

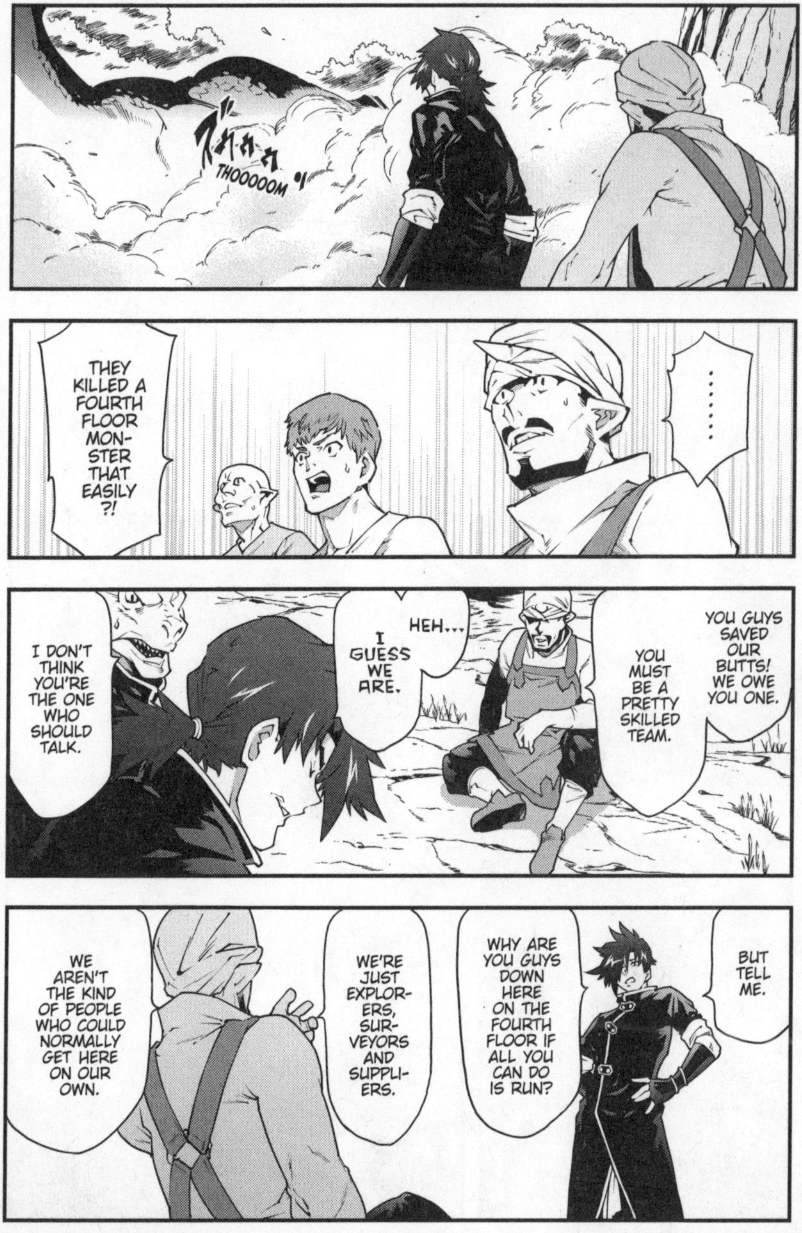
THOOOOM
......
THEY KILLED A FOURTH FLOOR MON-STER THAT EASILY?!
YOU GUYS SAVED OUR BUTTS! WE OWE YOU ONE.
YOU MUST BE A PRETTY SKILLED TEAM.
HEH... I GUESS WE ARE.
I DON'T THINK YOU'RE THE ONE WHO SHOULD TALK.
BUT TELL ME.
WHY ARE YOU GUYS DOWN HERE ON THE FOURTH FLOOR IF ALL YOU CAN DO IS RUN?
WE'RE JUST EXPLOR-ERS, SUR-VEYORS AND SUPPLI-ERS.
WE AREN'T THE KIND OF PEOPLE WHO COULD NORMALLY GET HERE ON OUR OWN.

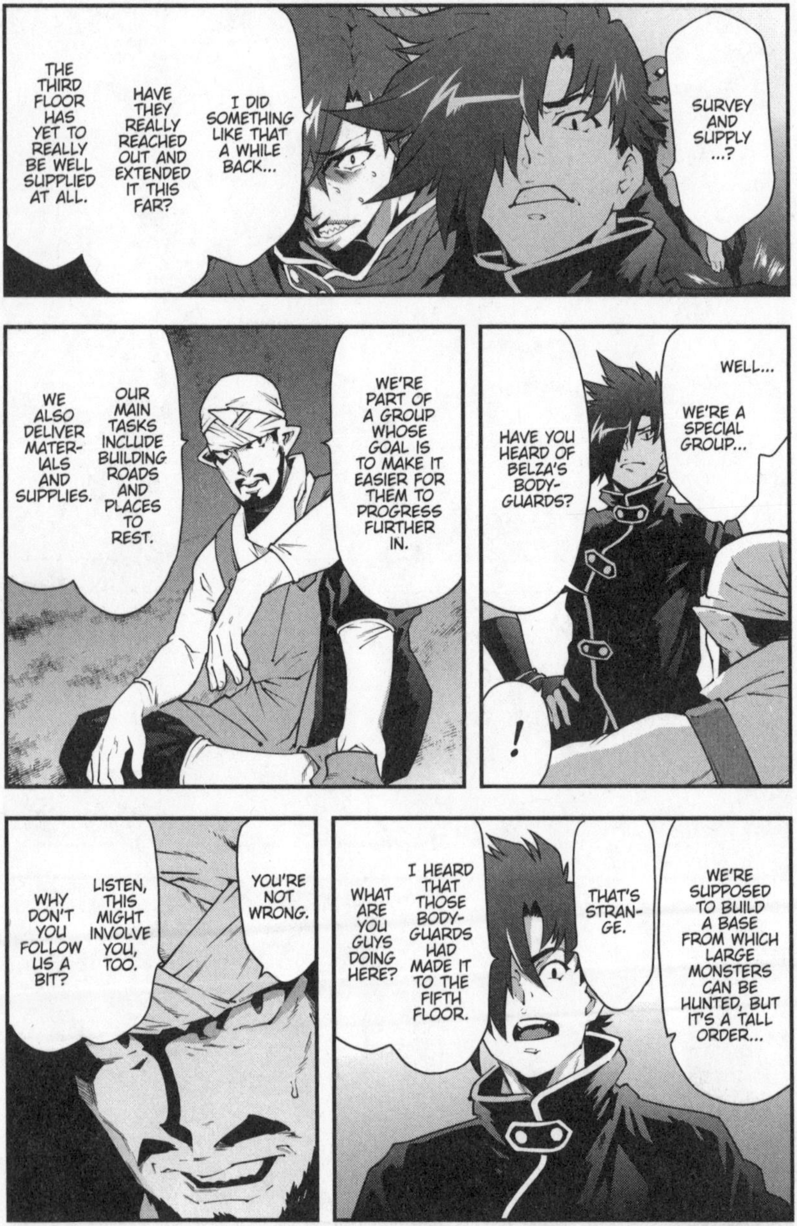
SURVEY AND SUPPLY ...?
I DID SOMETHING LIKE THAT A WHILE BACK...
HAVE THEY REALLY REACHED OUT AND EXTENDED IT THIS FAR?
THE THIRD FLOOR HAS YET TO REALLY BE WELL SUPPLIED AT ALL.
WELL...
WE'RE A SPECIAL GROUP...
HAVE YOU HEARD OF BELZA'S BODY-GUARDS?
!
WE'RE PART OF A GROUP WHOSE GOAL IS TO MAKE IT EASIER FOR THEM TO PROGRESS FURTHER IN.
OUR MAIN TASKS INCLUDE BUILDING ROADS AND PLACES TO REST.
WE ALSO DELIVER MATER-IALS AND SUPPLIES.
WE'RE SUPPOSED TO BUILD A BASE FROM WHICH LARGE MONSTERS CAN BE HUNTED, BUT IT'S A TALL ORDER...
THAT'S STRAN-GE.
I HEARD THAT THOSE BODY-GUARDS HAD MADE IT TO THE FIFTH FLOOR.
WHAT ARE YOU GUYS DOING HERE?
YOU'RE NOT WRONG.
LISTEN, THIS MIGHT INVOLVE YOU, TOO.
WHY DON'T YOU FOLLOW US A BIT?

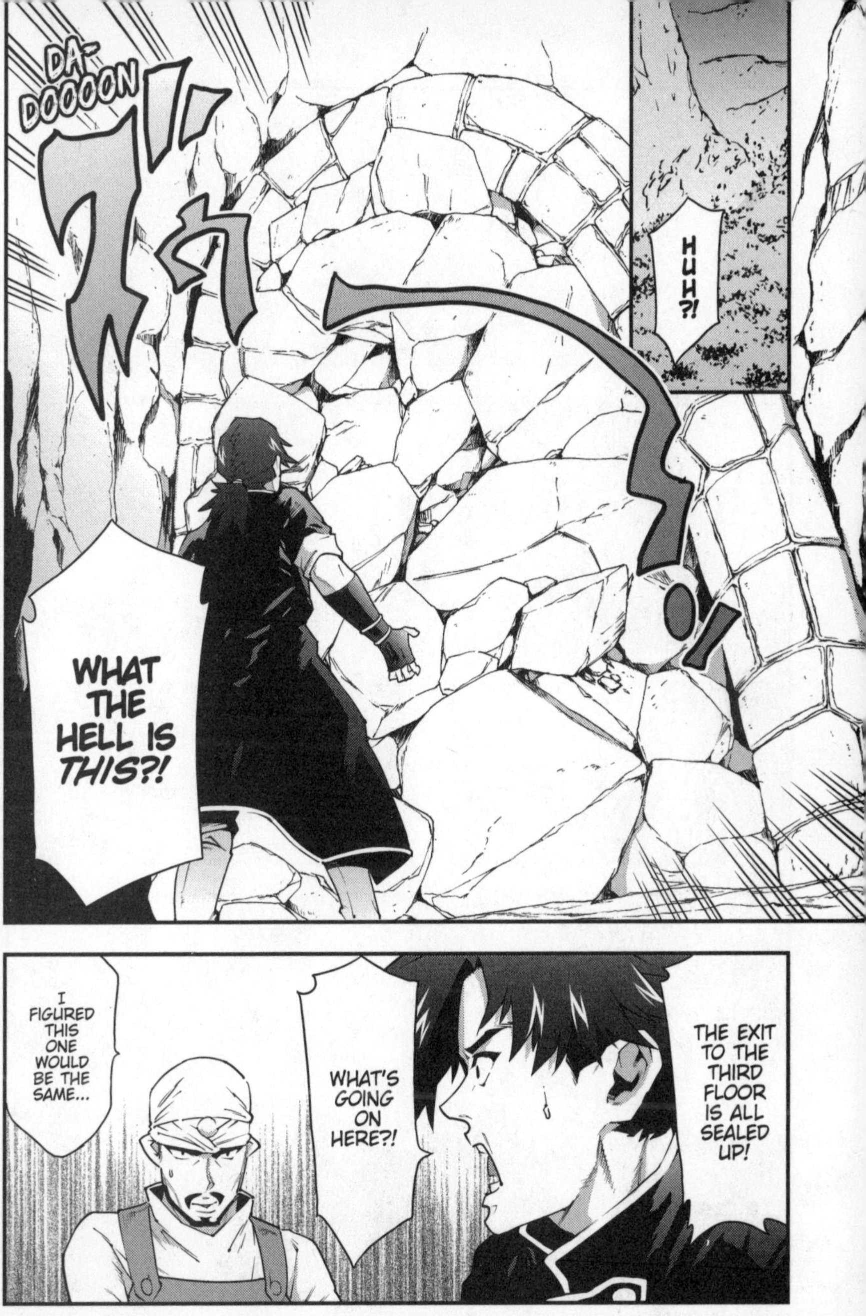
HUH?!
DA-DOOOON
WHAT THE HELL IS *THIS?!*
THE EXIT TO THE THIRD FLOOR IS ALL SEALED UP!
WHAT'S GOING ON HERE?!
I FIGURED THIS ONE WOULD BE THE SAME...

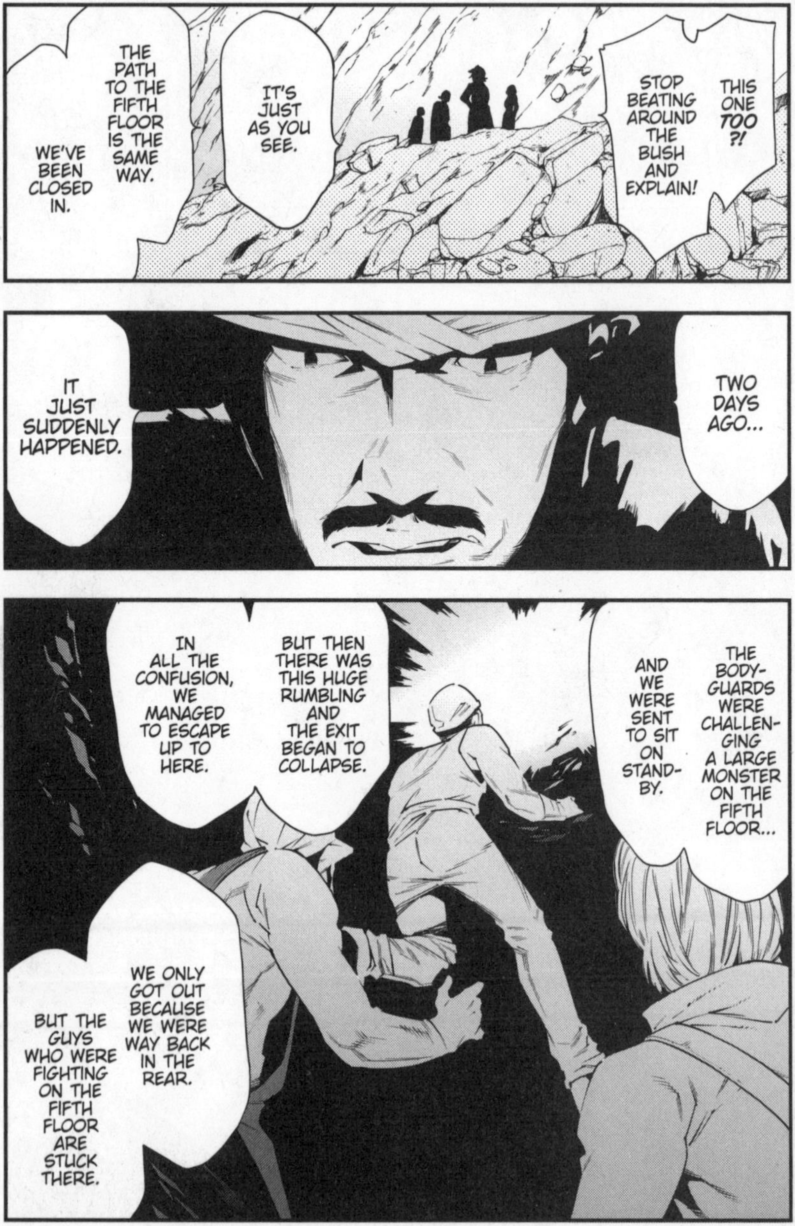
THIS ONE TOO?!
STOP BEATING AROUND THE BUSH AND EXPLAIN!
IT'S JUST AS YOU SEE.
THE PATH TO THE FIFTH FLOOR IS THE SAME WAY.
WE'VE BEEN CLOSED IN.
TWO DAYS AGO...
IT JUST SUDDENLY HAPPENED.
THE BODYGUARDS WERE CHALLENGING A LARGE MONSTER ON THE FIFTH FLOOR...
AND WE WERE SENT TO SIT ON STANDBY.
BUT THEN THERE WAS THIS HUGE RUMBLING AND THE EXIT BEGAN TO COLLAPSE.
IN ALL THE CONFUSION, WE MANAGED TO ESCAPE UP TO HERE.
WE ONLY GOT OUT BECAUSE WE WERE WAY BACK IN THE REAR.
BUT THE GUYS WHO WERE FIGHTING ON THE FIFTH FLOOR ARE STUCK THERE.

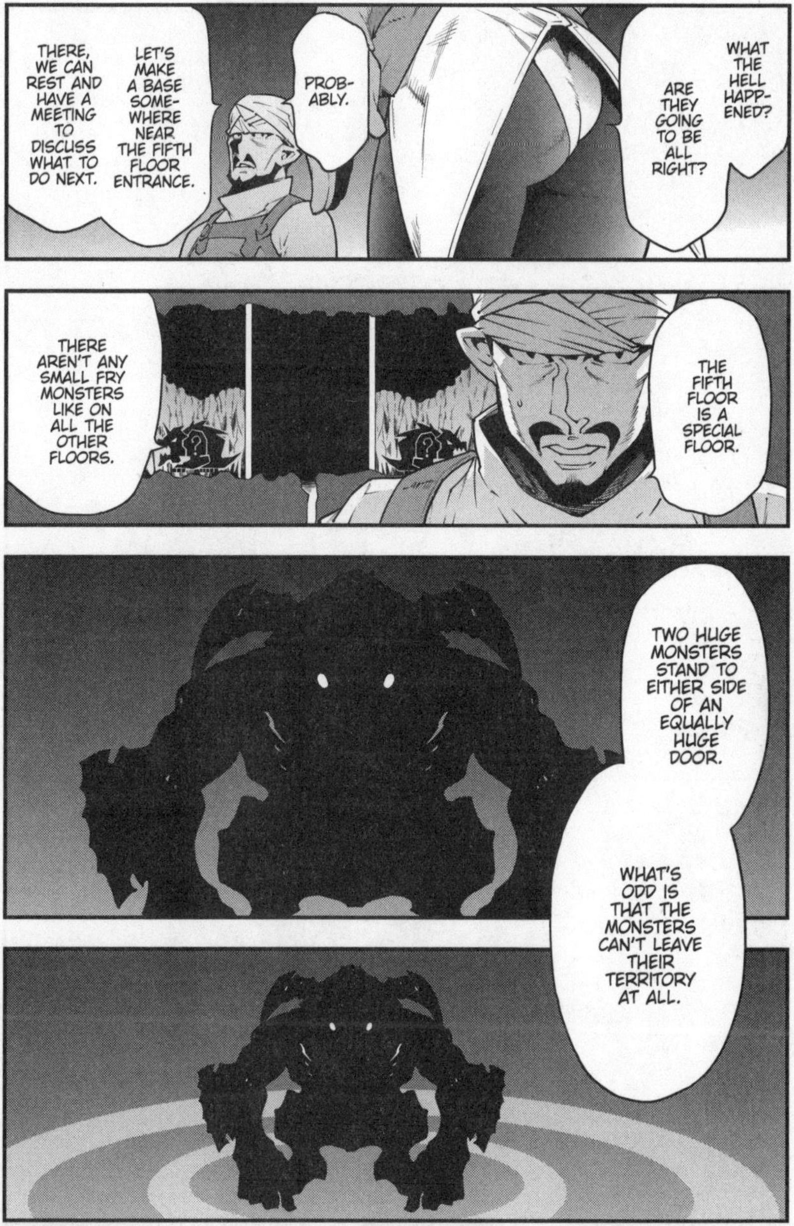
WHAT THE HELL HAPPENED?
ARE THEY GOING TO BE ALL RIGHT?
PROBABLY.
LET'S MAKE A BASE SOMEWHERE NEAR THE FIFTH FLOOR ENTRANCE.
THERE, WE CAN REST AND HAVE A MEETING TO DISCUSS WHAT TO DO NEXT.
THE FIFTH FLOOR IS A SPECIAL FLOOR.
THERE AREN'T ANY SMALL FRY MONSTERS LIKE ON ALL THE OTHER FLOORS.
TWO HUGE MONSTERS STAND TO EITHER SIDE OF AN EQUALLY HUGE DOOR.
WHAT'S ODD IS THAT THE MONSTERS CAN'T LEAVE THEIR TERRITORY AT ALL.

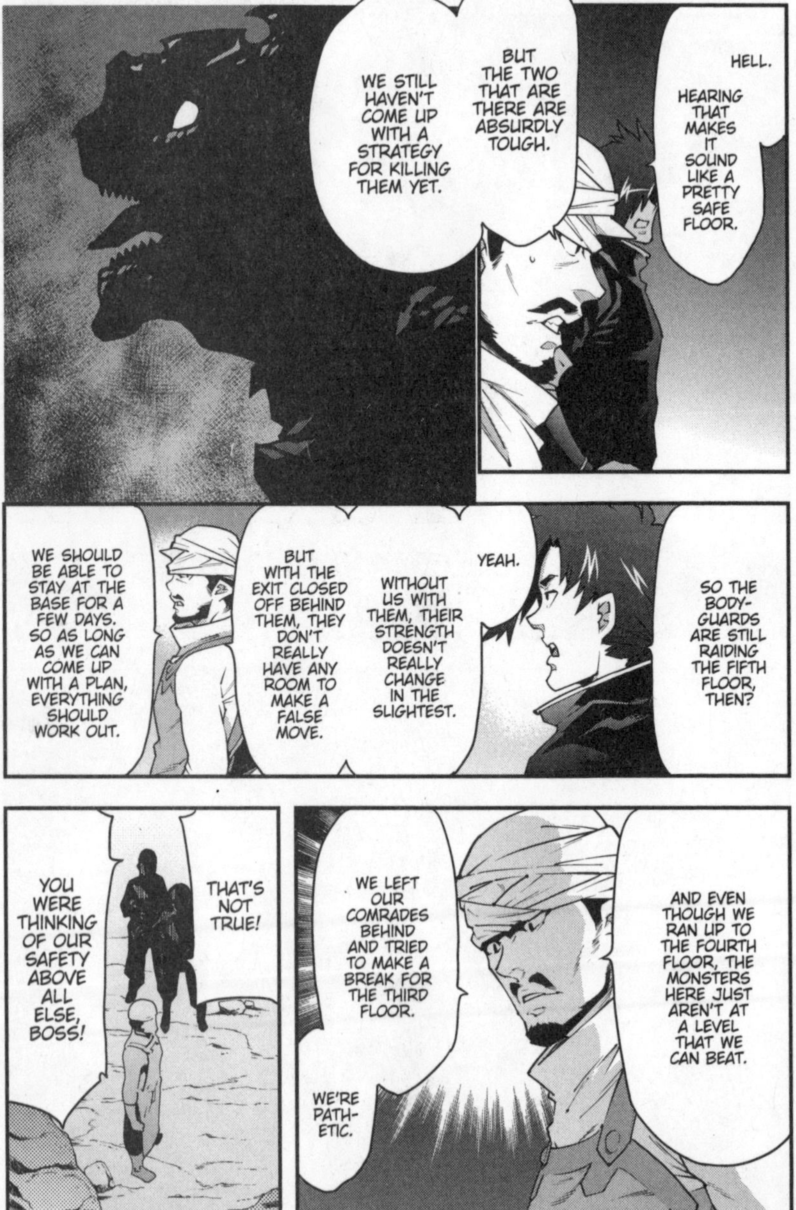
HELL.
HEARING THAT MAKES IT SOUND LIKE A PRETTY SAFE FLOOR.
BUT THE TWO THAT ARE THERE ARE ABSURDLY TOUGH.
WE STILL HAVEN'T COME UP WITH A STRATEGY FOR KILLING THEM YET.
SO THE BODY-GUARDS ARE STILL RAIDING THE FIFTH FLOOR, THEN?
YEAH.
WITHOUT US WITH THEM, THEIR STRENGTH DOESN'T REALLY CHANGE IN THE SLIGHTEST.
BUT WITH THE EXIT CLOSED OFF BEHIND THEM, THEY DON'T REALLY HAVE ANY ROOM TO MAKE A FALSE MOVE.
WE SHOULD BE ABLE TO STAY AT THE BASE FOR A FEW DAYS. SO AS LONG AS WE CAN COME UP WITH A PLAN, EVERYTHING SHOULD WORK OUT.
AND EVEN THOUGH WE RAN UP TO THE FOURTH FLOOR, THE MONSTERS HERE JUST AREN'T AT A LEVEL THAT WE CAN BEAT.
WE LEFT OUR COMRADES BEHIND AND TRIED TO MAKE A BREAK FOR THE THIRD FLOOR.
WE'RE PATH-ETIC.
THAT'S NOT TRUE!
YOU WERE THINKING OF OUR SAFETY ABOVE ALL ELSE, BOSS!

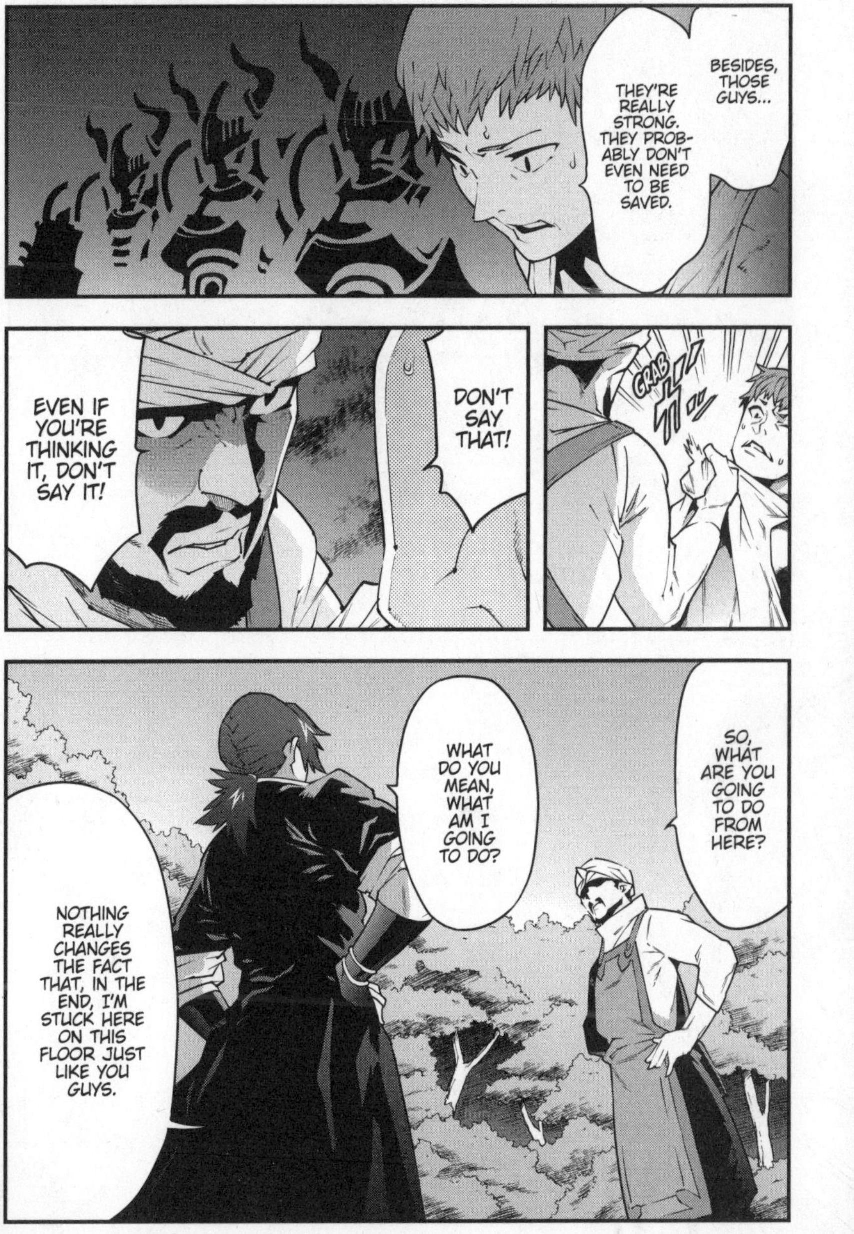
BESIDES, THOSE GUYS...
THEY'RE REALLY STRONG. THEY PROB-ABLY DON'T EVEN NEED TO BE SAVED.
GRAB
DON'T SAY THAT!
EVEN IF YOU'RE THINKING IT, DON'T SAY IT!
SO, WHAT ARE YOU GOING TO DO FROM HERE?
WHAT DO YOU MEAN, WHAT AM I GOING TO DO?
NOTHING REALLY CHANGES THE FACT THAT, IN THE END, I'M STUCK HERE ON THIS FLOOR JUST LIKE YOU GUYS.

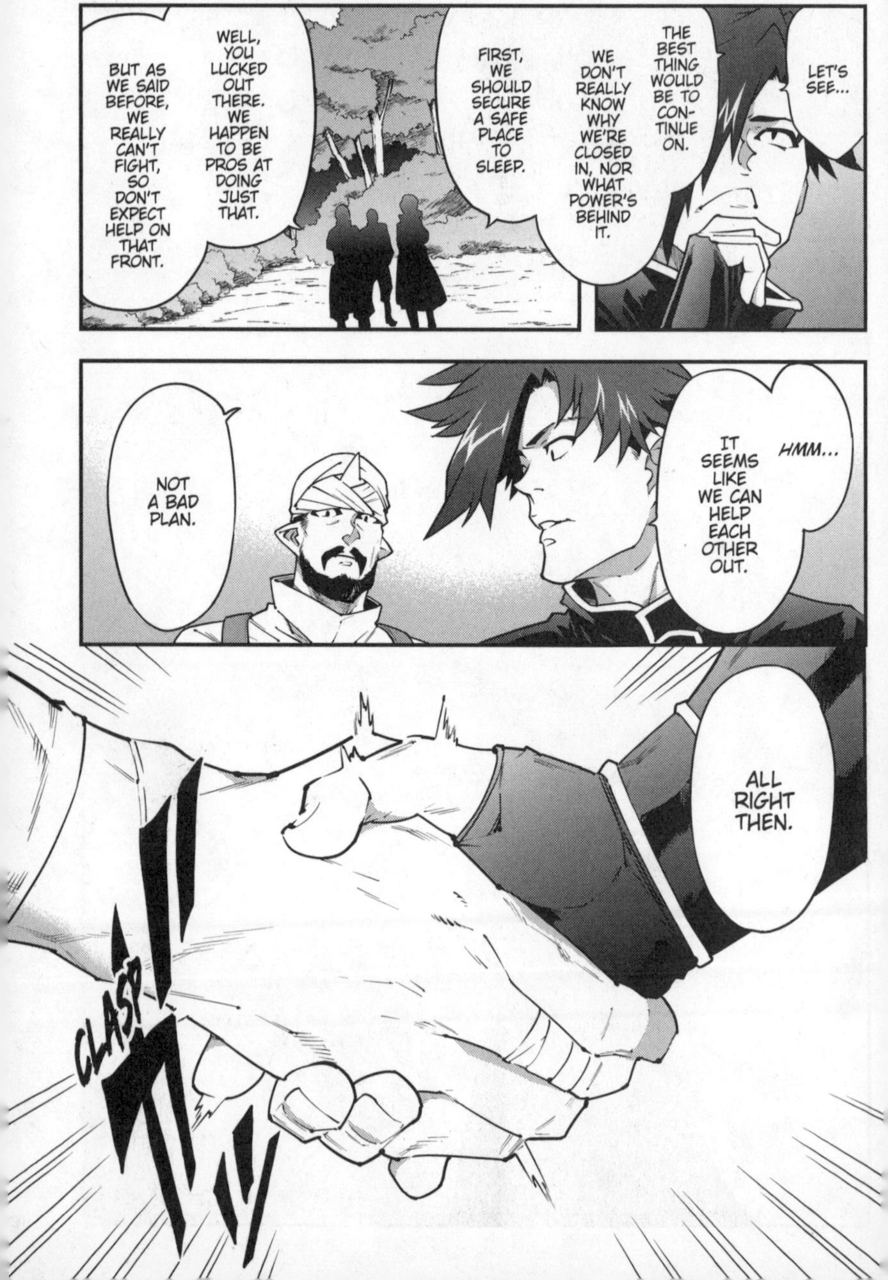
LET'S SEE...
THE BEST THING WOULD BE TO CON-TINUE ON.
WE DON'T REALLY KNOW WHY WE'RE CLOSED IN, NOR WHAT POWER'S BEHIND IT.
FIRST, WE SHOULD SECURE A SAFE PLACE TO SLEEP.
WELL, YOU LUCKED OUT THERE. WE HAPPEN TO BE PROS AT DOING JUST THAT.
BUT AS WE SAID BEFORE, WE REALLY CAN'T FIGHT, SO DON'T EXPECT HELP ON THAT FRONT.
HMM...
IT SEEMS LIKE WE CAN HELP EACH OTHER OUT.
NOT A BAD PLAN.
ALL RIGHT THEN.
CLASP

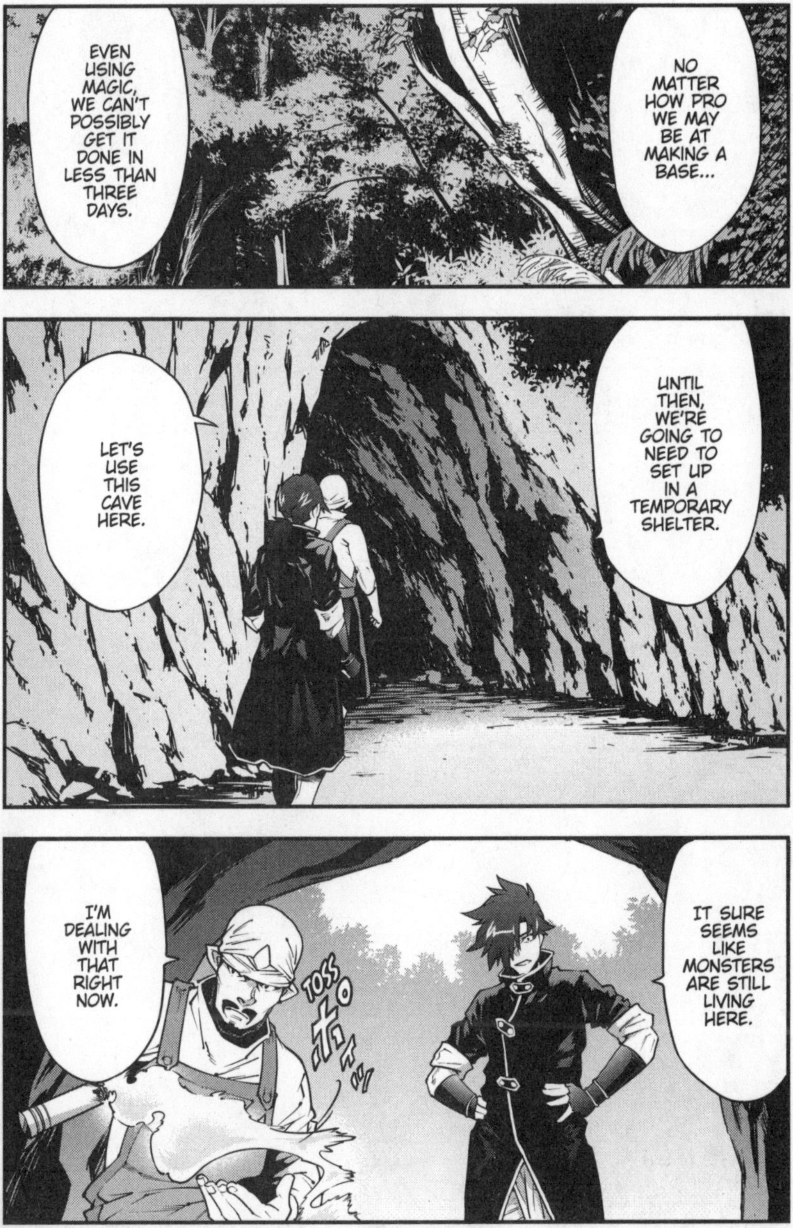
NO MATTER HOW PRO WE MAY BE AT MAKING A BASE...
EVEN USING MAGIC, WE CAN'T POSSIBLY GET IT DONE IN LESS THAN THREE DAYS.
UNTIL THEN, WE'RE GOING TO NEED TO SET UP IN A TEMPORARY SHELTER.
LET'S USE THIS CAVE HERE.
IT SURE SEEMS LIKE MONSTERS ARE STILL LIVING HERE.
I'M DEALING WITH THAT RIGHT NOW.
TOSS

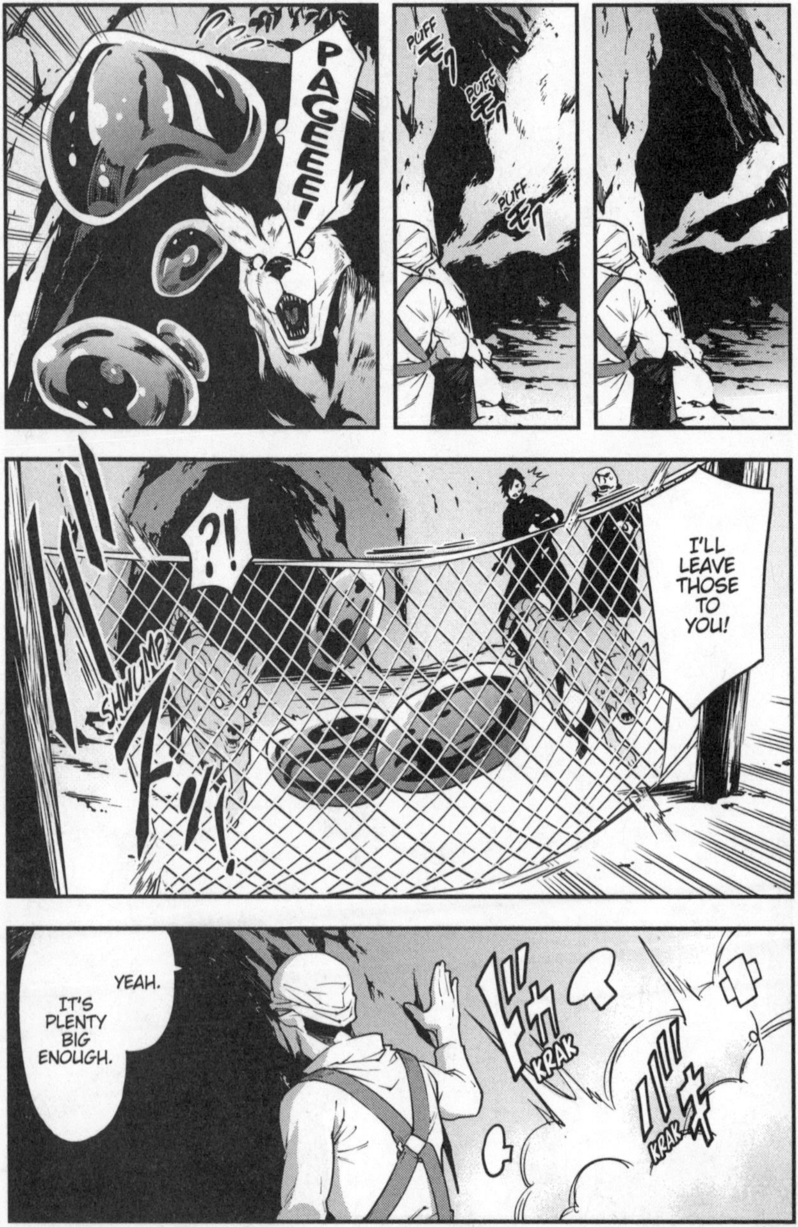

PUFF
PUFF
PUFF
PAGEEE!
I'LL LEAVE THOSE TO YOU!
?!
SHWUMP
KRAK
KRAK
YEAH.
IT'S PLENTY BIG ENOUGH.

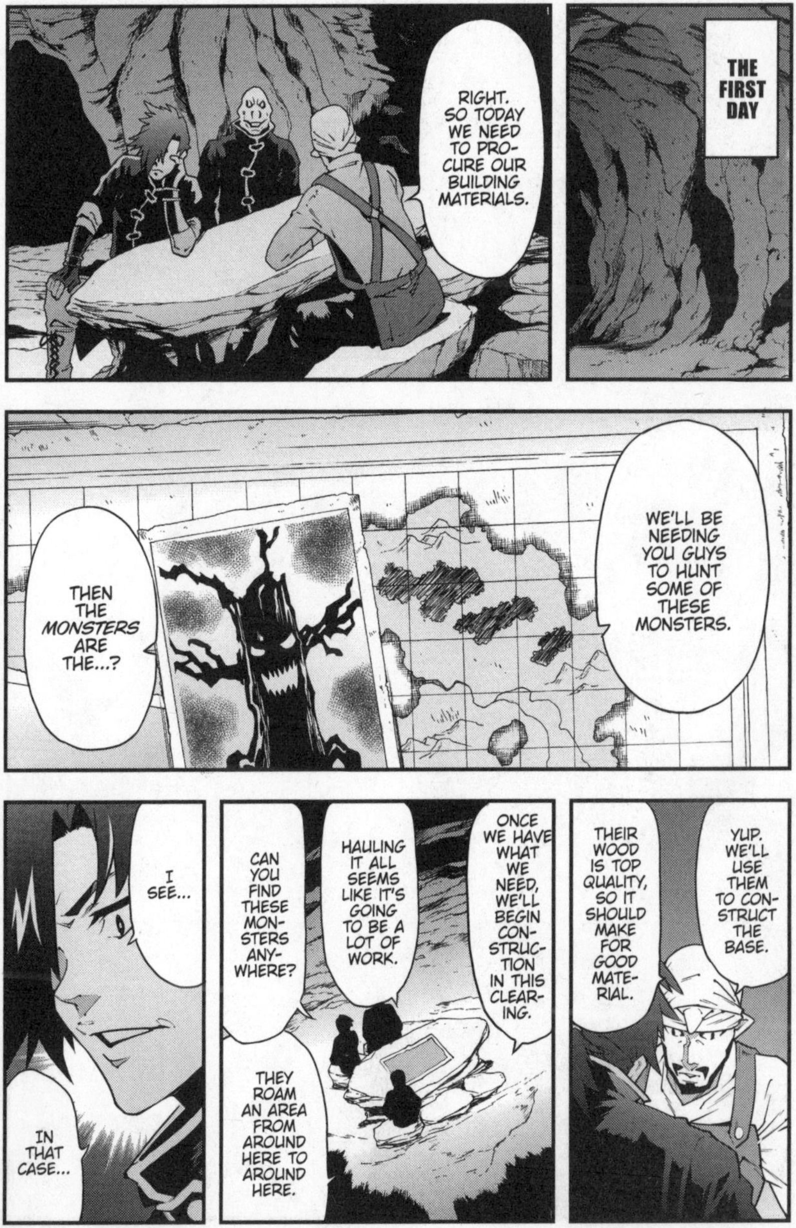
THE FIRST DAY
RIGHT. SO TODAY WE NEED TO PROCURE OUR BUILDING MATERIALS.
WE'LL BE NEEDING YOU GUYS TO HUNT SOME OF THESE MONSTERS.
THEN THE *MONSTERS* ARE THE...?
YUP. WE'LL USE THEM TO CONSTRUCT THE BASE.
THEIR WOOD IS TOP QUALITY, SO IT SHOULD MAKE FOR GOOD MATERIAL.
ONCE WE HAVE WHAT WE NEED, WE'LL BEGIN CONSTRUCTION IN THIS CLEARING.
HAULING IT ALL SEEMS LIKE IT'S GOING TO BE A LOT OF WORK.
CAN YOU FIND THESE MONSTERS ANYWHERE?
THEY ROAM AN AREA FROM AROUND HERE TO AROUND HERE.
I SEE...
IN THAT CASE...

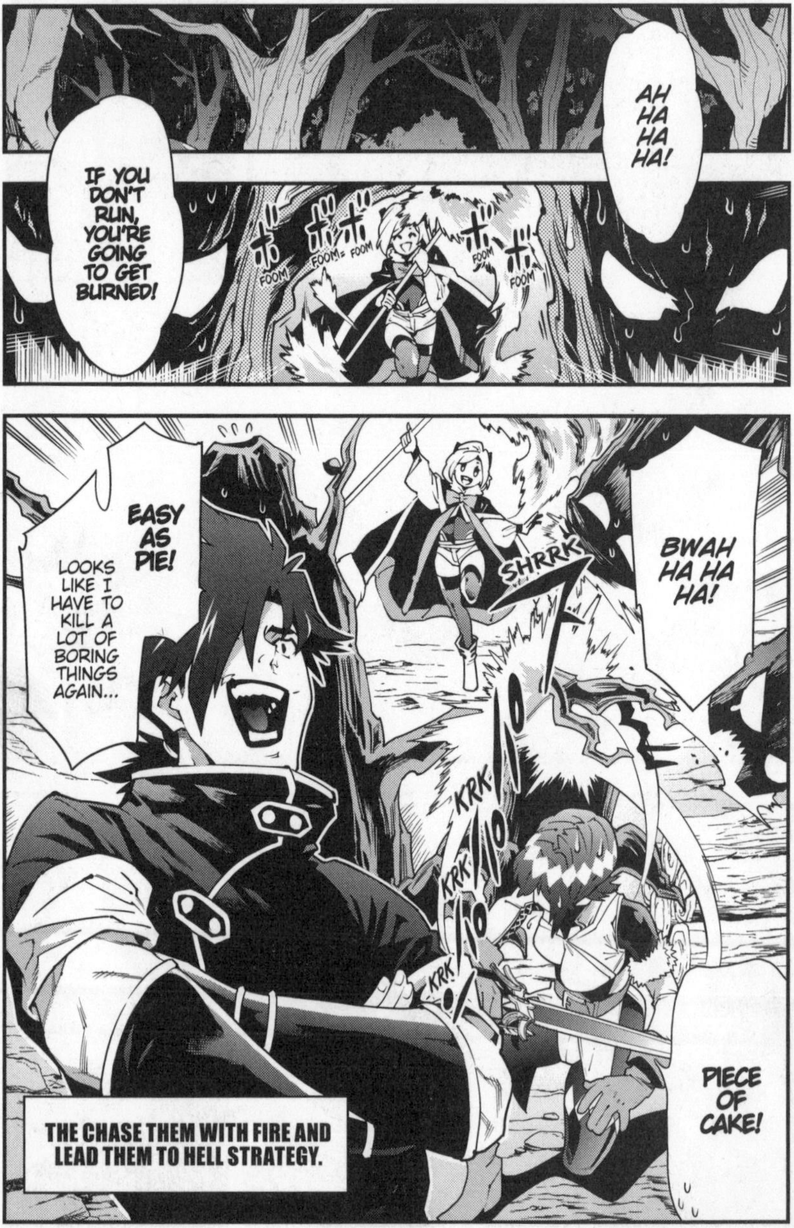
AH HA HA HA!
IF YOU DON'T RUN, YOU'RE GOING TO GET BURNED!
FOOM
FOOM
FOOM
FOOM
FOOM
BWAH HA HA HA!
SHRRK
EASY AS PIE!
LOOKS LIKE I HAVE TO KILL A LOT OF BORING THINGS AGAIN...
KRK
KRK
KRK
PIECE OF CAKE!
THE CHASE THEM WITH FIRE AND LEAD THEM TO HELL STRATEGY.

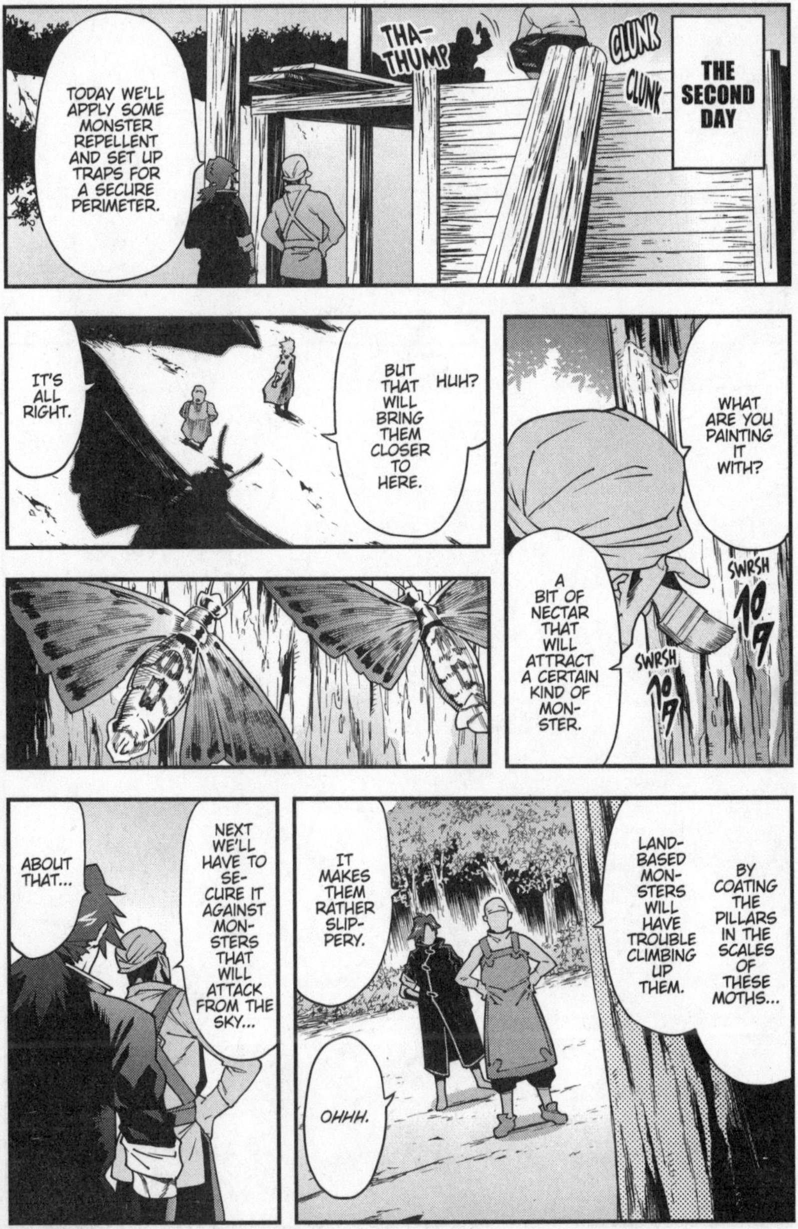
THE SECOND DAY
CLUNK
CLUNK
THA-THUMP
TODAY WE'LL APPLY SOME MONSTER REPELLENT AND SET UP TRAPS FOR A SECURE PERIMETER.
WHAT ARE YOU PAINTING IT WITH?
SWRSH
SWRSH
A BIT OF NECTAR THAT WILL ATTRACT A CERTAIN KIND OF MON-STER.
HUH?
BUT THAT WILL BRING THEM CLOSER TO HERE.
IT'S ALL RIGHT.
BY COATING THE PILLARS IN THE SCALES OF THESE MOTHS...
LAND-BASED MON-STERS WILL HAVE TROUBLE CLIMBING UP THEM.
IT MAKES THEM RATHER SLIP-PERY.
OHHH.
NEXT WE'LL HAVE TO SE-CURE IT AGAINST MON-STERS THAT WILL ATTACK FROM THE SKY...
ABOUT THAT...

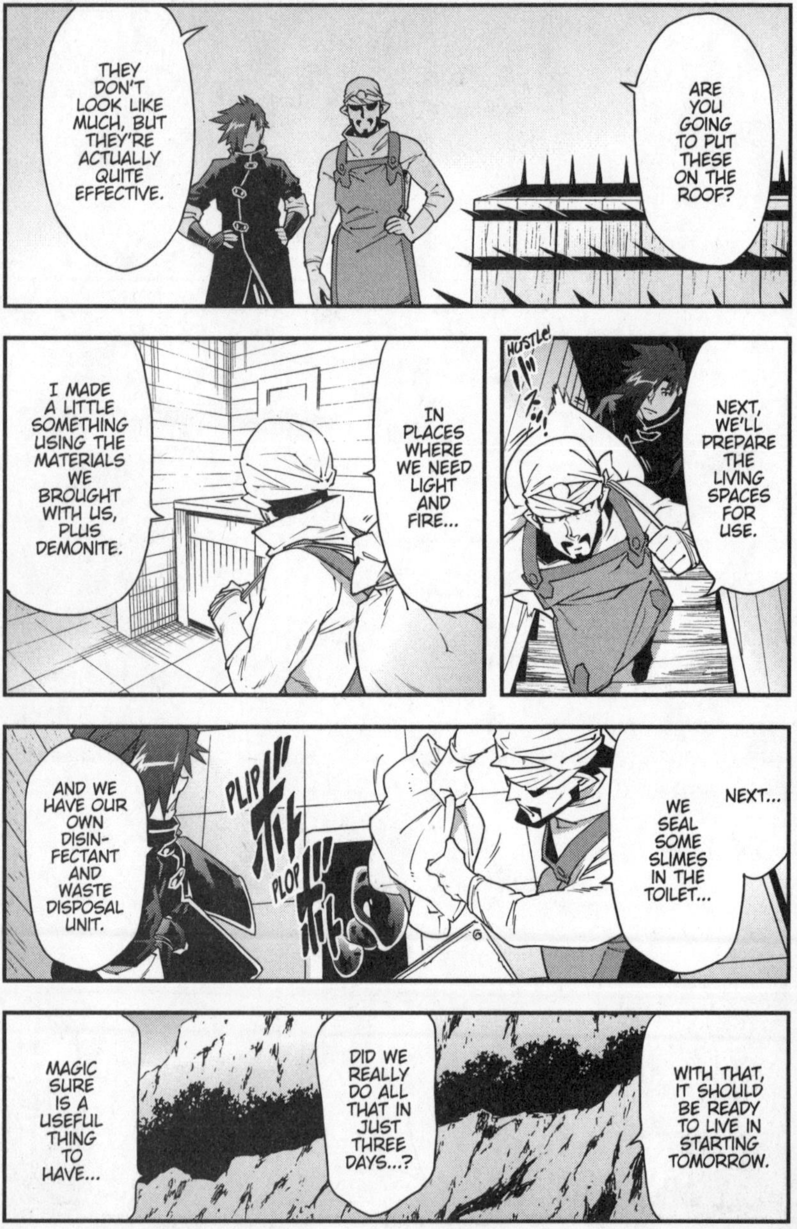
ARE YOU GOING TO PUT THESE ON THE ROOF?
THEY DON'T LOOK LIKE MUCH, BUT THEY'RE ACTUALLY QUITE EFFECTIVE.
HUSTLE!
NEXT, WE'LL PREPARE THE LIVING SPACES FOR USE.
IN PLACES WHERE WE NEED LIGHT AND FIRE...
I MADE A LITTLE SOMETHING USING THE MATERIALS WE BROUGHT WITH US, PLUS DEMONITE.
NEXT...
WE SEAL SOME SLIMES IN THE TOILET...
PLIP
PLOP
AND WE HAVE OUR OWN DISIN-FECTANT AND WASTE DISPOSAL UNIT.
WITH THAT, IT SHOULD BE READY TO LIVE IN STARTING TOMORROW.
DID WE REALLY DO ALL THAT IN JUST THREE DAYS...?
MAGIC SURE IS A USEFUL THING TO HAVE...

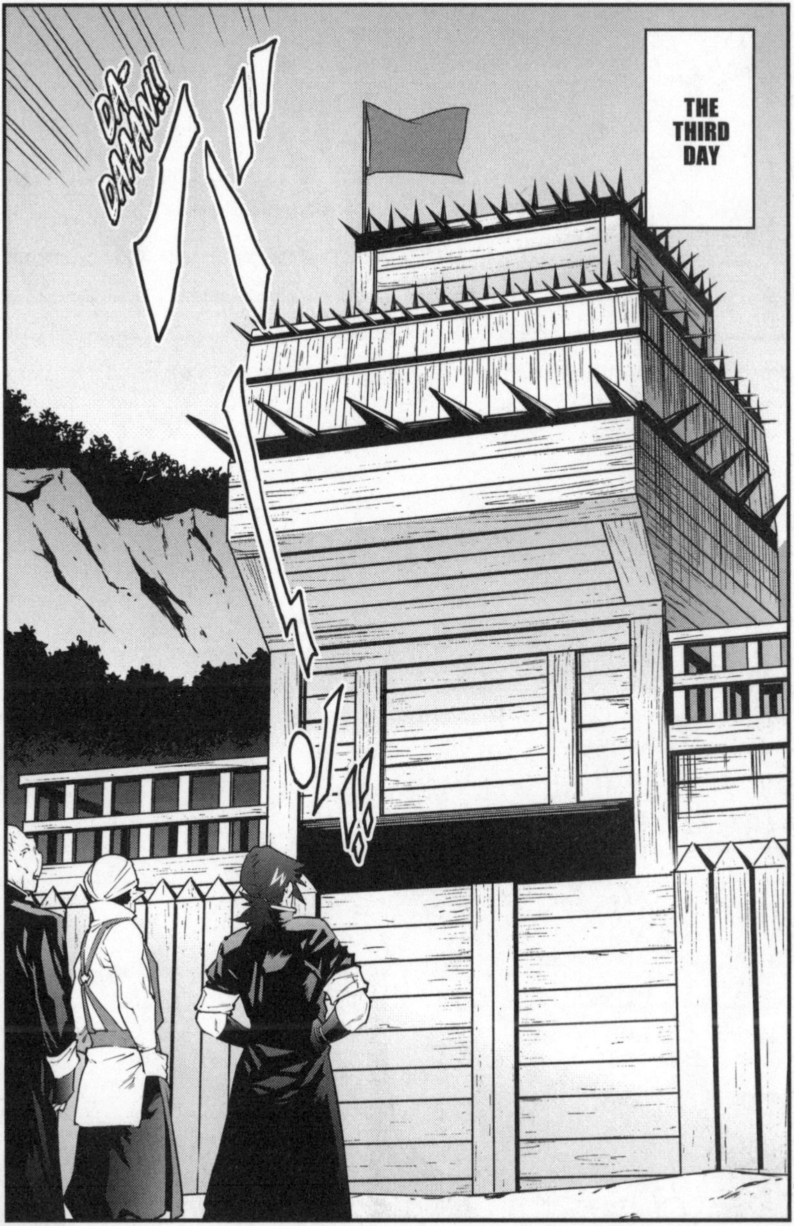
THE THIRD DAY
DA-DAAAN!!

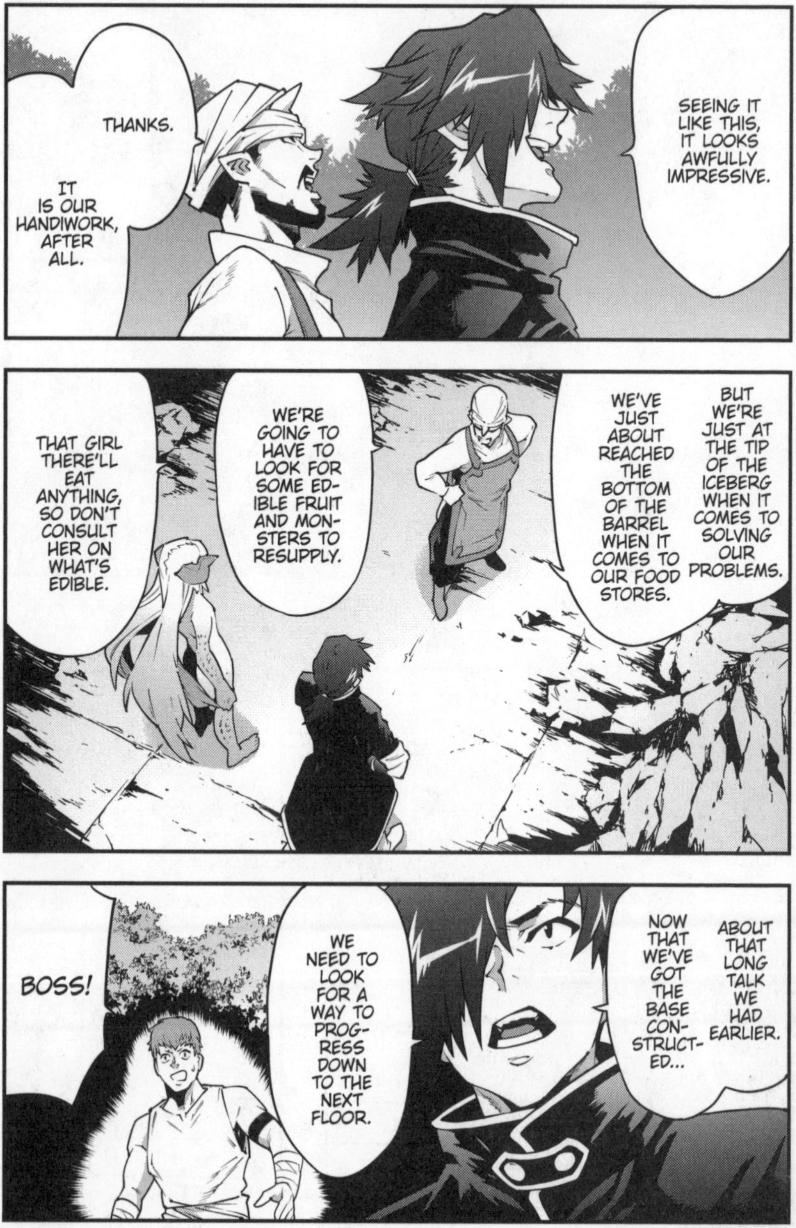
SEEING IT LIKE THIS, IT LOOKS AWFULLY IMPRESSIVE.
THANKS.
IT IS OUR HANDIWORK, AFTER ALL.
BUT WE'RE JUST AT THE TIP OF THE ICEBERG WHEN IT COMES TO SOLVING OUR PROBLEMS.
WE'VE JUST ABOUT REACHED THE BOTTOM OF THE BARREL WHEN IT COMES TO OUR FOOD STORES.
WE'RE GOING TO HAVE TO LOOK FOR SOME EDIBLE FRUIT AND MONSTERS TO RESUPPLY.
THAT GIRL THERE'LL EAT ANYTHING, SO DON'T CONSULT HER ON WHAT'S EDIBLE.
ABOUT THAT LONG TALK WE HAD EARLIER.
NOW THAT WE'VE GOT THE BASE CONSTRUCTED...
WE NEED TO LOOK FOR A WAY TO PROGRESS DOWN TO THE NEXT FLOOR.
BOSS!

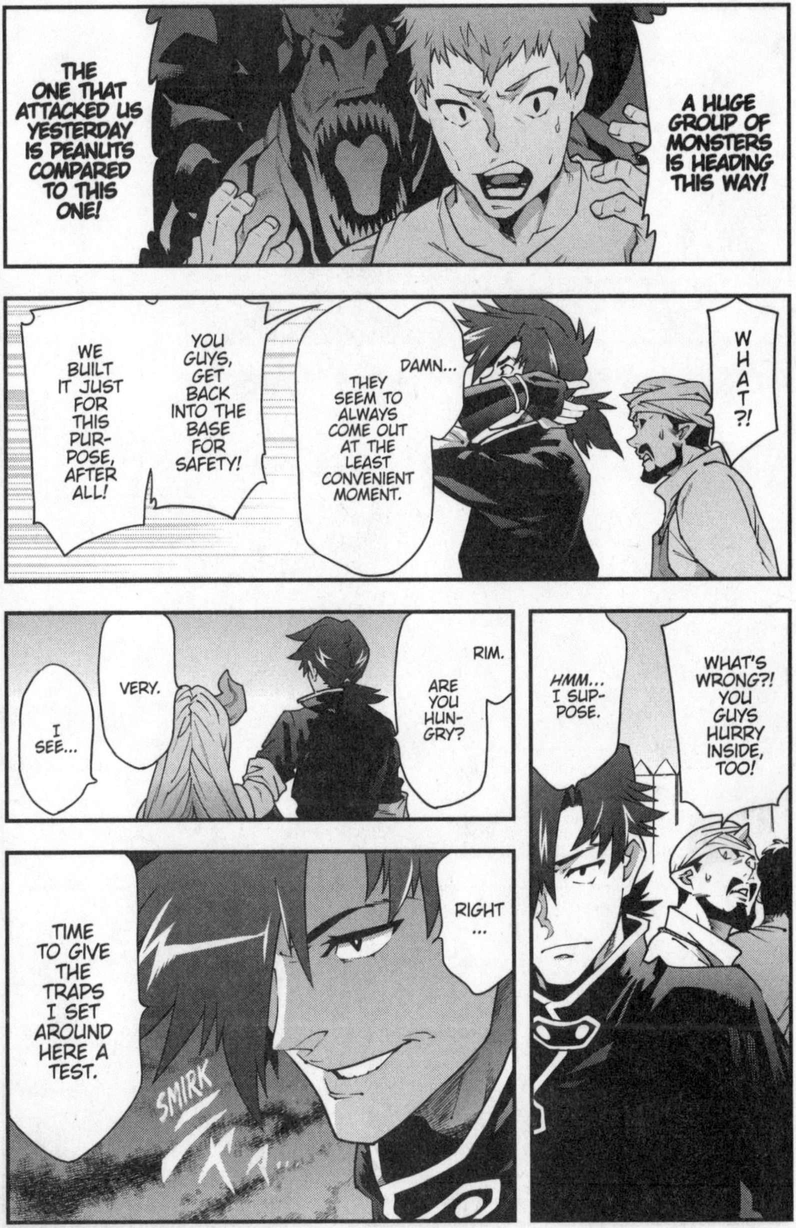
A HUGE GROUP OF MONSTERS IS HEADING THIS WAY!
THE ONE THAT ATTACKED US YESTERDAY IS PEANUTS COMPARED TO THIS ONE!
WHAT?!
DAMN...
THEY SEEM TO ALWAYS COME OUT AT THE LEAST CONVENIENT MOMENT.
YOU GUYS, GET BACK INTO THE BASE FOR SAFETY!
WE BUILT IT JUST FOR THIS PURPOSE, AFTER ALL!
WHAT'S WRONG?! YOU GUYS HURRY INSIDE, TOO!
HMM... I SUPPOSE.
RIM.
ARE YOU HUNGRY?
VERY.
I SEE...
RIGHT...
TIME TO GIVE THE TRAPS I SET AROUND HERE A TEST.
SMIRK

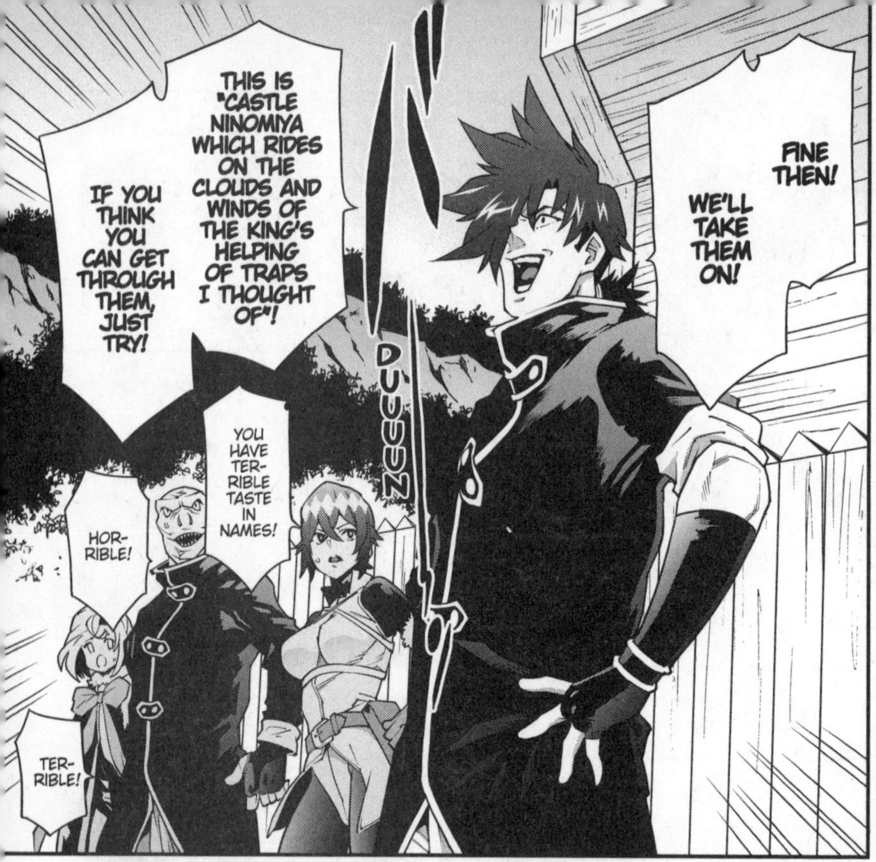
FINE THEN!
WE'LL TAKE THEM ON!
THIS IS "CASTLE NINOMIYA WHICH RIDES ON THE CLOUDS AND WINDS OF THE KING'S HELPING OF TRAPS I THOUGHT OF"!
IF YOU THINK YOU CAN GET THROUGH THEM, JUST TRY!
DUUUN
YOU HAVE TER-RIBLE TASTE IN NAMES!
HOR-RIBLE!
TER-RIBLE!
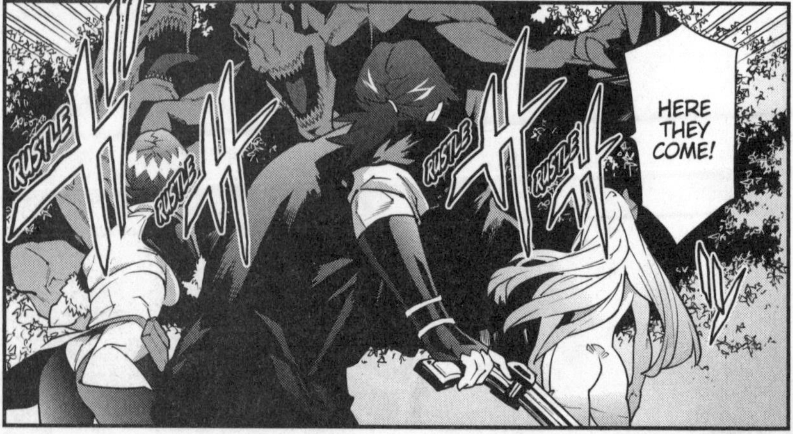
HERE THEY COME!
RUSTLE
RUSTLE
RUSTLE
RUSTLE

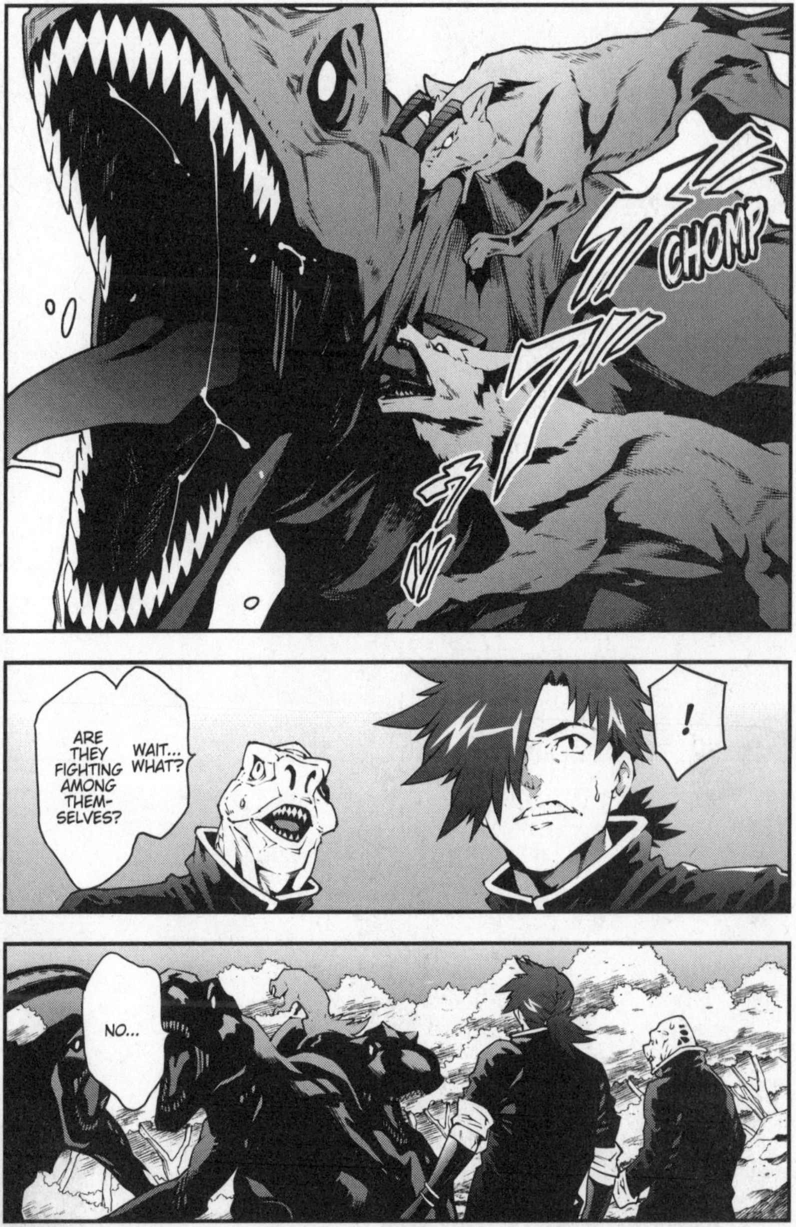
CHOMP
!
WAIT... WHAT?
ARE THEY FIGHTING AMONG THEM-SELVES?
NO...

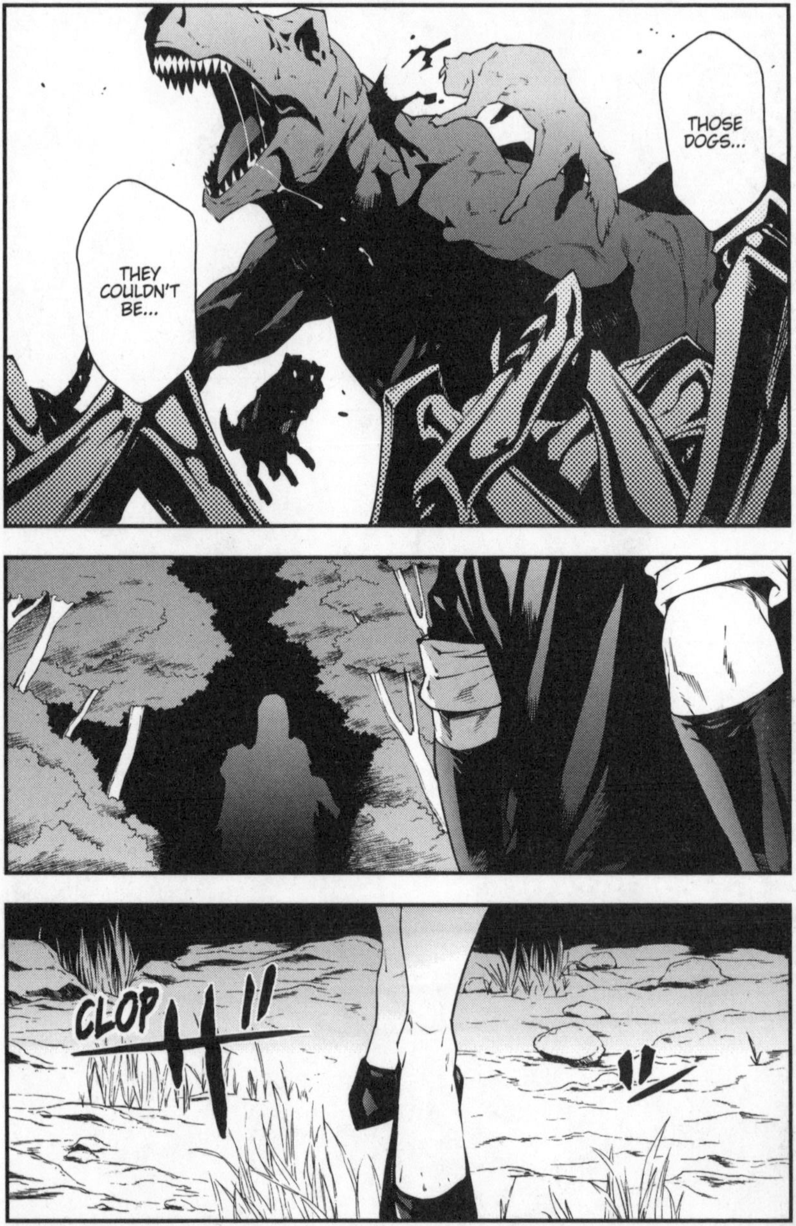
THOSE DOGS...
THEY COULDN'T BE...
CLOP

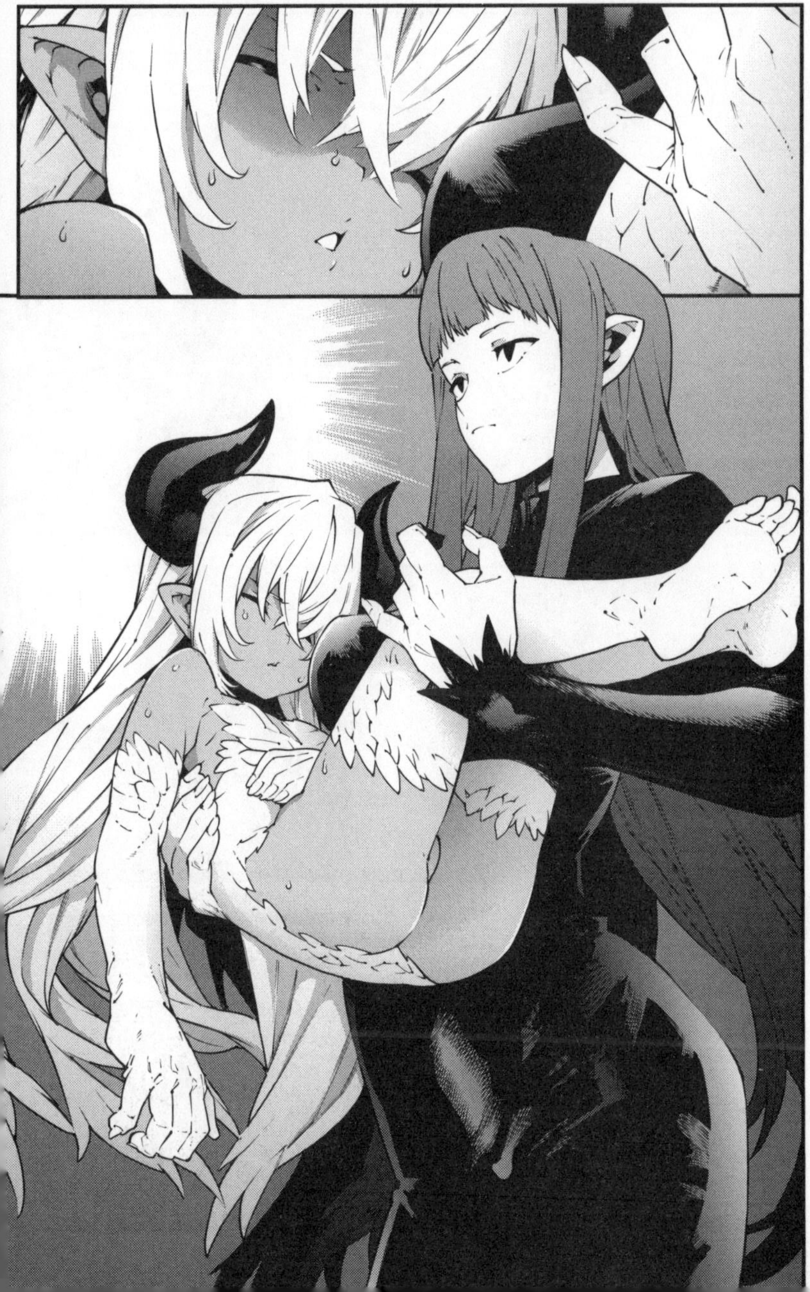

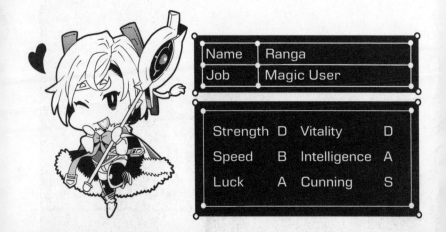

Name	Ranga
Job	Magic User

Strength	D	Vitality	D
Speed	B	Intelligence	A
Luck	A	Cunning	S

THE DUNGEON OF
BLACK COMPANY

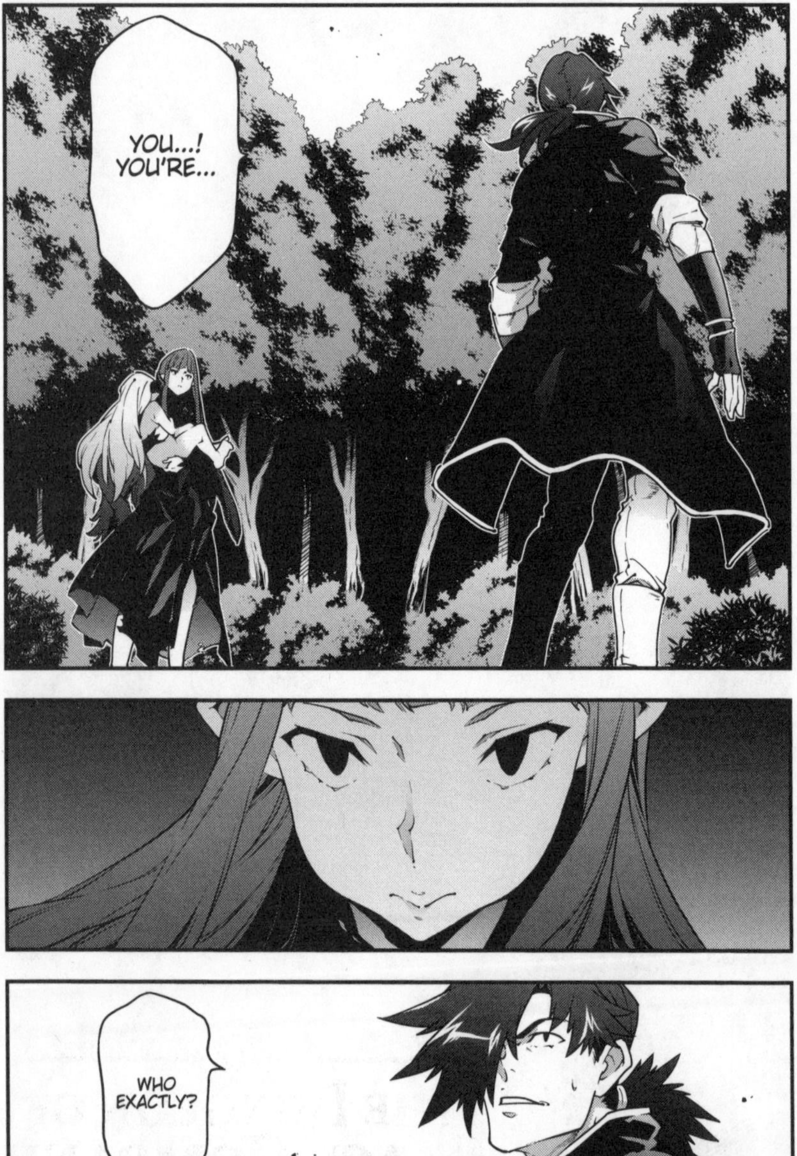
YOU...! YOU'RE...
WHO EXACTLY?

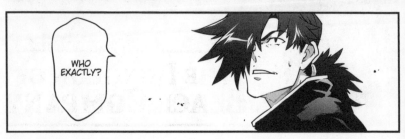

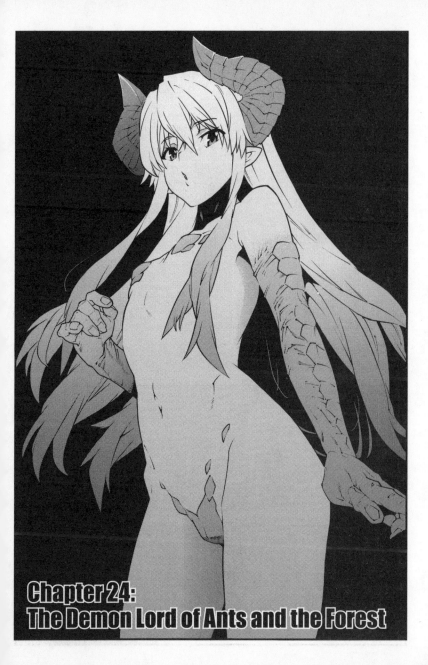

Chapter 24:
The Demon Lord of Ants and the Forest

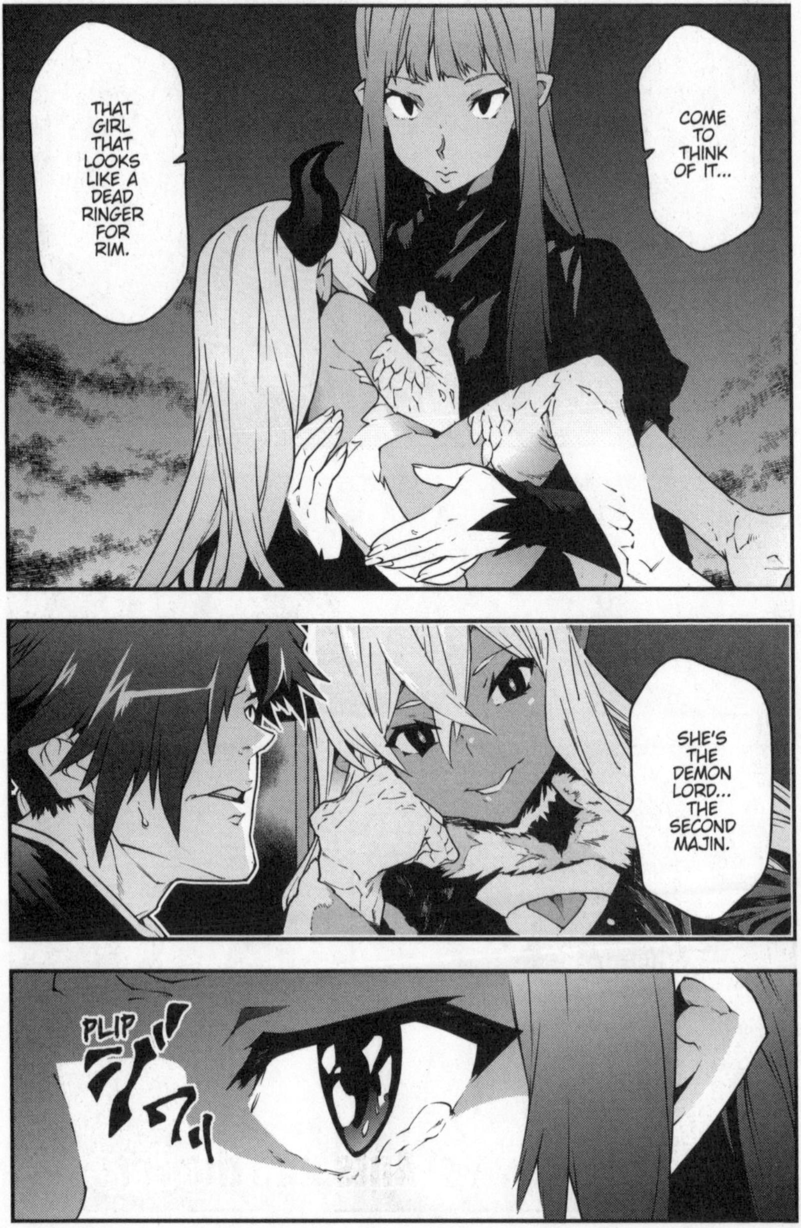
COME TO THINK OF IT...
THAT GIRL THAT LOOKS LIKE A DEAD RINGER FOR RIM.
SHE'S THE DEMON LORD... THE SECOND MAJIN.
PLIP

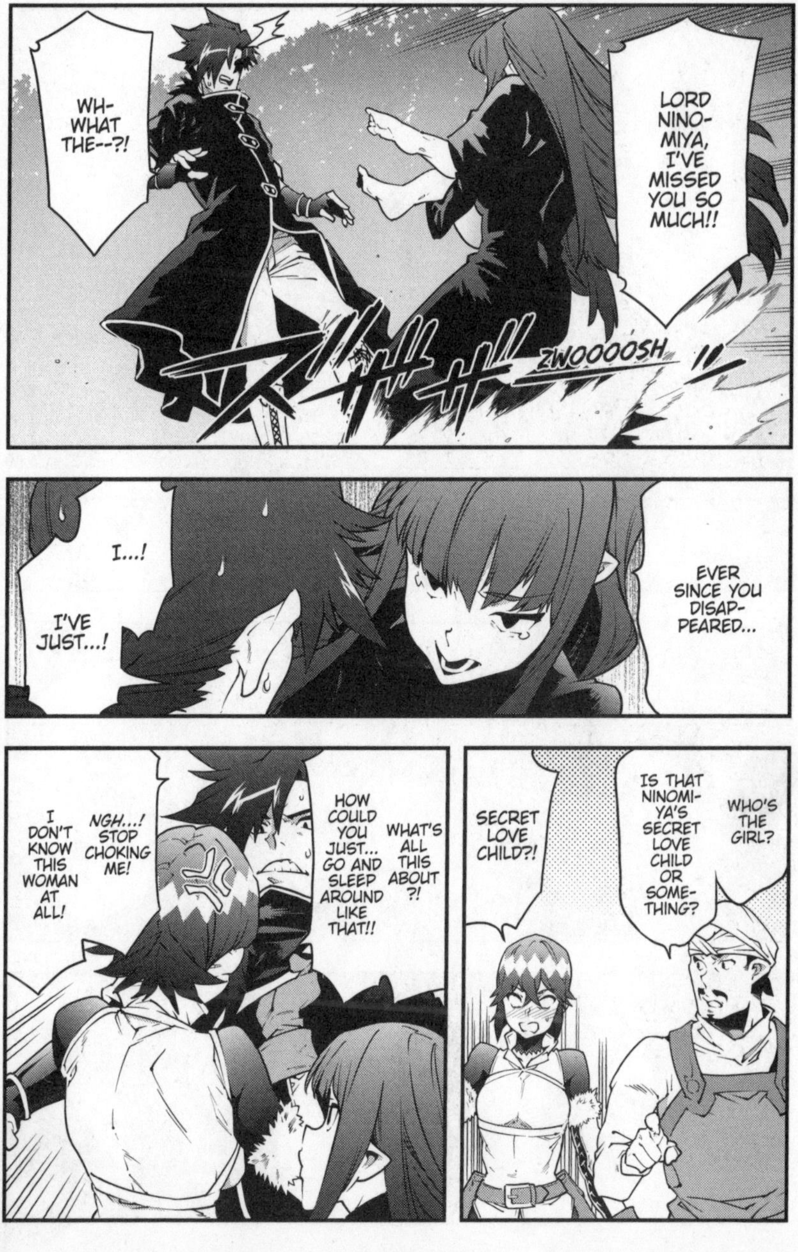
LORD NINOMIYA, I'VE MISSED YOU SO MUCH!!
WH-WHAT THE--?!
ZWOOOOSH
EVER SINCE YOU DISAPPEARED...
I...!
I'VE JUST...!
WHO'S THE GIRL?
IS THAT NINOMIYA'S SECRET LOVE CHILD OR SOMETHING?
SECRET LOVE CHILD?!
WHAT'S ALL THIS ABOUT?!
HOW COULD YOU JUST... GO AND SLEEP AROUND LIKE THAT!!
NGH...! STOP CHOKING ME!
I DON'T KNOW THIS WOMAN AT ALL!

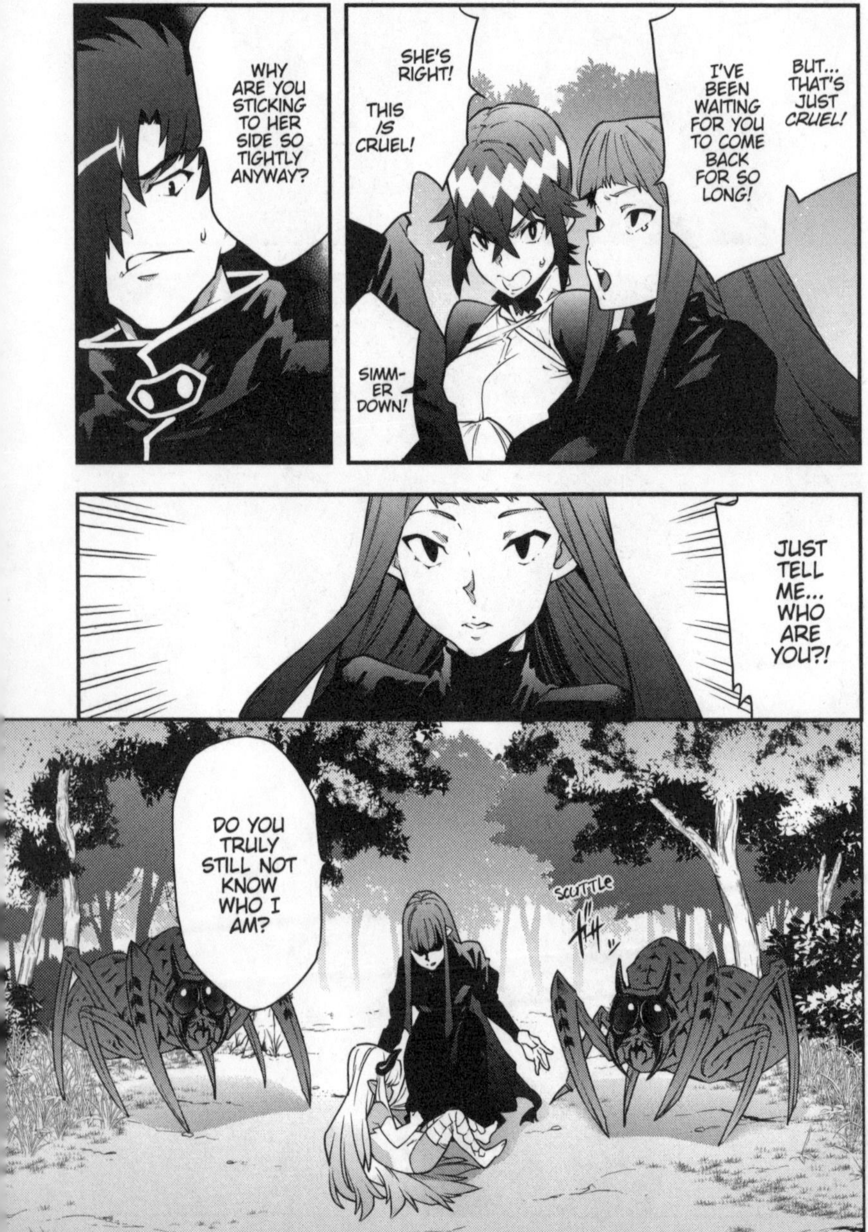
BUT... THAT'S JUST CRUEL!
I'VE BEEN WAITING FOR YOU TO COME BACK FOR SO LONG!
SHE'S RIGHT!
THIS IS CRUEL!
SIMMER-DOWN!
WHY ARE YOU STICKING TO HER SIDE SO TIGHTLY ANYWAY?
JUST TELL ME... WHO ARE YOU?!
DO YOU TRULY STILL NOT KNOW WHO I AM?
SCUTTLE

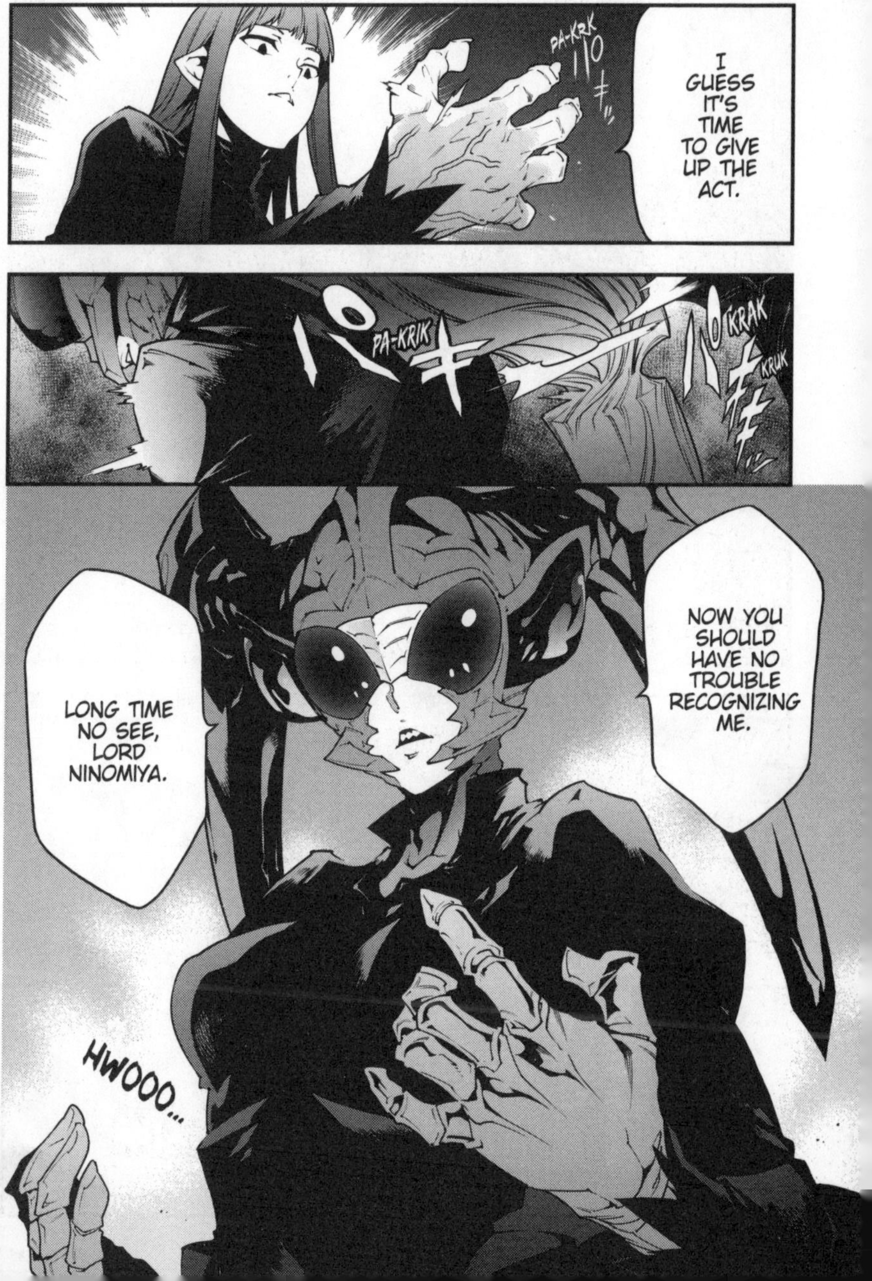
I GUESS IT'S TIME TO GIVE UP THE ACT.
PA-KRK
KRAK
KRUK
PA-KRIK
NOW YOU SHOULD HAVE NO TROUBLE RECOGNIZING ME.
LONG TIME NO SEE, LORD NINOMIYA.
HWOOO...

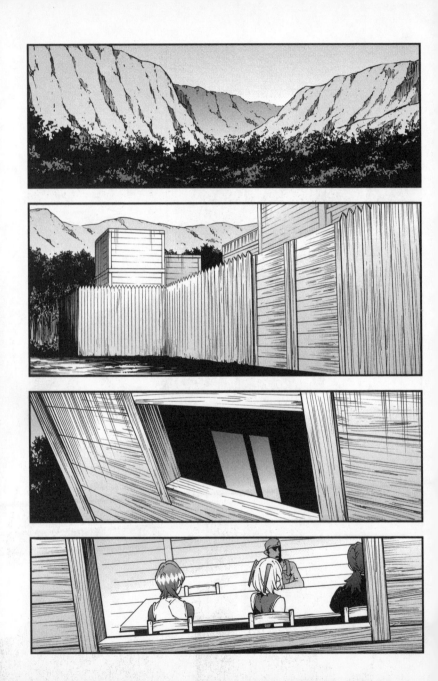

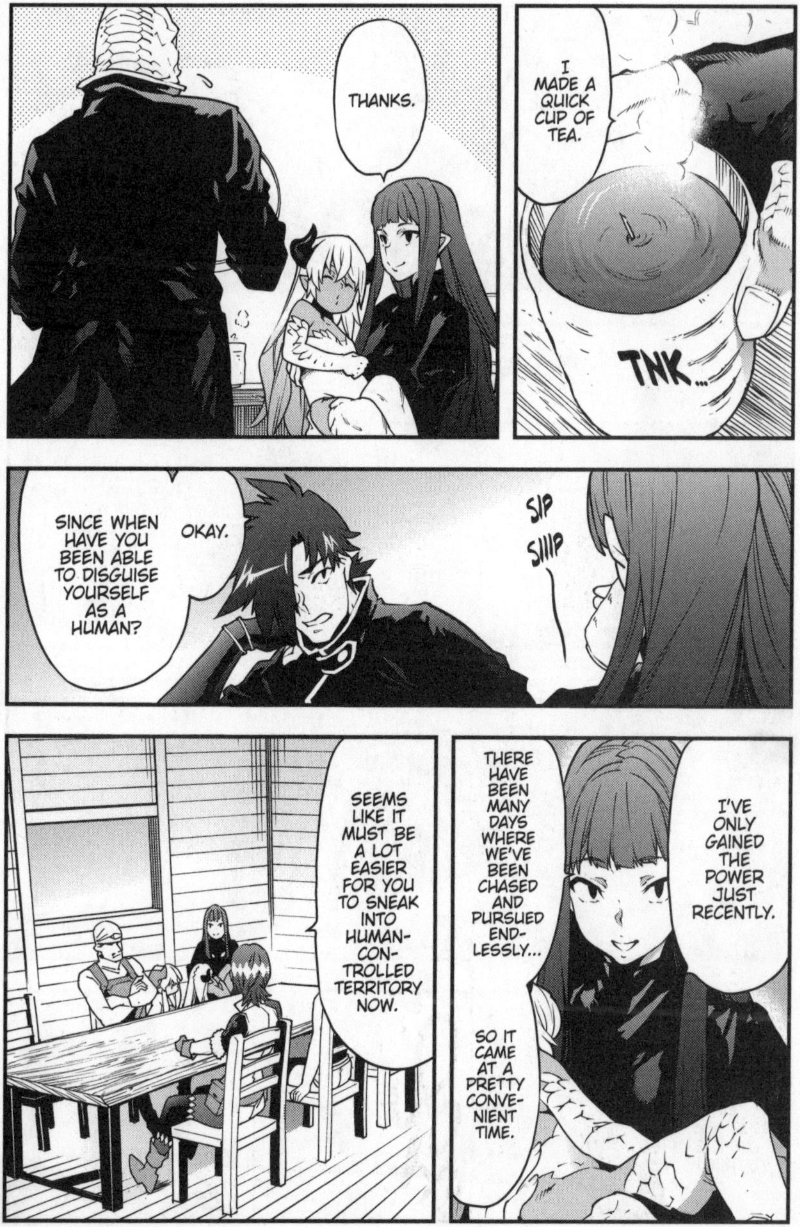
I MADE A QUICK CUP OF TEA.
TNK...
THANKS.
SIP
SIIIP
OKAY.
SINCE WHEN HAVE YOU BEEN ABLE TO DISGUISE YOURSELF AS A HUMAN?
I'VE ONLY GAINED THE POWER JUST RECENTLY.
THERE HAVE BEEN MANY DAYS WHERE WE'VE BEEN CHASED AND PURSUED END-LESSLY...
SO IT CAME AT A PRETTY CONVE-NIENT TIME.
SEEMS LIKE IT MUST BE A LOT EASIER FOR YOU TO SNEAK INTO HUMAN-CON-TROLLED TERRITORY NOW.

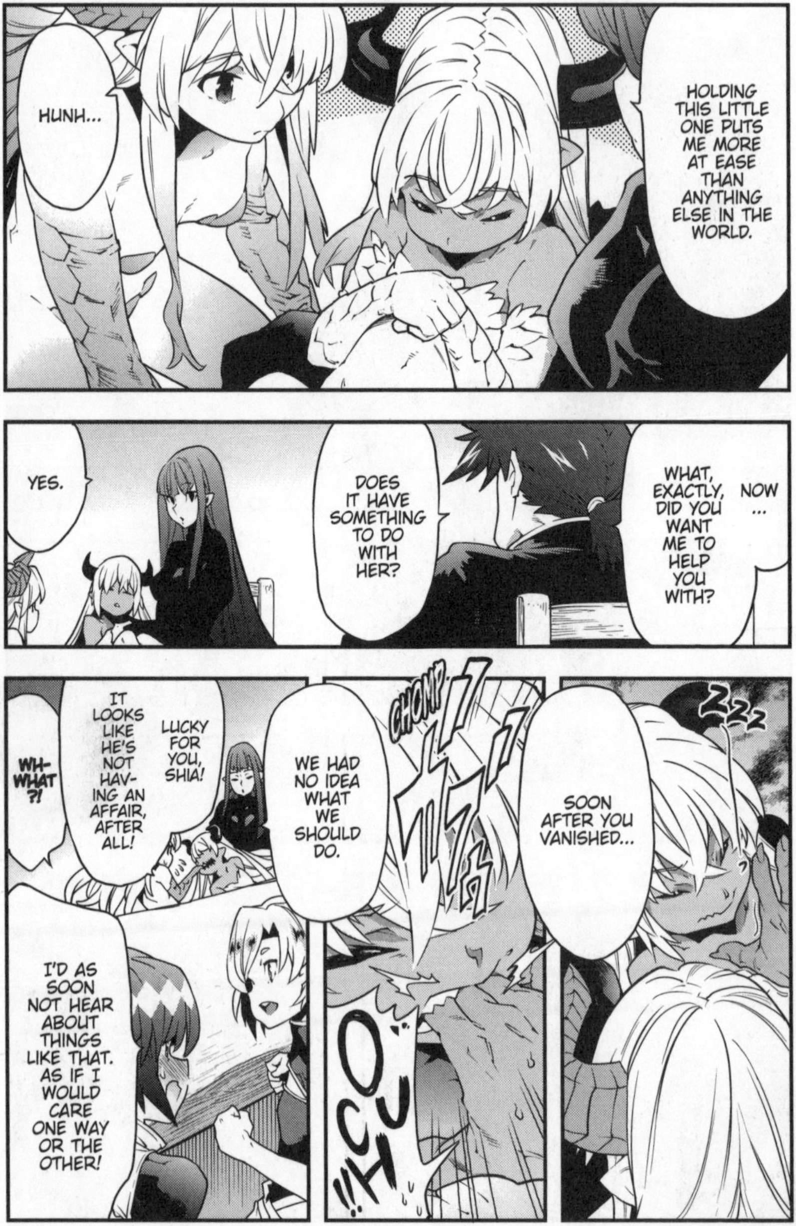
HOLDING THIS LITTLE ONE PUTS ME MORE AT EASE THAN ANYTHING ELSE IN THE WORLD.
HUNH...
NOW ...
WHAT, EXACTLY, DID YOU WANT ME TO HELP YOU WITH?
DOES IT HAVE SOMETHING TO DO WITH HER?
YES.
ZZZ
SOON AFTER YOU VANISHED...
CHOMP
OUCH!!
WE HAD NO IDEA WHAT WE SHOULD DO.
LUCKY FOR YOU, SHIA!
IT LOOKS LIKE HE'S NOT HAVING AN AFFAIR, AFTER ALL!
WH-WHAT?!
I'D AS SOON NOT HEAR ABOUT THINGS LIKE THAT. AS IF I WOULD CARE ONE WAY OR THE OTHER!

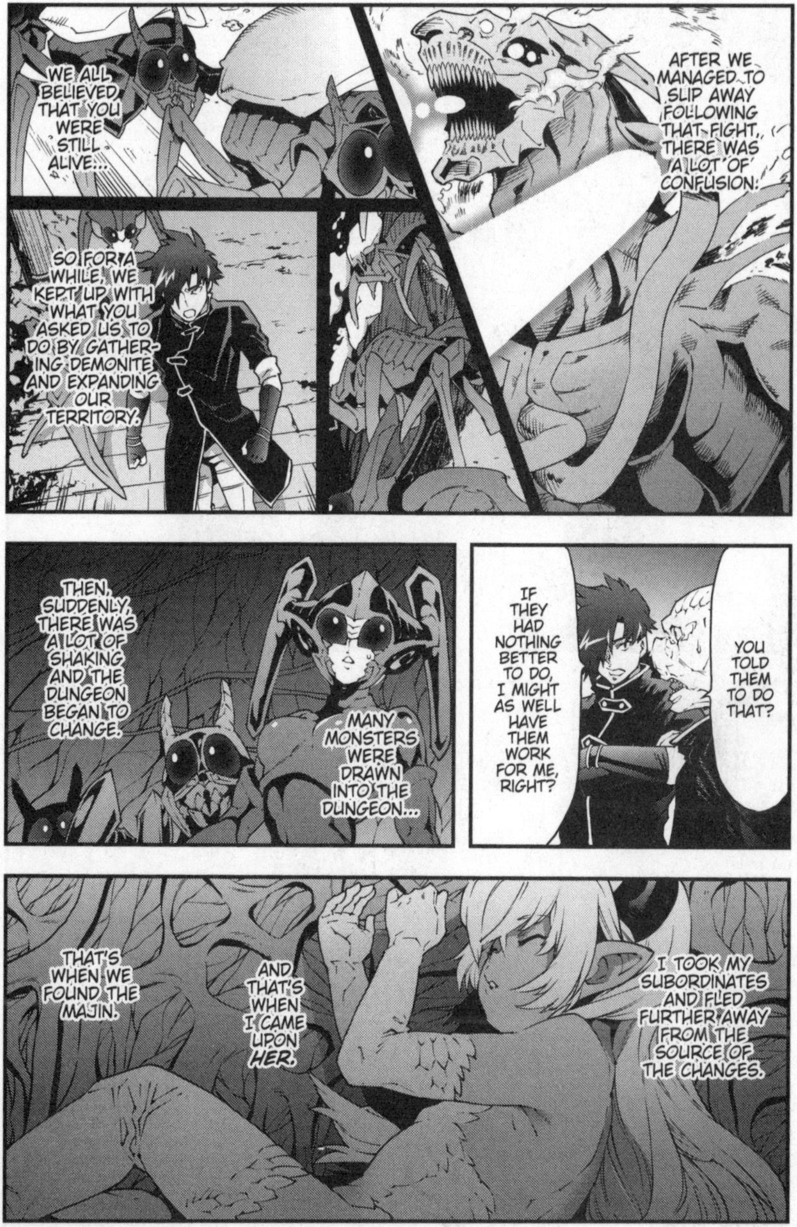
AFTER WE MANAGED TO SLIP AWAY FOLLOWING THAT FIGHT, THERE WAS A LOT OF CONFUSION.
WE ALL BELIEVED THAT YOU WERE STILL ALIVE...
SO FOR A WHILE, WE KEPT UP WITH WHAT YOU ASKED US TO DO BY GATHERING DEMONITE AND EXPANDING OUR TERRITORY.
YOU TOLD THEM TO DO THAT?
IF THEY HAD NOTHING BETTER TO DO, I MIGHT AS WELL HAVE THEM WORK FOR ME, RIGHT?
THEN, SUDDENLY, THERE WAS A LOT OF SHAKING AND THE DUNGEON BEGAN TO CHANGE.
MANY MONSTERS WERE DRAWN INTO THE DUNGEON...
I TOOK MY SUBORDINATES AND FLED FURTHER AWAY FROM THE SOURCE OF THE CHANGES.
THAT'S WHEN WE FOUND THE MAJIN.
AND THAT'S WHEN I CAME UPON HER.

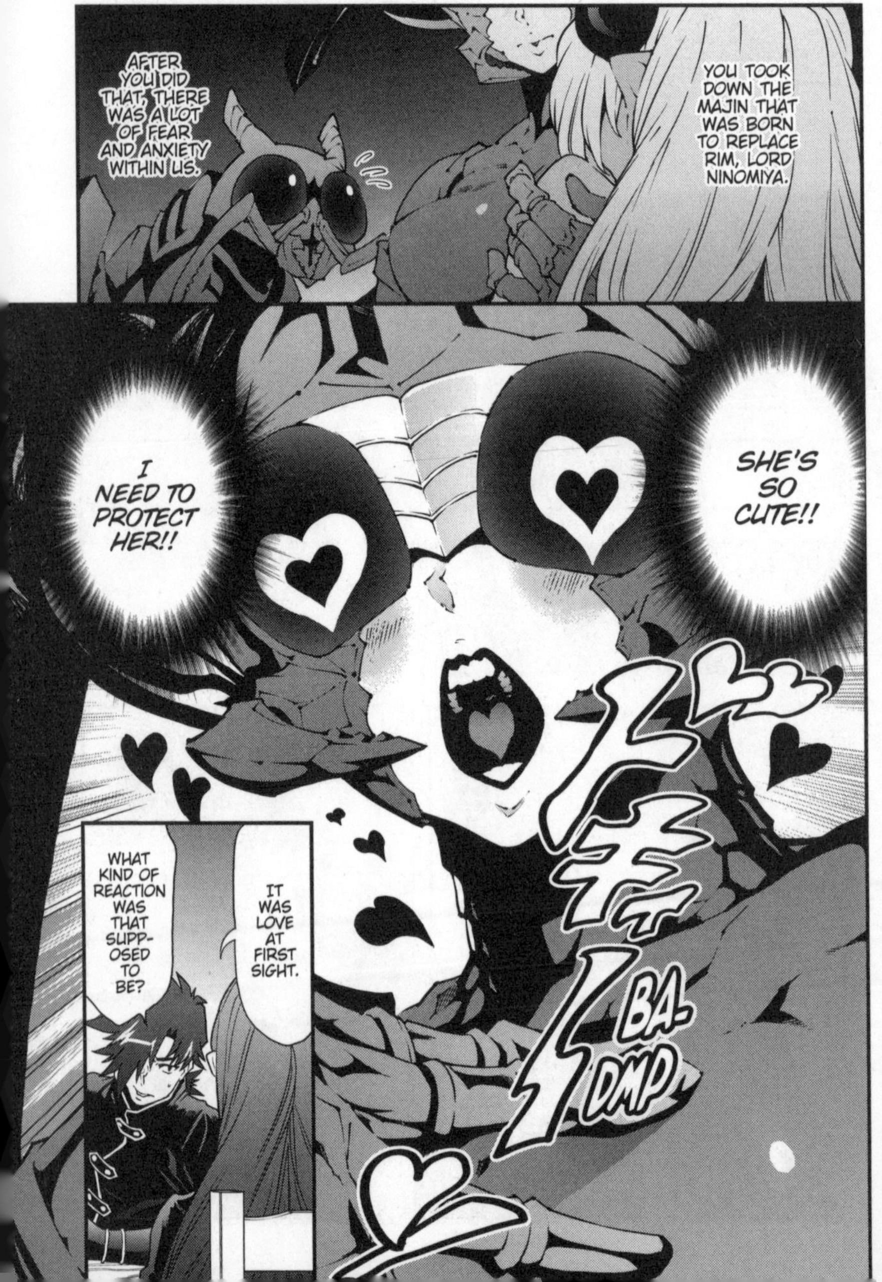
YOU TOOK DOWN THE MAJIN THAT WAS BORN TO REPLACE RIM, LORD NINOMIYA.
AFTER YOU DID THAT, THERE WAS A LOT OF FEAR AND ANXIETY WITHIN US.
SHE'S SO CUTE!!
I NEED TO PROTECT HER!!
BA-DMP
IT WAS LOVE AT FIRST SIGHT.
WHAT KIND OF REACTION WAS THAT SUPP-OSED TO BE?

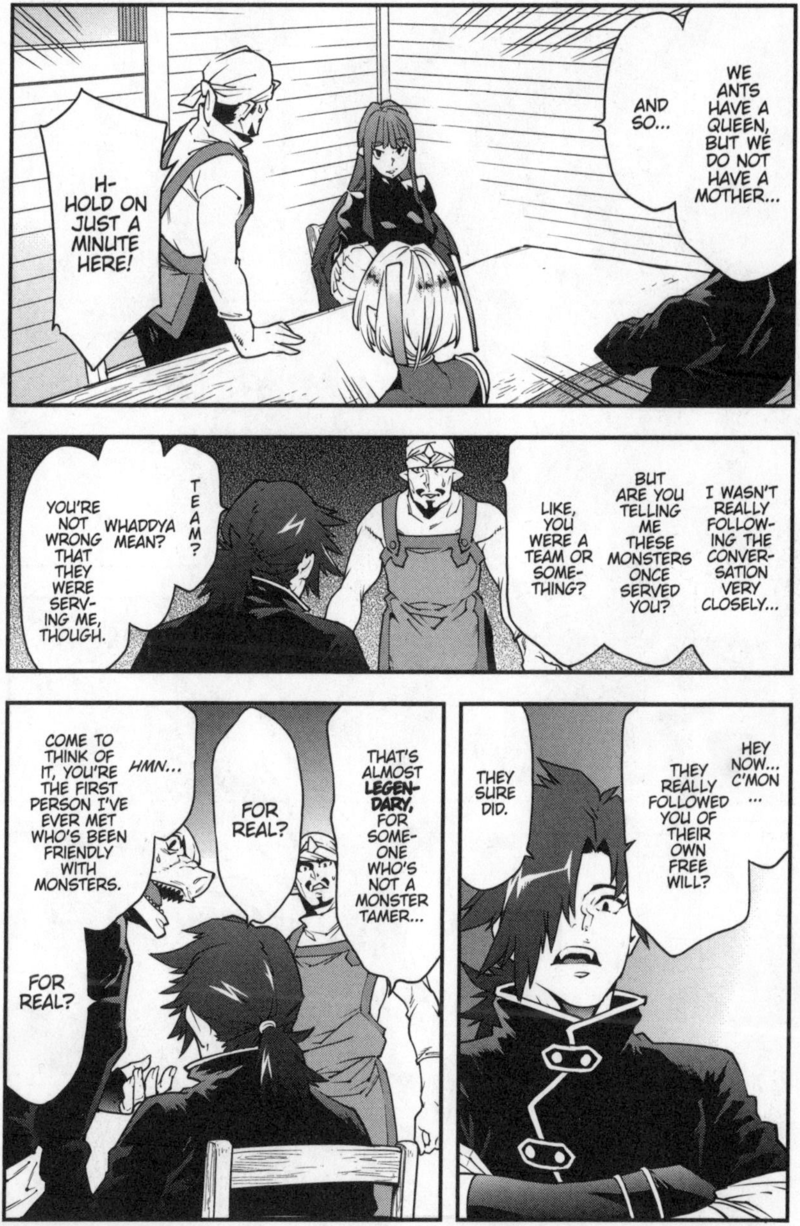
WE ANTS HAVE A QUEEN, BUT WE DO NOT HAVE A MOTHER...
AND SO...
H-HOLD ON JUST A MINUTE HERE!
I WASN'T REALLY FOLLOWING THE CONVERSATION VERY CLOSELY...
BUT ARE YOU TELLING ME THESE MONSTERS ONCE SERVED YOU?
LIKE, YOU WERE A TEAM OR SOMETHING?
TEAM?
WHADDYA MEAN?
YOU'RE NOT WRONG THAT THEY WERE SERVING ME, THOUGH.
HEY NOW... C'MON...
THEY REALLY FOLLOWED YOU OF THEIR OWN FREE WILL?
THEY SURE DID.
THAT'S ALMOST LEGENDARY, FOR SOMEONE WHO'S NOT A MONSTER TAMER...
FOR REAL?
HMN...
COME TO THINK OF IT, YOU'RE THE FIRST PERSON I'VE EVER MET WHO'S BEEN FRIENDLY WITH MONSTERS.
FOR REAL?

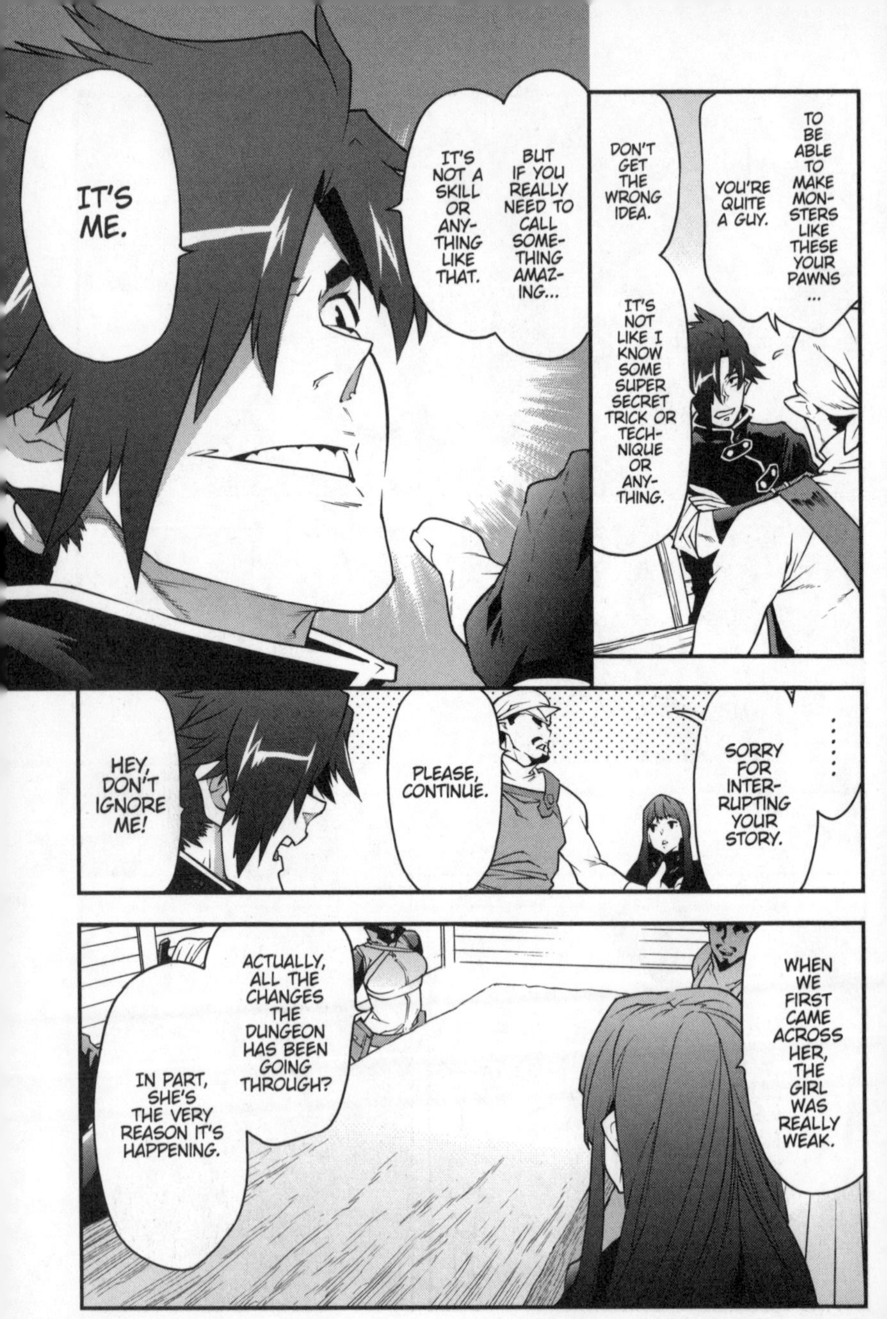
TO BE ABLE TO MAKE MONSTERS LIKE THESE YOUR PAWNS...
YOU'RE QUITE A GUY.
DON'T GET THE WRONG IDEA.
IT'S NOT LIKE I KNOW SOME SUPER SECRET TRICK OR TECHNIQUE OR ANYTHING.
BUT IF YOU REALLY NEED TO CALL SOMETHING AMAZING...
IT'S NOT A SKILL OR ANYTHING LIKE THAT.
IT'S ME.
......
SORRY FOR INTERRUPTING YOUR STORY.
PLEASE, CONTINUE.
HEY, DON'T IGNORE ME!
WHEN WE FIRST CAME ACROSS HER, THE GIRL WAS REALLY WEAK.
ACTUALLY, ALL THE CHANGES THE DUNGEON HAS BEEN GOING THROUGH?
IN PART, SHE'S THE VERY REASON IT'S HAPPENING.

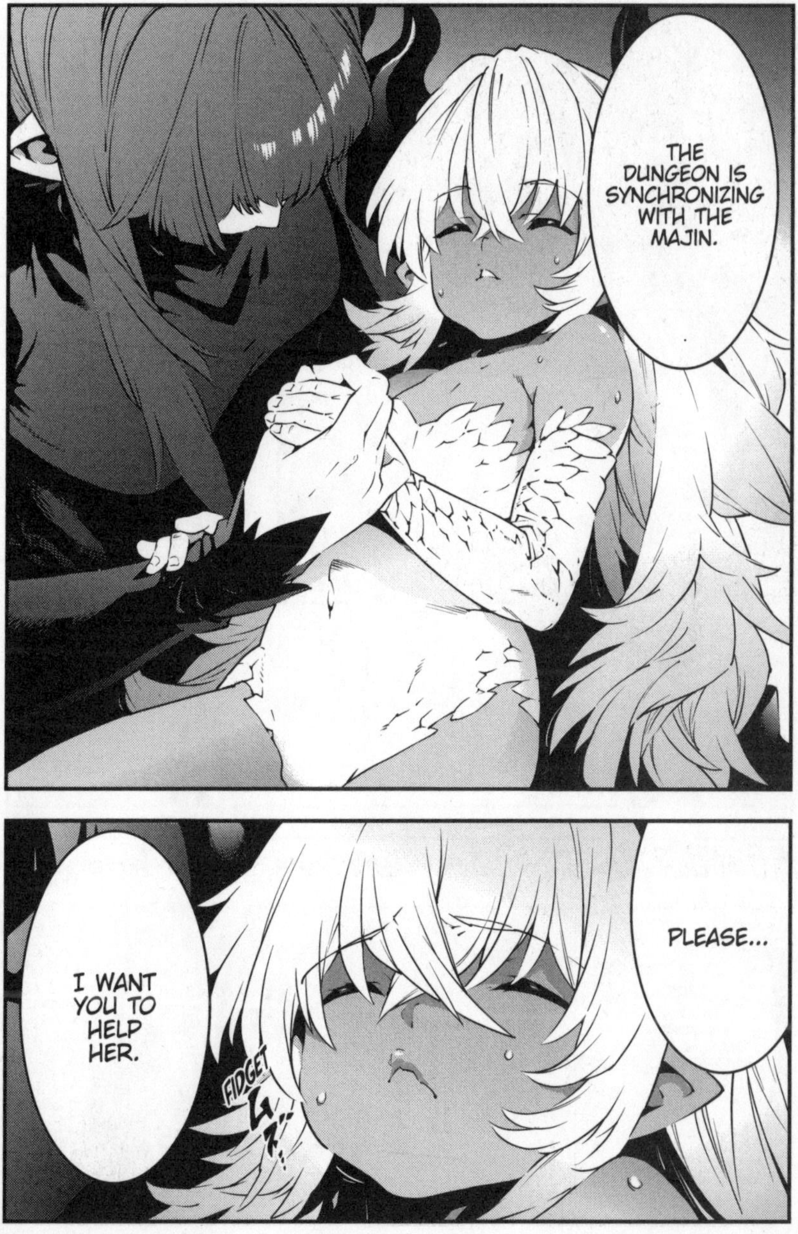
THE DUNGEON IS SYNCHRONIZING WITH THE MAJIN.
PLEASE...
I WANT YOU TO HELP HER.
FIDGET

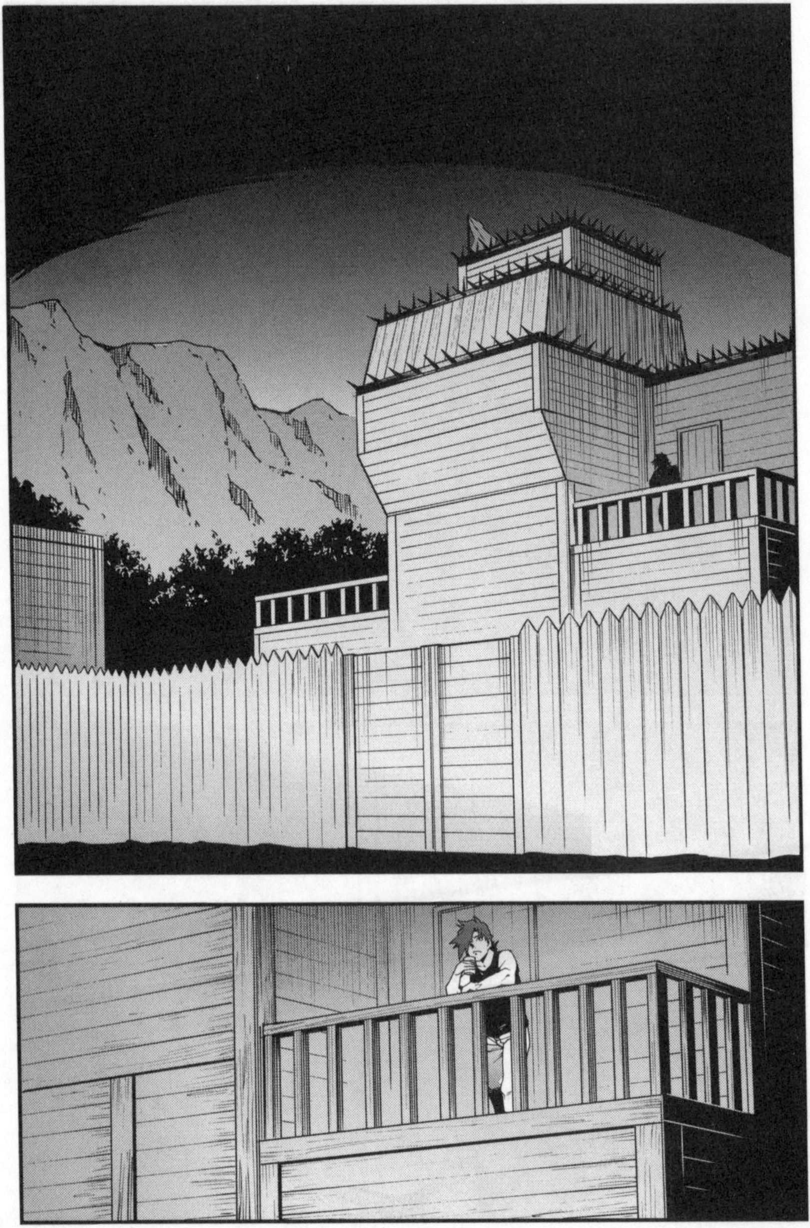

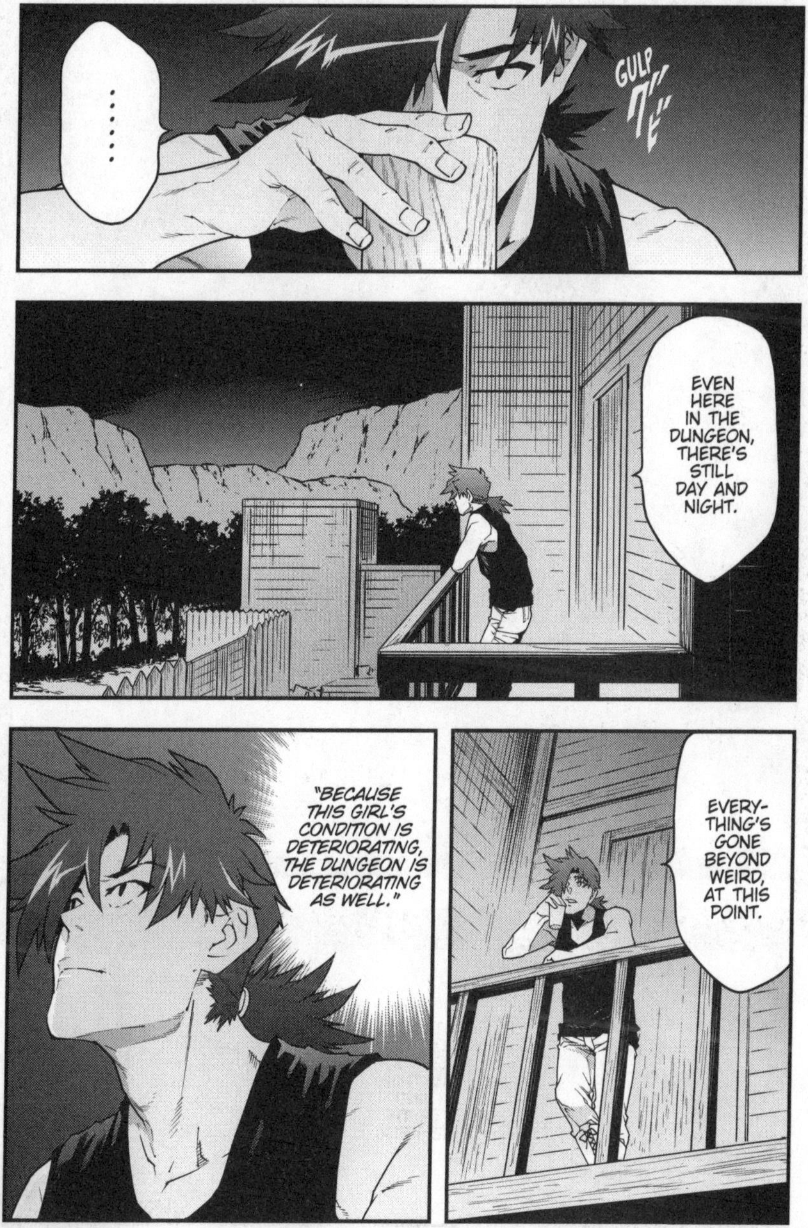
GULP
......
EVEN HERE IN THE DUNGEON, THERE'S STILL DAY AND NIGHT.
EVERY-THING'S GONE BEYOND WEIRD, AT THIS POINT.
"BECAUSE THIS GIRL'S CONDITION IS DETERIORATING, THE DUNGEON IS DETERIORATING AS WELL."

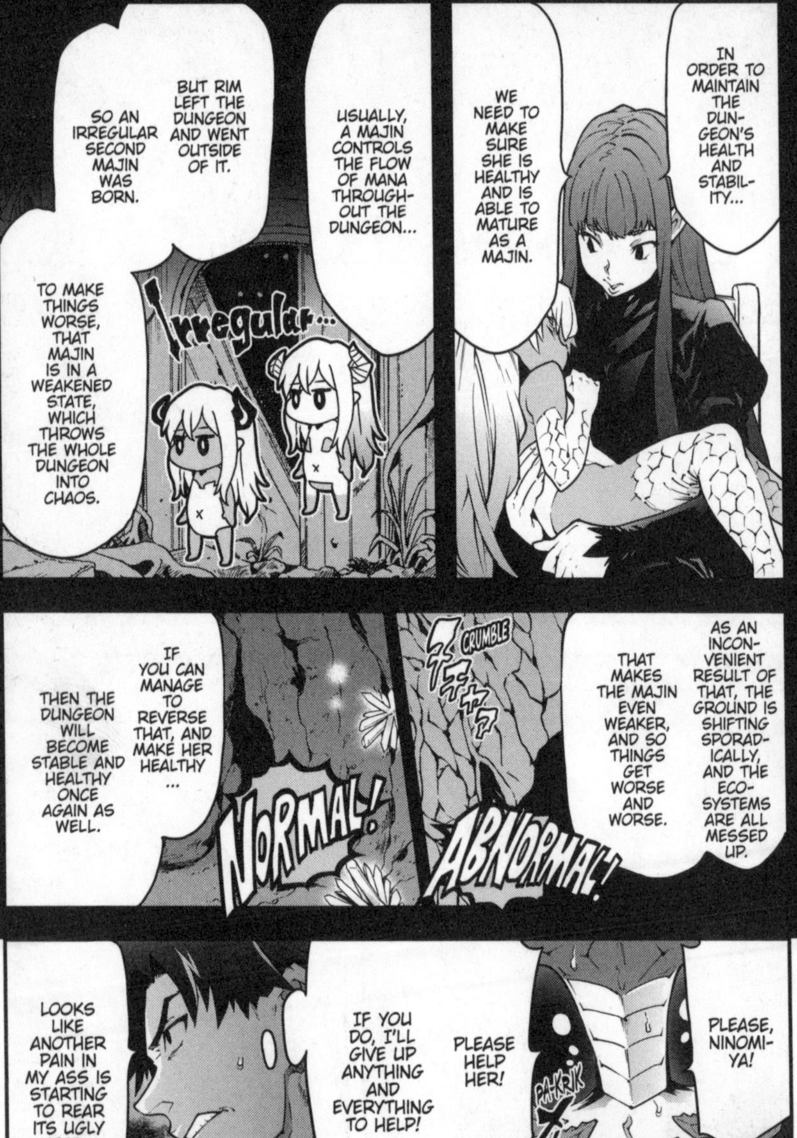
IN ORDER TO MAINTAIN THE DUNGEON'S HEALTH AND STABILITY...
WE NEED TO MAKE SURE SHE IS HEALTHY AND IS ABLE TO MATURE AS A MAJIN.
USUALLY, A MAJIN CONTROLS THE FLOW OF MANA THROUGHOUT THE DUNGEON...
BUT RIM LEFT THE DUNGEON AND WENT OUTSIDE OF IT.
SO AN IRREGULAR SECOND MAJIN WAS BORN.
Irregular...
TO MAKE THINGS WORSE, THAT MAJIN IS IN A WEAKENED STATE, WHICH THROWS THE WHOLE DUNGEON INTO CHAOS.
AS AN INCONVENIENT RESULT OF THAT, THE GROUND IS SHIFTING SPORADICALLY, AND THE ECOSYSTEMS ARE ALL MESSED UP.
CRUMBLE
THAT MAKES THE MAJIN EVEN WEAKER, AND SO THINGS GET WORSE AND WORSE.
ABNORMAL!
IF YOU CAN MANAGE TO REVERSE THAT, AND MAKE HER HEALTHY...
THEN THE DUNGEON WILL BECOME STABLE AND HEALTHY ONCE AGAIN AS WELL.
NORMAL!
PLEASE, NINOMIYA!
PAKRIK
PLEASE HELP HER!
IF YOU DO, I'LL GIVE UP ANYTHING AND EVERYTHING TO HELP!
LOOKS LIKE ANOTHER PAIN IN MY ASS IS STARTING TO REAR ITS UGLY HEAD...

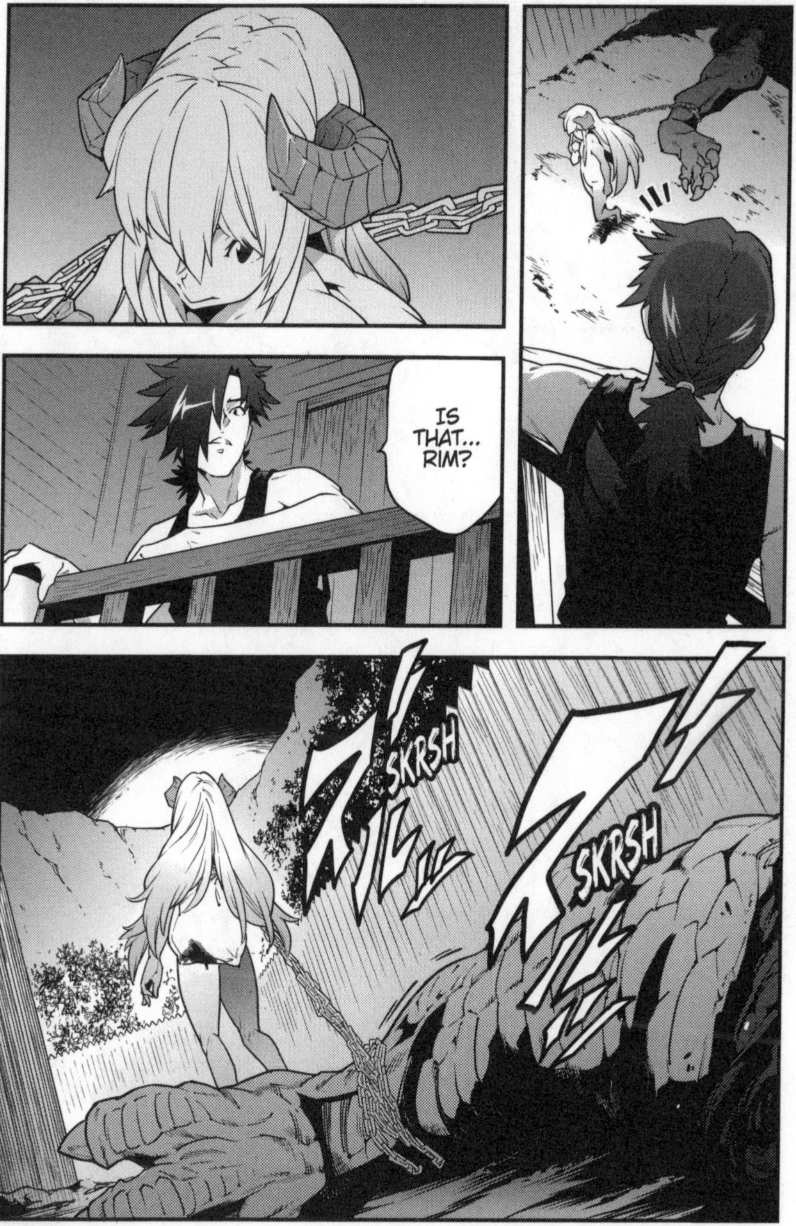
IS THAT... RIM?
SKRSH
SKRSH

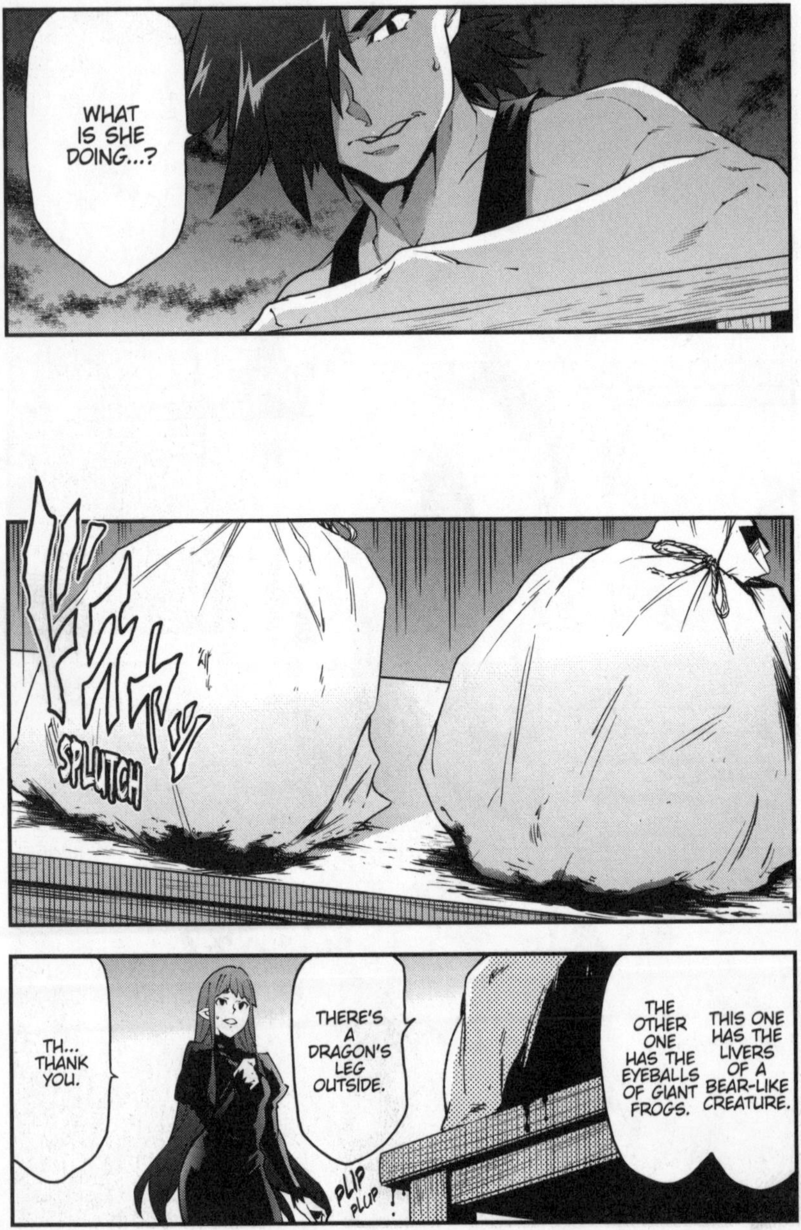
WHAT IS SHE DOING...?
SPLUTCH
THIS ONE HAS THE LIVERS OF A BEAR-LIKE CREATURE.
THE OTHER ONE HAS THE EYEBALLS OF GIANT FROGS.
THERE'S A DRAGON'S LEG OUTSIDE.
PLIP PLUP
TH... THANK YOU.

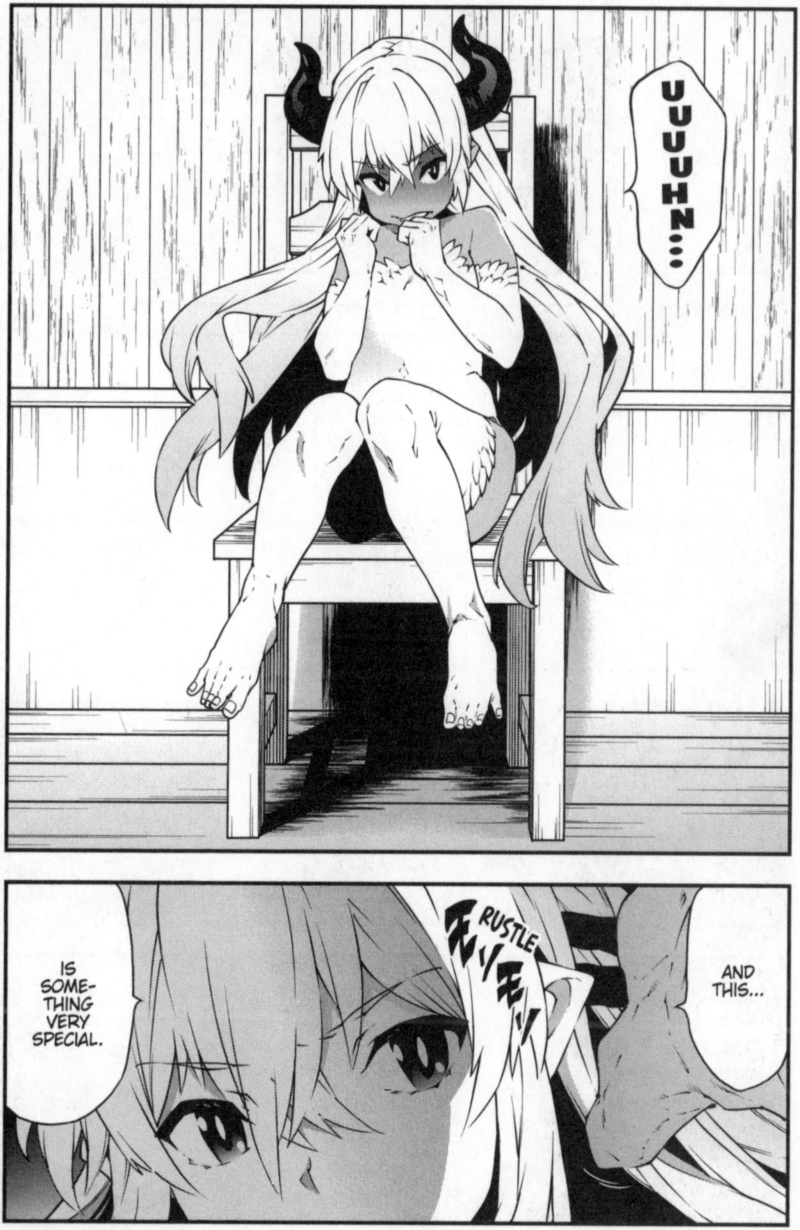
UUUHN...
AND THIS...
RUSTLE
IS SOME-THING VERY SPECIAL.

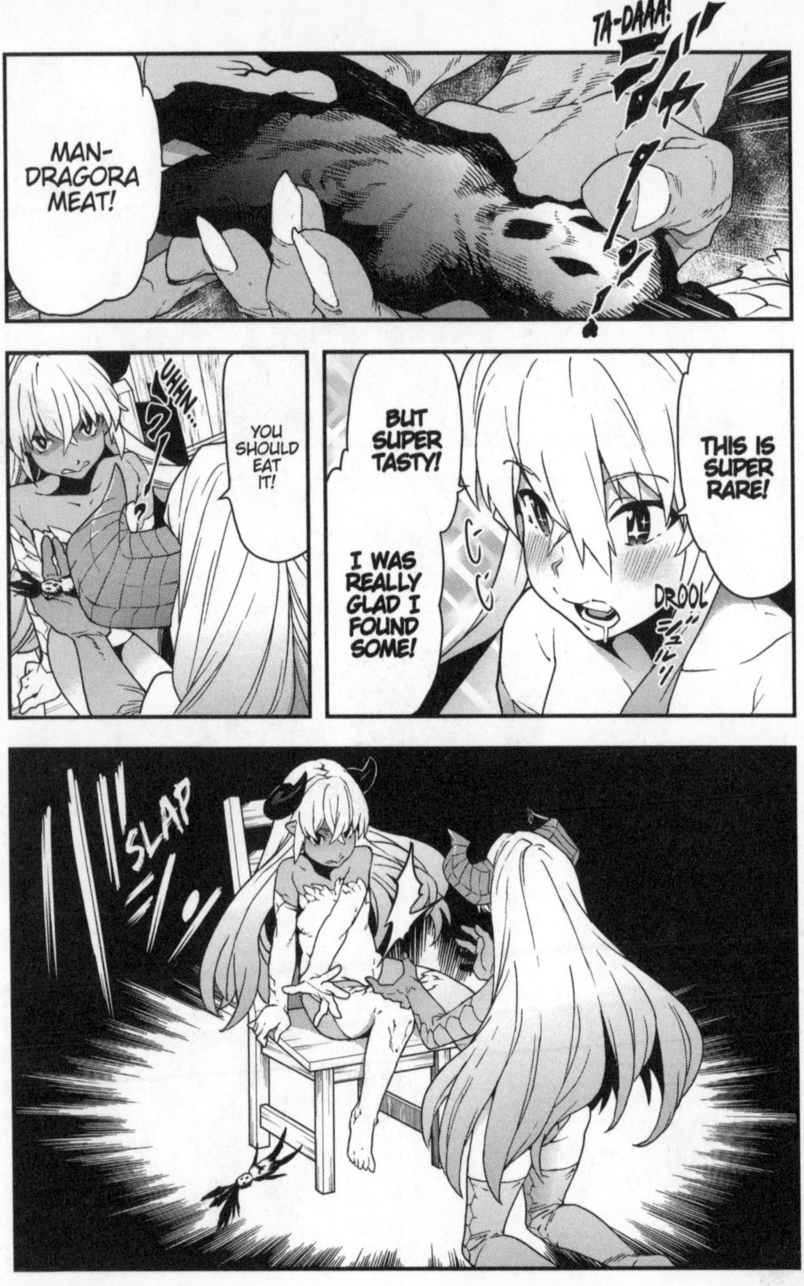
TA-DAAA!
MAN-DRAGORA MEAT!
THIS IS SUPER RARE!
DROOL
BUT SUPER TASTY!
I WAS REALLY GLAD I FOUND SOME!
YOU SHOULD EAT IT!
UHHN...
SLAP

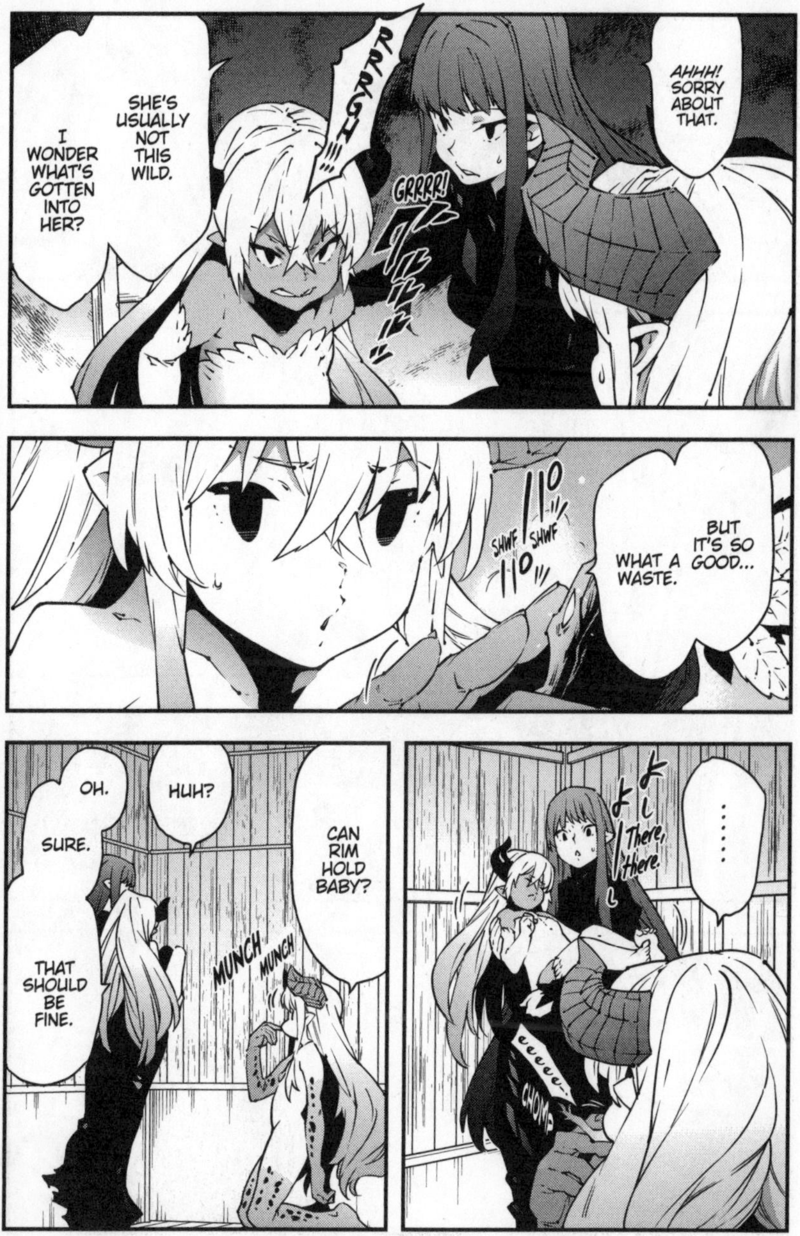
AHHH! SORRY ABOUT THAT.
RRRRGH!!!
GRRRR!
SHE'S USUALLY NOT THIS WILD.
I WONDER WHAT'S GOTTEN INTO HER?
BUT IT'S SO GOOD...
WHAT A WASTE.
SHWF SHWF
......
よし よし
There, there.
eeeee...
CHOMP
CAN RIM HOLD BABY?
MUNCH MUNCH
HUH?
OH.
SURE.
THAT SHOULD BE FINE.

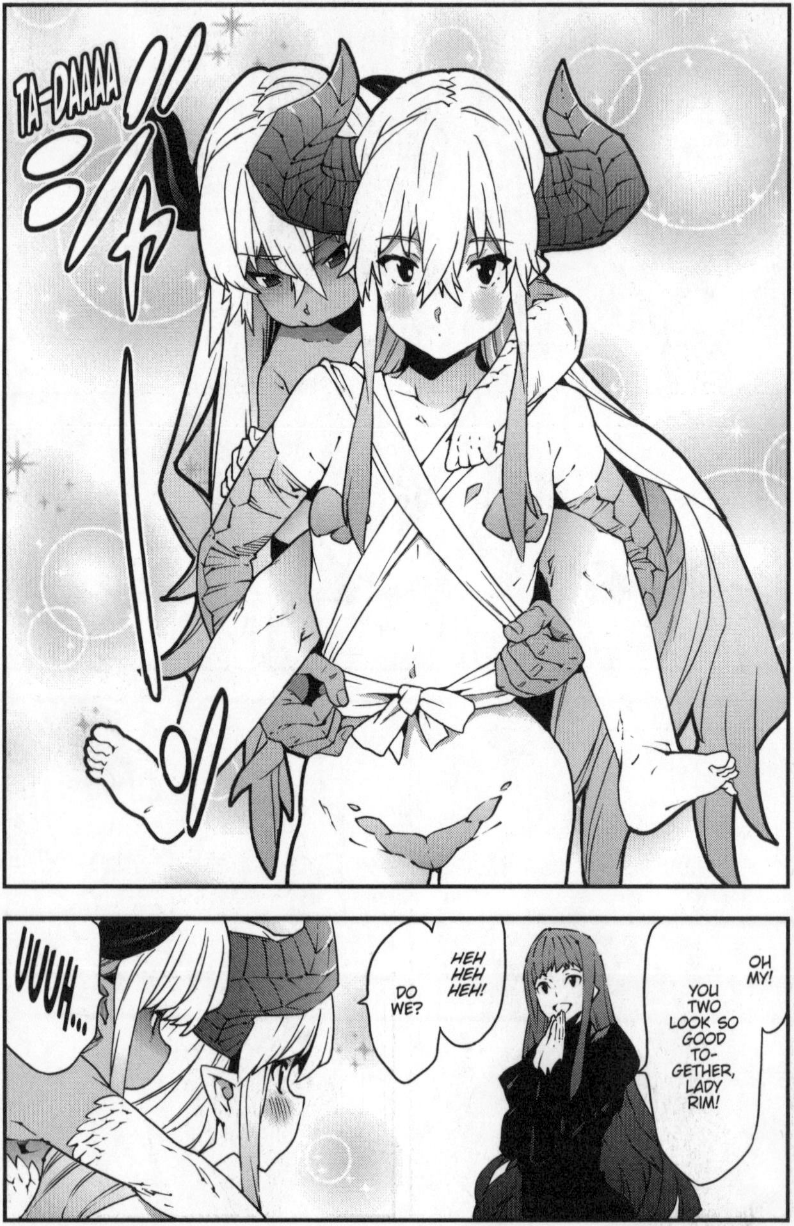
TA-DAAAA
OH MY!
YOU TWO LOOK SO GOOD TO-GETHER, LADY RIM!
HEH HEH HEH!
DO WE?
UUUH...

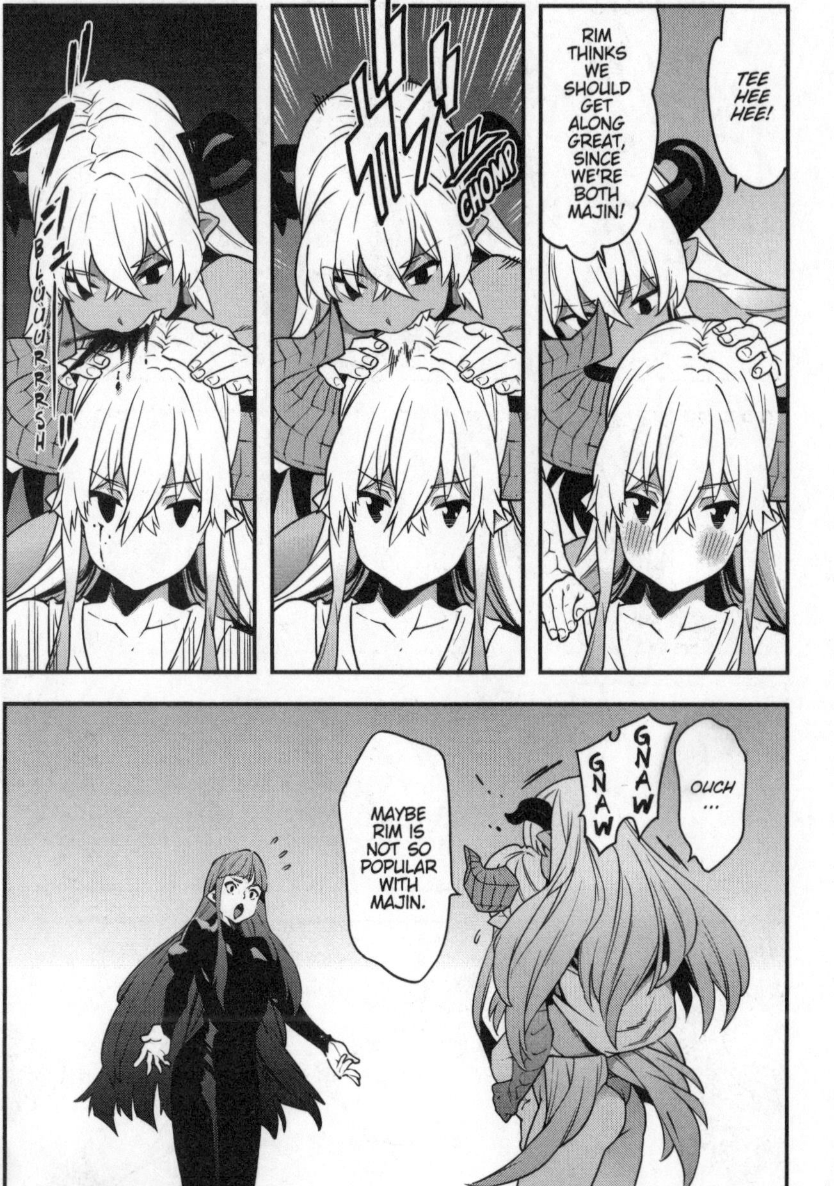
TEE HEE HEE!
RIM THINKS WE SHOULD GET ALONG GREAT, SINCE WE'RE BOTH MAJIN!
CHOMP
BLUUURRRSH
OUCH...
GNAW GNAW
MAYBE RIM IS NOT SO POPULAR WITH MAJIN.

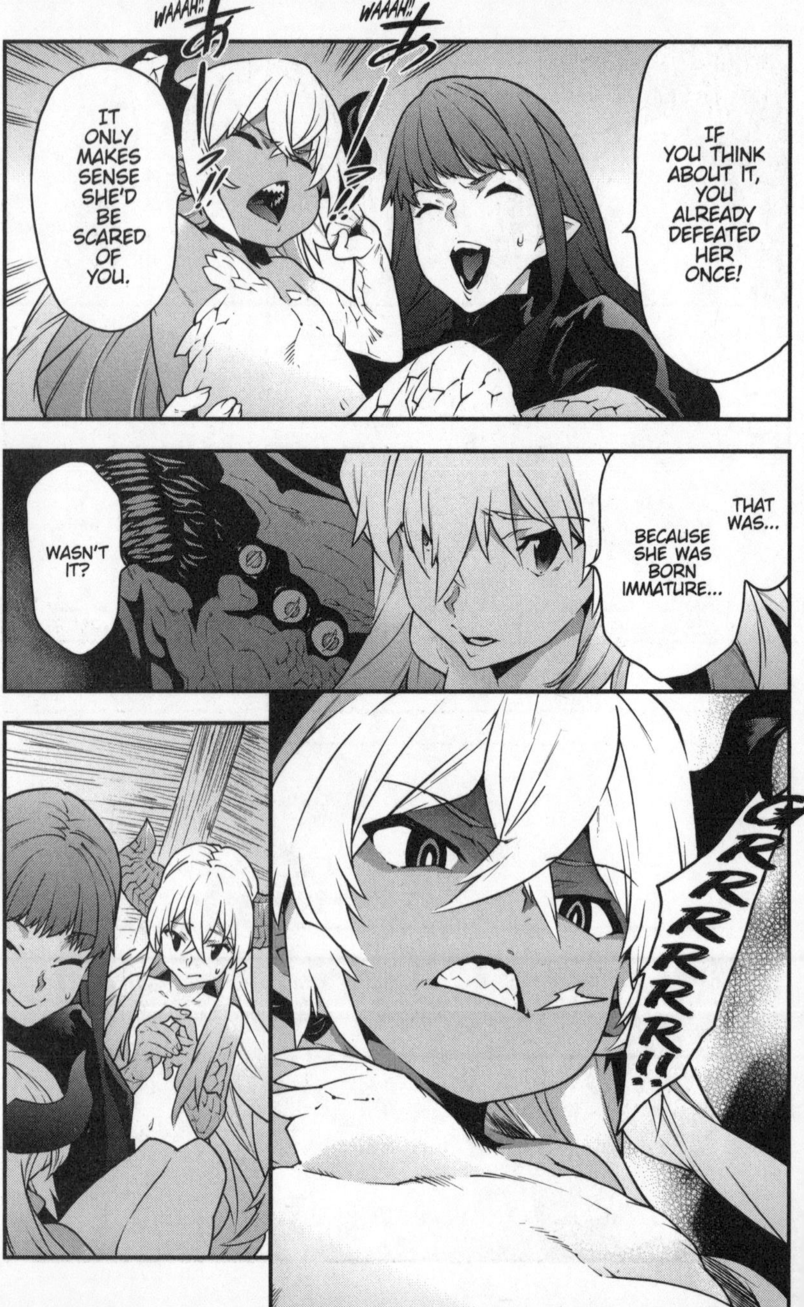

WAAAH!!
IF YOU THINK ABOUT IT, YOU ALREADY DEFEATED HER ONCE!
WAAAH!!
IT ONLY MAKES SENSE SHE'D BE SCARED OF YOU.
THAT WAS...
BECAUSE SHE WAS BORN IMMATURE...
WASN'T IT?
GRRRRRR!!

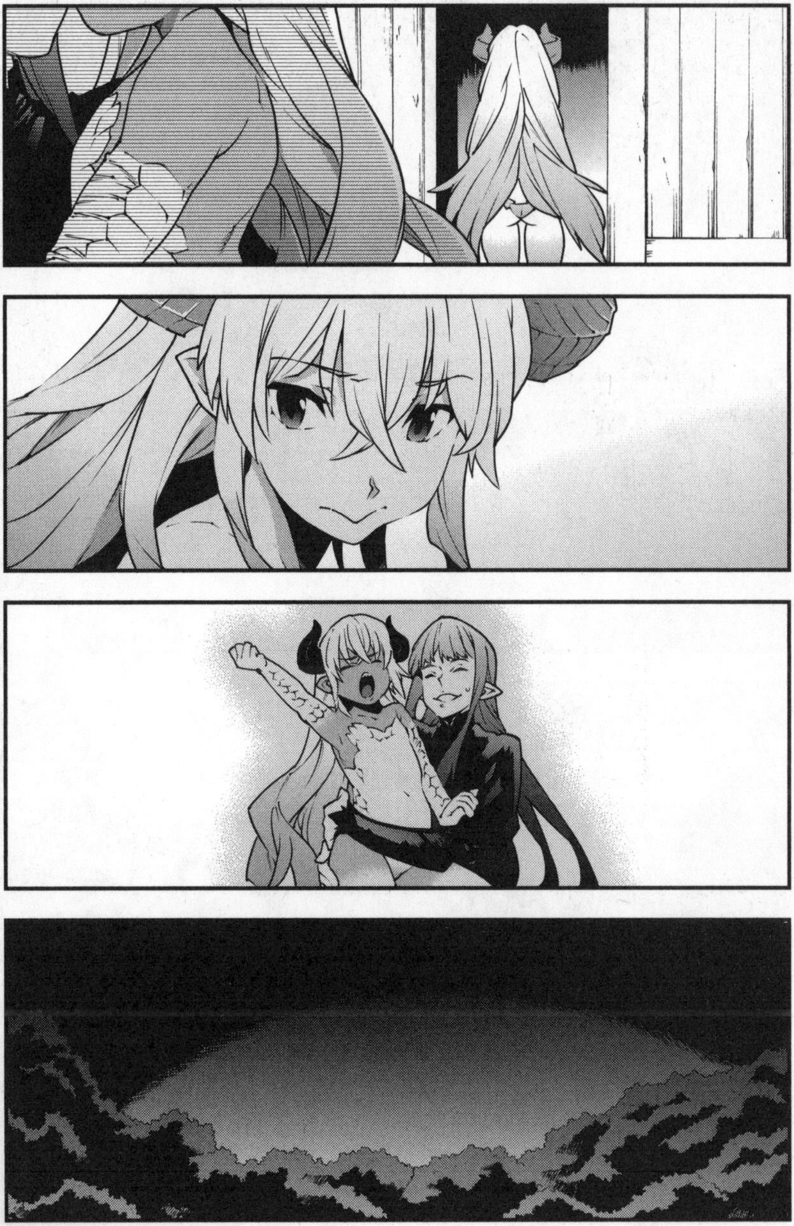

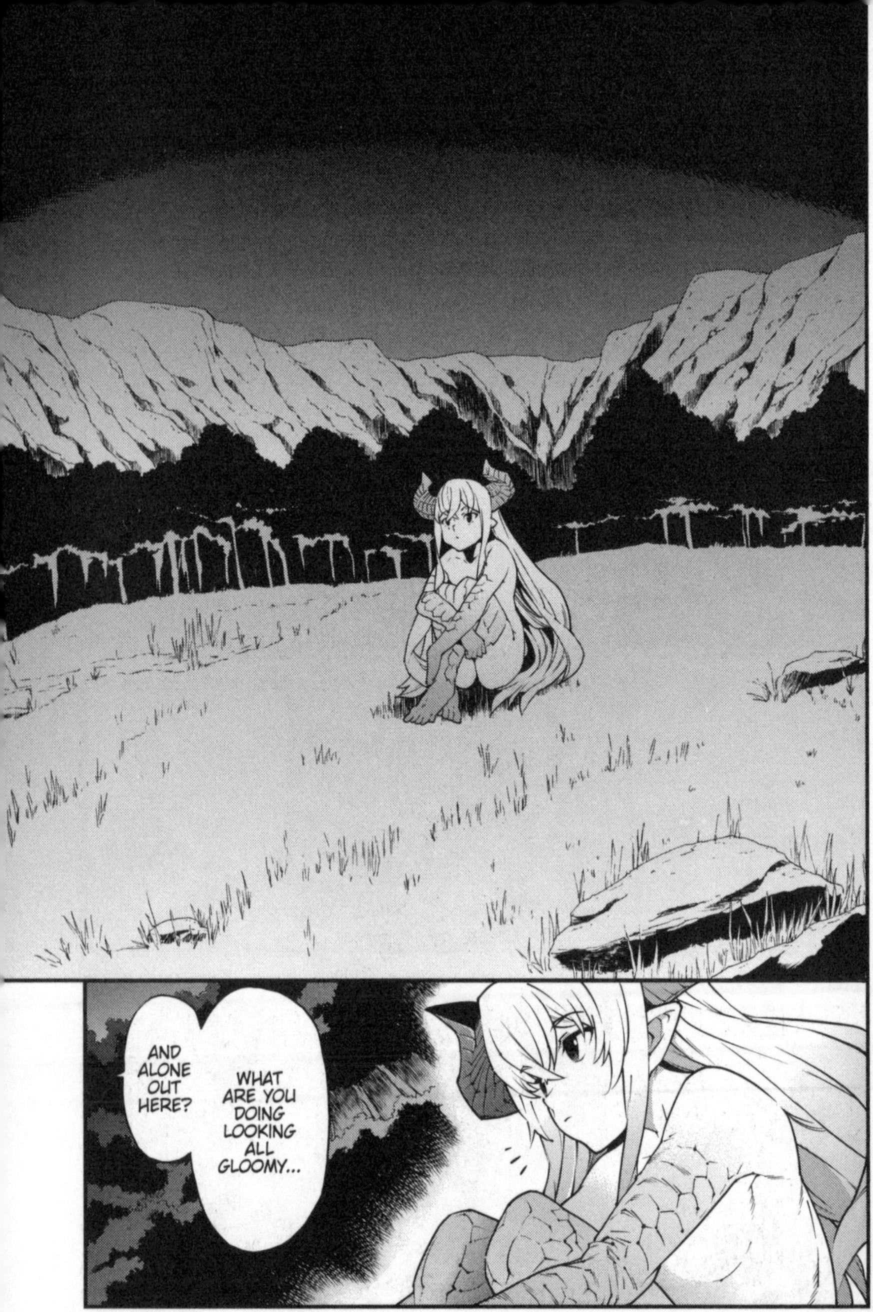
WHAT ARE YOU DOING LOOKING ALL GLOOMY...
AND ALONE OUT HERE?

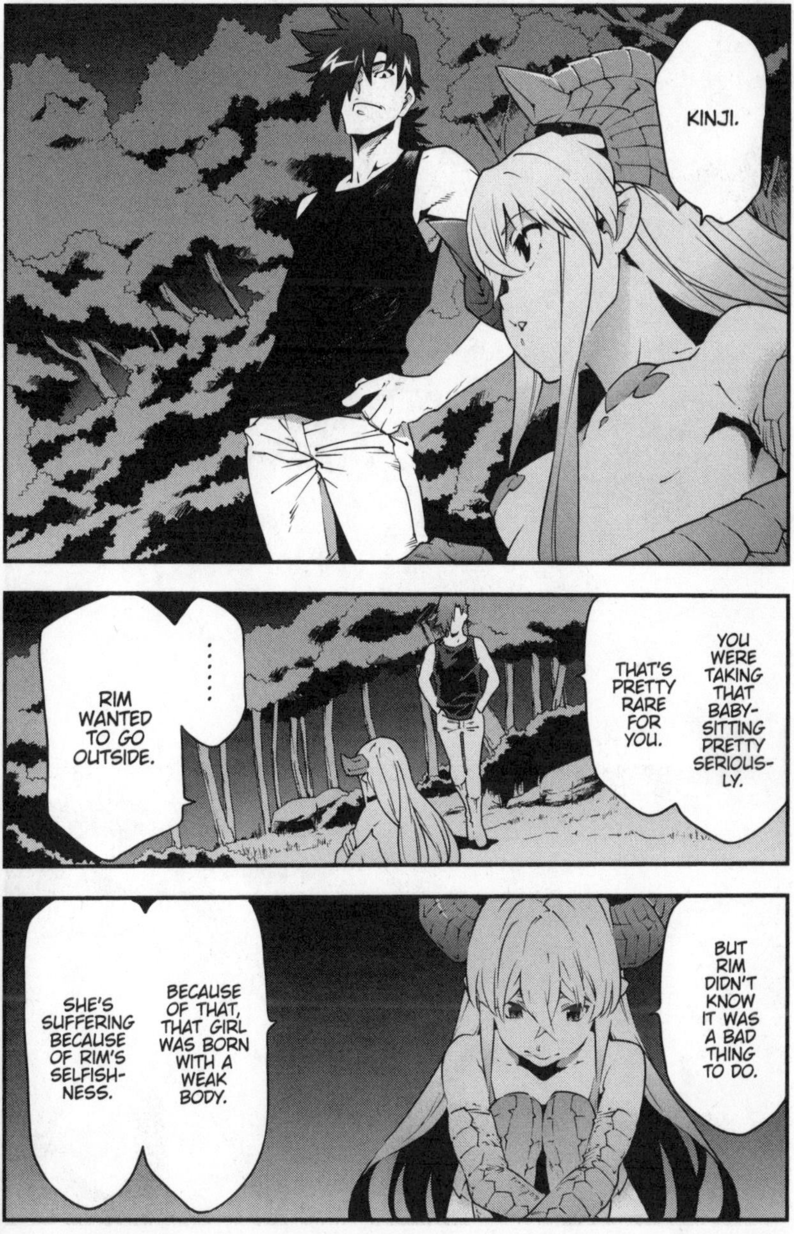
KINJI.
YOU WERE TAKING THAT BABY-SITTING PRETTY SERIOUS-LY.
THAT'S PRETTY RARE FOR YOU.
......
RIM WANTED TO GO OUTSIDE.
BUT RIM DIDN'T KNOW IT WAS A BAD THING TO DO.
BECAUSE OF THAT, THAT GIRL WAS BORN WITH A WEAK BODY.
SHE'S SUFFERING BECAUSE OF RIM'S SELFISH-NESS.

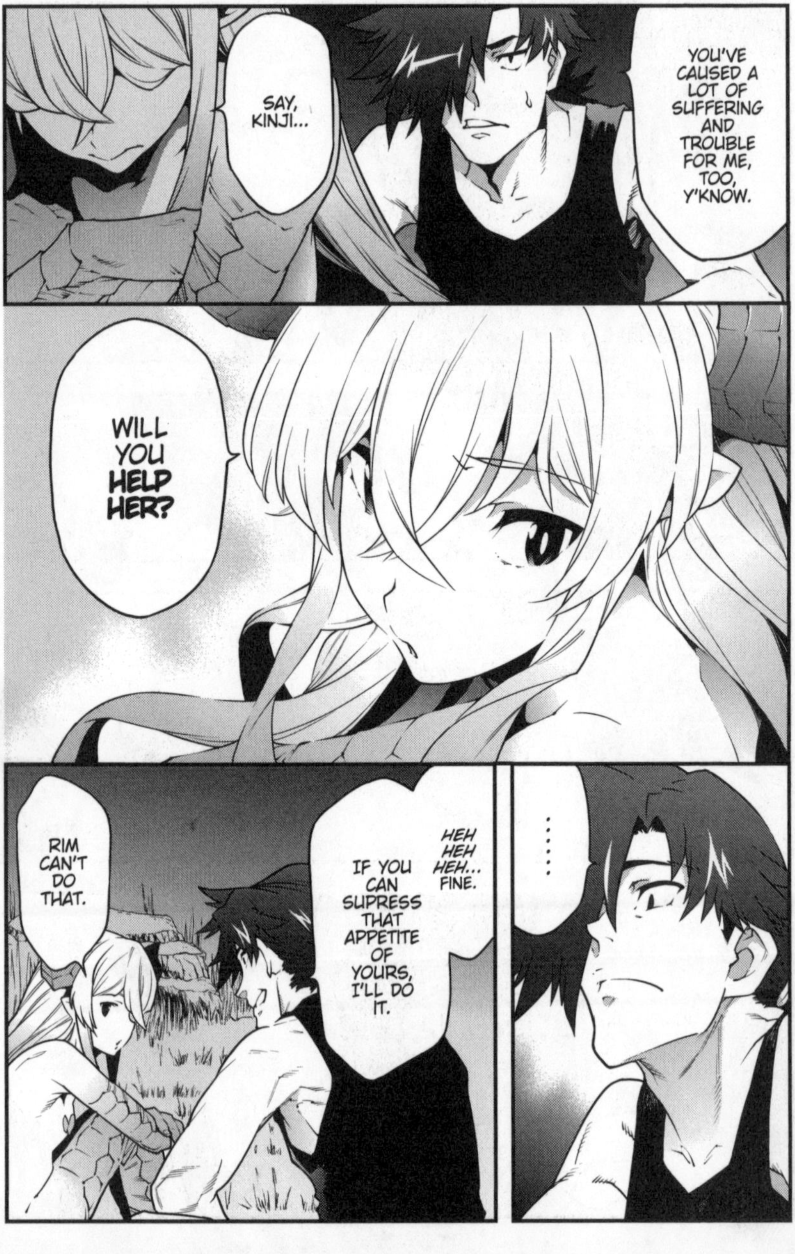
YOU'VE CAUSED A LOT OF SUFFERING AND TROUBLE FOR ME, TOO, Y'KNOW.
SAY, KINJI...
WILL YOU HELP HER?
......
HEH HEH HEH... FINE.
IF YOU CAN SUPRESS THAT APPETITE OF YOURS, I'LL DO IT.
RIM CAN'T DO THAT.

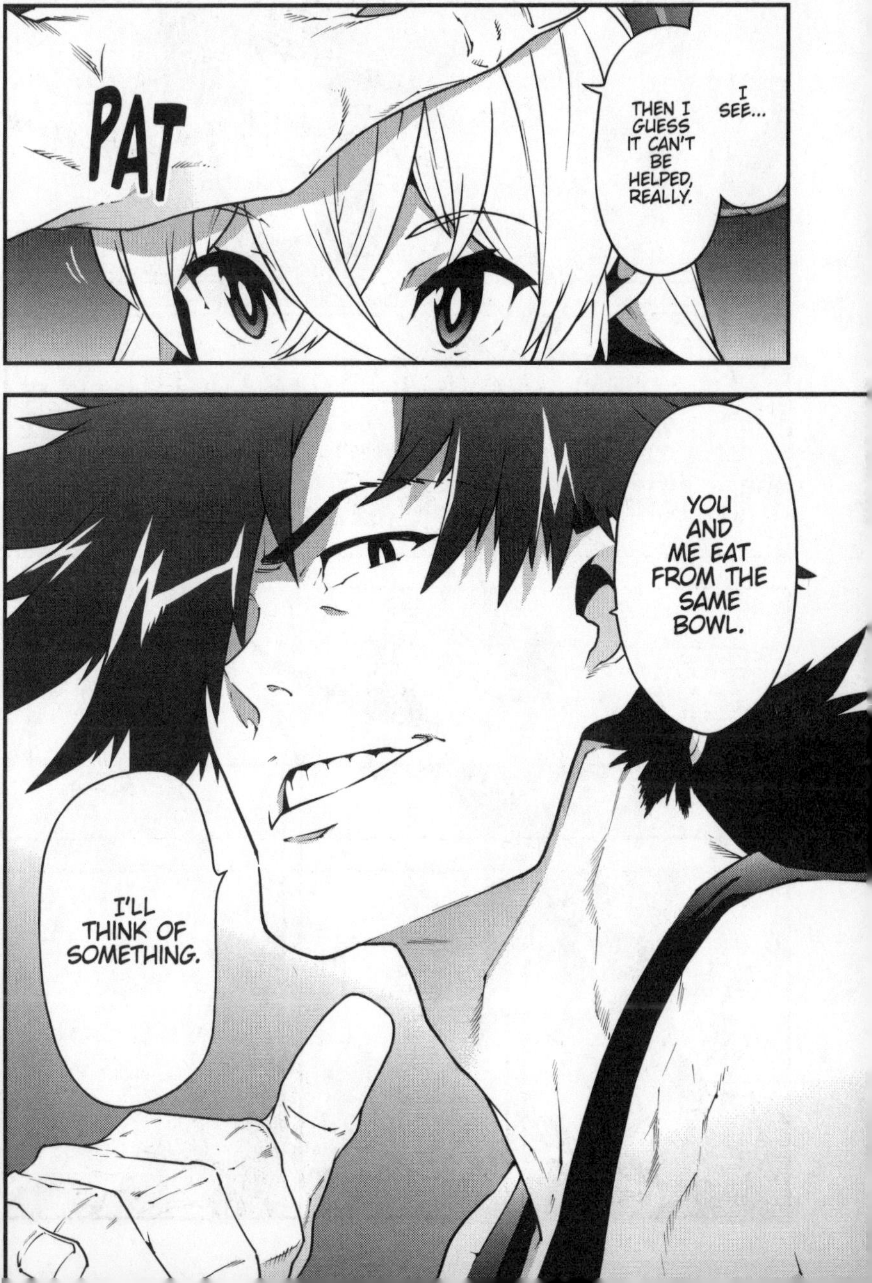
I SEE...
THEN I GUESS IT CAN'T BE HELPED, REALLY.
PAT
YOU AND ME EAT FROM THE SAME BOWL.
I'LL THINK OF SOMETHING.

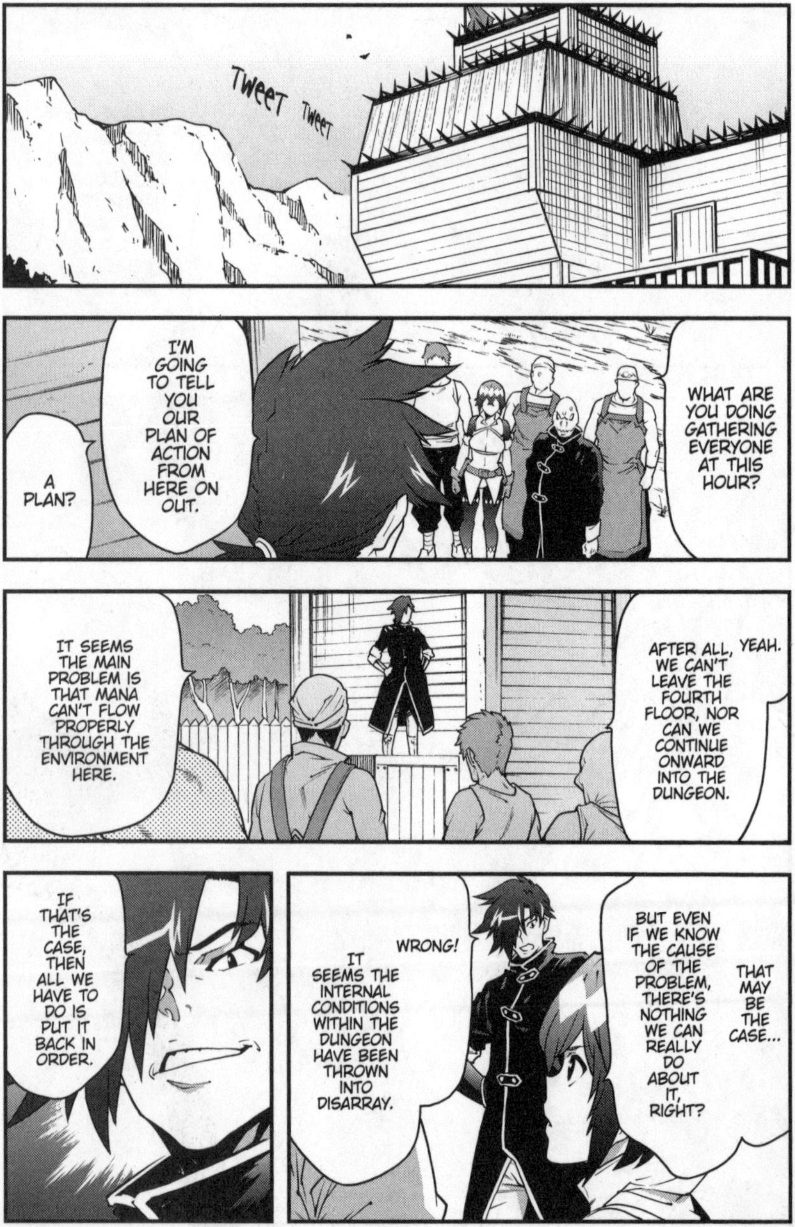
TWEET TWEET
WHAT ARE YOU DOING GATHERING EVERYONE AT THIS HOUR?
I'M GOING TO TELL YOU OUR PLAN OF ACTION FROM HERE ON OUT.
A PLAN?
YEAH.
AFTER ALL, WE CAN'T LEAVE THE FOURTH FLOOR, NOR CAN WE CONTINUE ONWARD INTO THE DUNGEON.
IT SEEMS THE MAIN PROBLEM IS THAT MANA CAN'T FLOW PROPERLY THROUGH THE ENVIRONMENT HERE.
THAT MAY BE THE CASE...
BUT EVEN IF WE KNOW THE CAUSE OF THE PROBLEM, THERE'S NOTHING WE CAN REALLY DO ABOUT IT, RIGHT?
WRONG!
IT SEEMS THE INTERNAL CONDITIONS WITHIN THE DUNGEON HAVE BEEN THROWN INTO DISARRAY.
IF THAT'S THE CASE, THEN ALL WE HAVE TO DO IS PUT IT BACK IN ORDER.

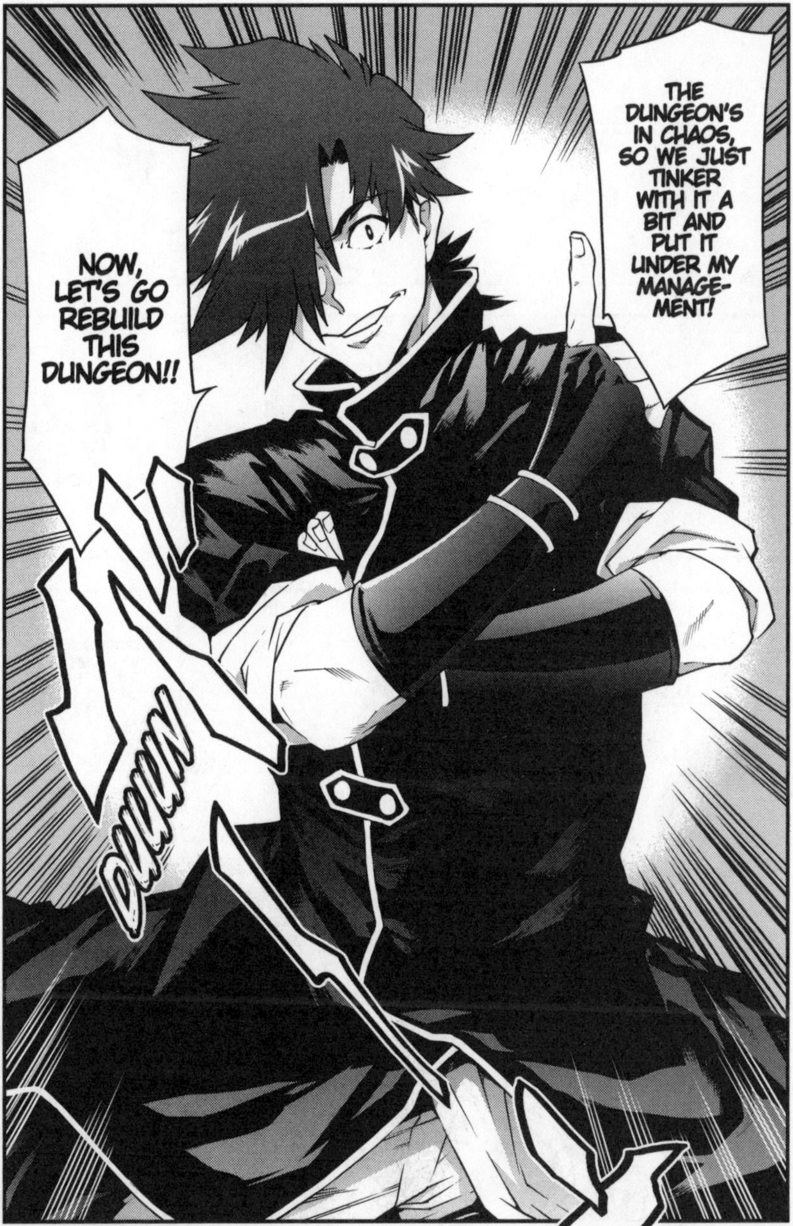
THE DUNGEON'S IN CHAOS, SO WE JUST TINKER WITH IT A BIT AND PUT IT UNDER MY MANAGE-MENT!
NOW, LET'S GO REBUILD THIS DUNGEON!!

DROOL...

PLUP

Name	Rim
Job	Majin

Strength	S	Vitality	S
Speed	S	Intelligence	D
Luck	B	Fuel Efficiency	E

THE DUNGEON OF
BLACK COMPANY

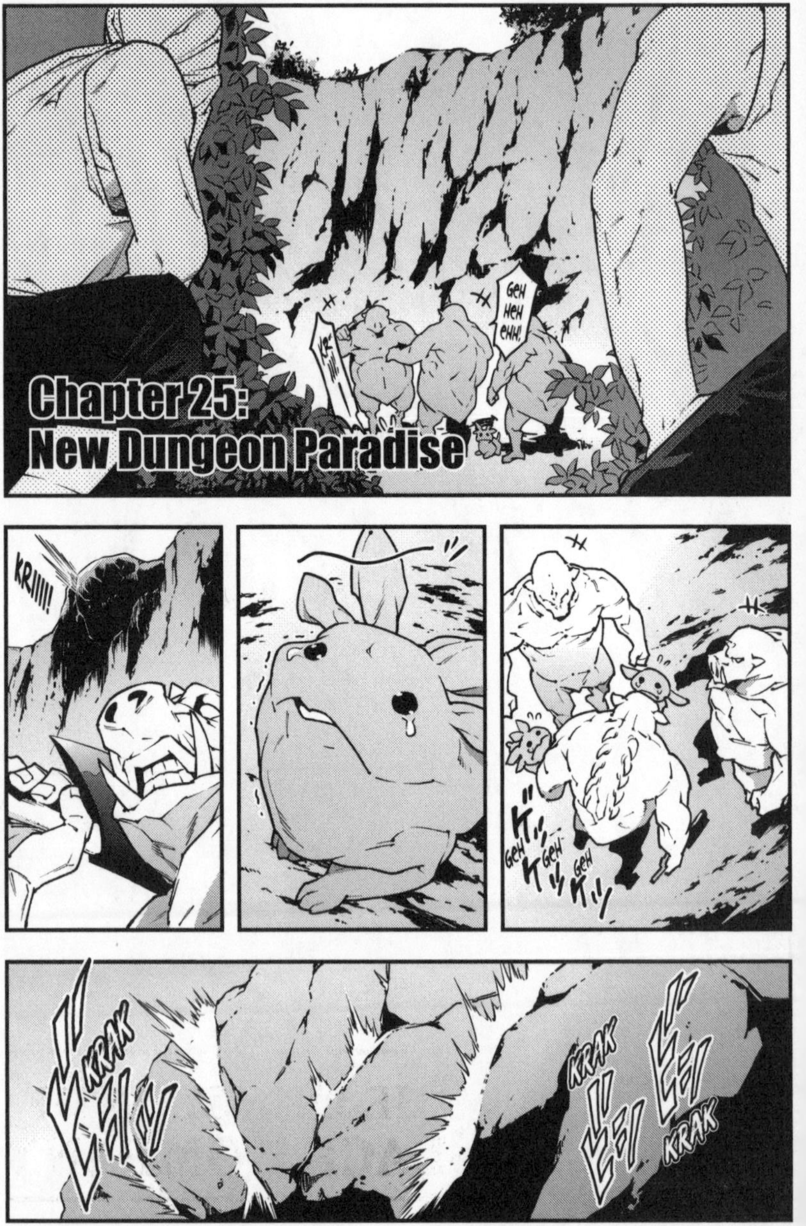
GEH HEH EHH!
KR-!!!
Chapter 25:
New Dungeon Paradise
GEH GEH GEH
KRIIIII!
KRAK
KRAK
KRAK

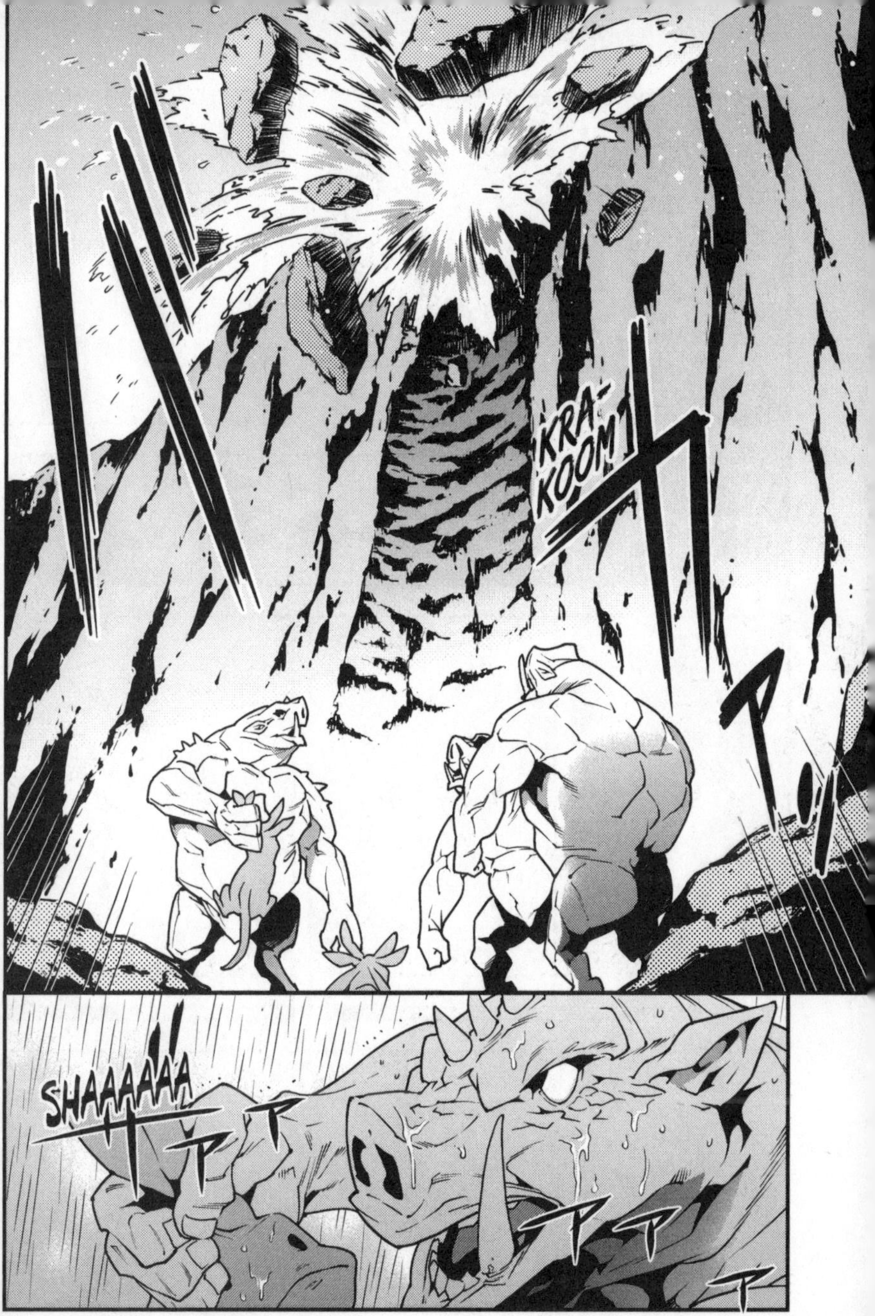

KRA-KOOM
SHAAAAAA

KRA-KOOM

KRA-KOOM

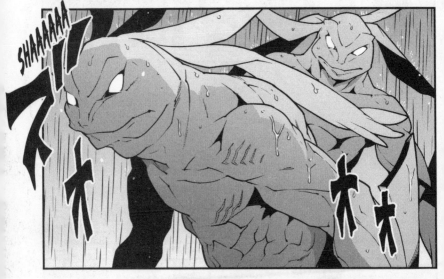
SHAAAAAAAA

IT WORK-ED!

ALL RIGHT!

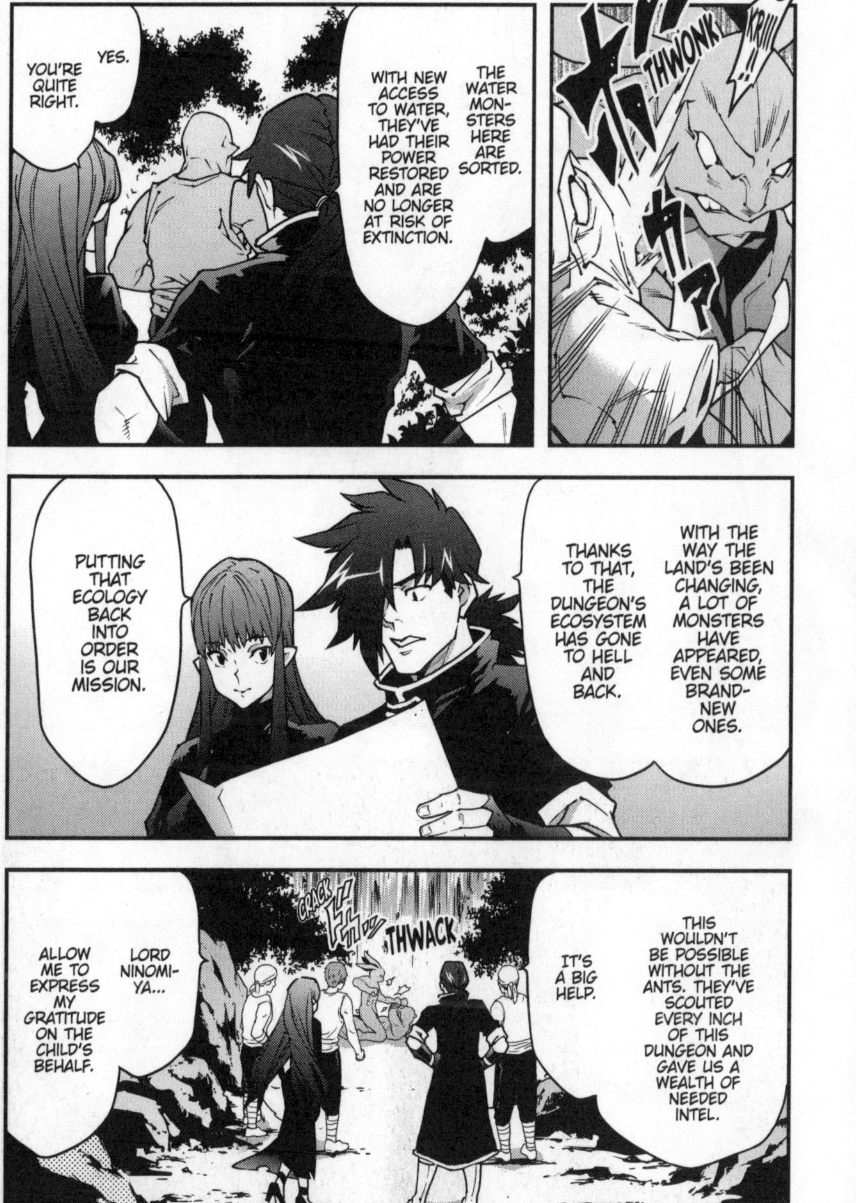
THWONK
KRIII!!
THE WATER MONSTERS HERE ARE SORTED.
WITH NEW ACCESS TO WATER, THEY'VE HAD THEIR POWER RESTORED AND ARE NO LONGER AT RISK OF EXTINCTION.
YES.
YOU'RE QUITE RIGHT.
WITH THE WAY THE LAND'S BEEN CHANGING, A LOT OF MONSTERS HAVE APPEARED, EVEN SOME BRAND-NEW ONES.
THANKS TO THAT, THE DUNGEON'S ECOSYSTEM HAS GONE TO HELL AND BACK.
PUTTING THAT ECOLOGY BACK INTO ORDER IS OUR MISSION.
THIS WOULDN'T BE POSSIBLE WITHOUT THE ANTS. THEY'VE SCOUTED EVERY INCH OF THIS DUNGEON AND GAVE US A WEALTH OF NEEDED INTEL.
IT'S A BIG HELP.
THWACK
CRACK
LORD NINOMIYA...
ALLOW ME TO EXPRESS MY GRATITUDE ON THE CHILD'S BEHALF.

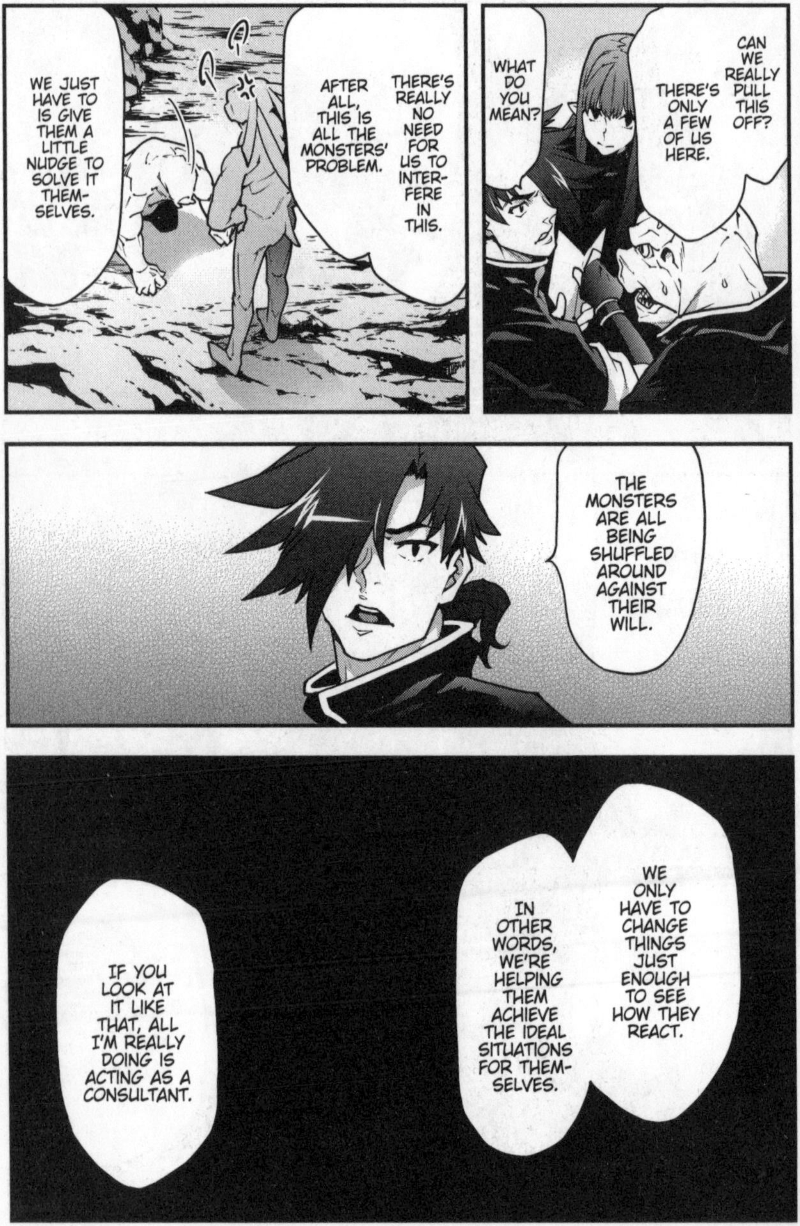
CAN WE REALLY PULL THIS OFF?
THERE'S ONLY A FEW OF US HERE.
WHAT DO YOU MEAN?
THERE'S REALLY NO NEED FOR US TO INTERFERE IN THIS.
AFTER ALL, THIS IS ALL THE MONSTERS' PROBLEM.
WE JUST HAVE TO IS GIVE THEM A LITTLE NUDGE TO SOLVE IT THEMSELVES.
THE MONSTERS ARE ALL BEING SHUFFLED AROUND AGAINST THEIR WILL.
WE ONLY HAVE TO CHANGE THINGS JUST ENOUGH TO SEE HOW THEY REACT.
IN OTHER WORDS, WE'RE HELPING THEM ACHIEVE THE IDEAL SITUATIONS FOR THEMSELVES.
IF YOU LOOK AT IT LIKE THAT, ALL I'M REALLY DOING IS ACTING AS A CONSULTANT.

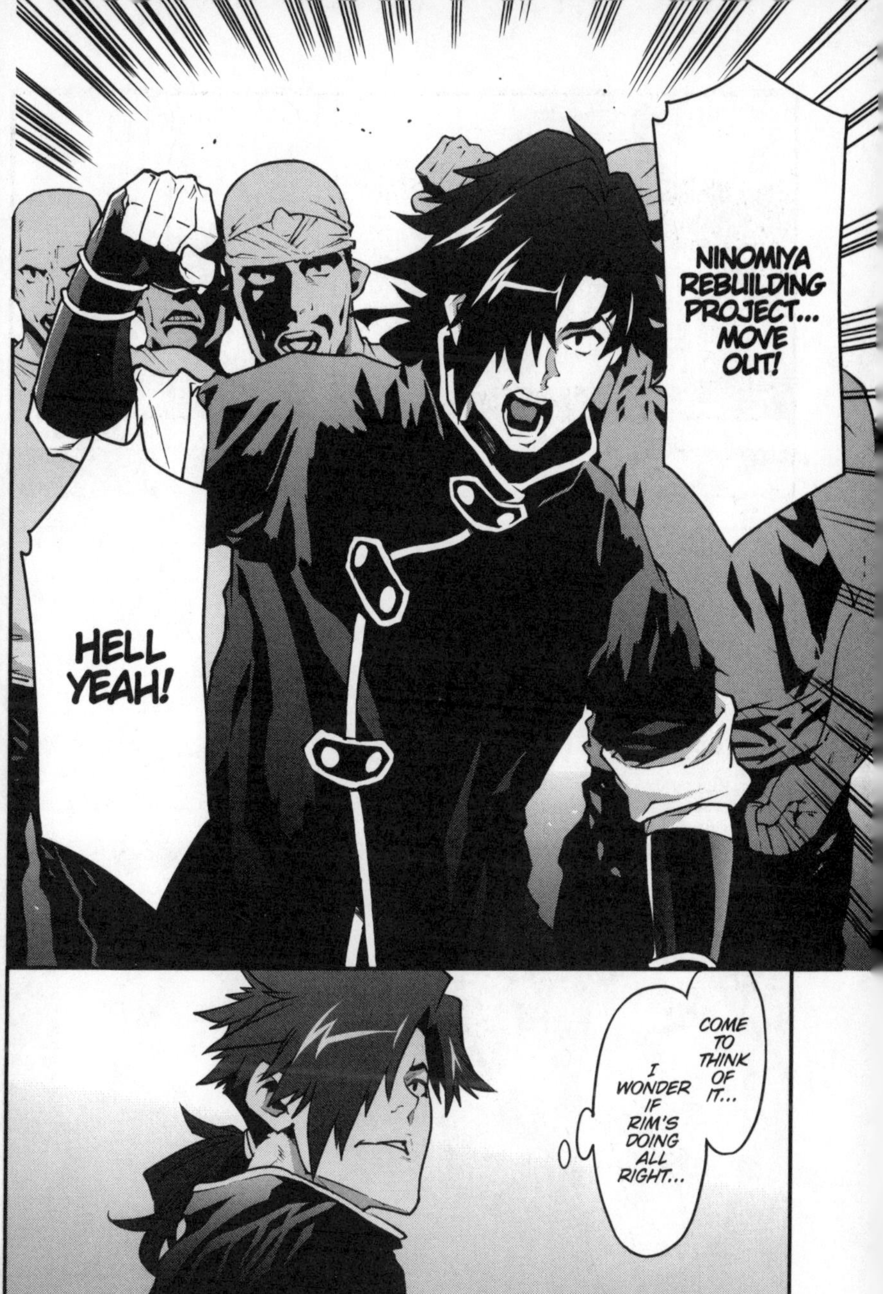
NINOMIYA REBUILDING PROJECT... MOVE OUT!
HELL YEAH!
COME TO THINK OF IT...
I WONDER IF RIM'S DOING ALL RIGHT...

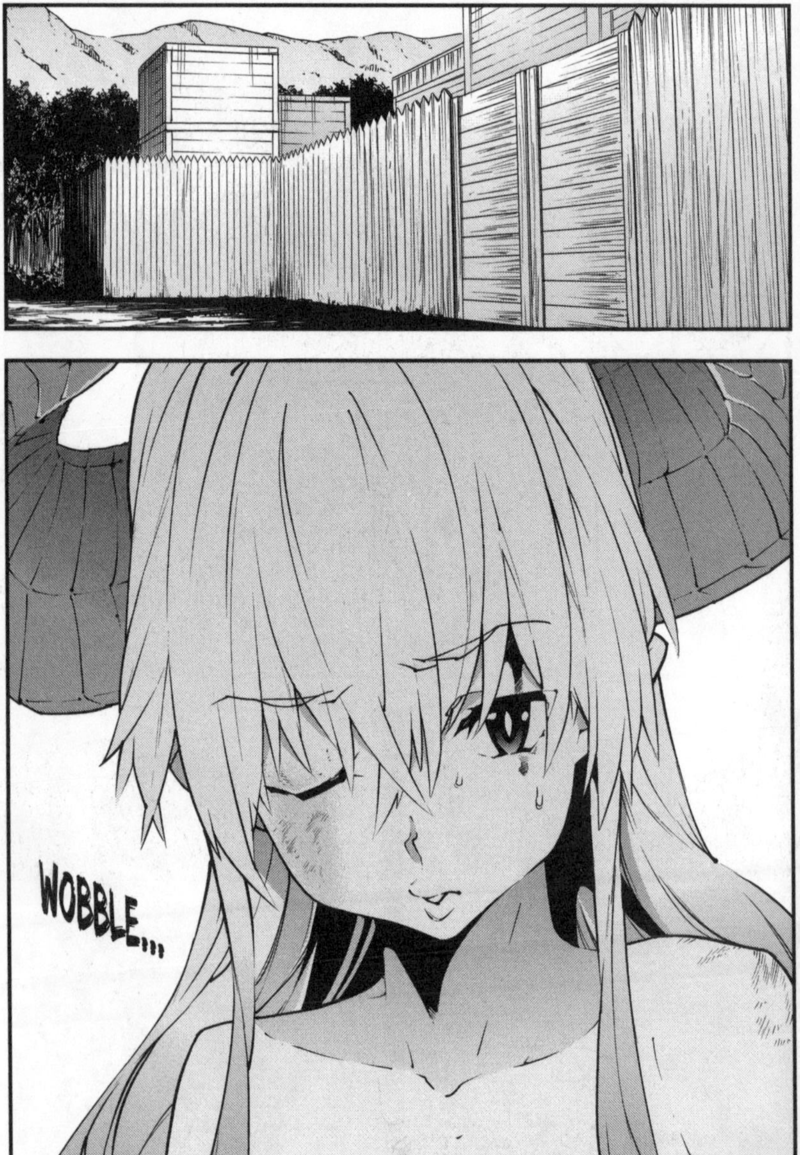
WOBBLE...

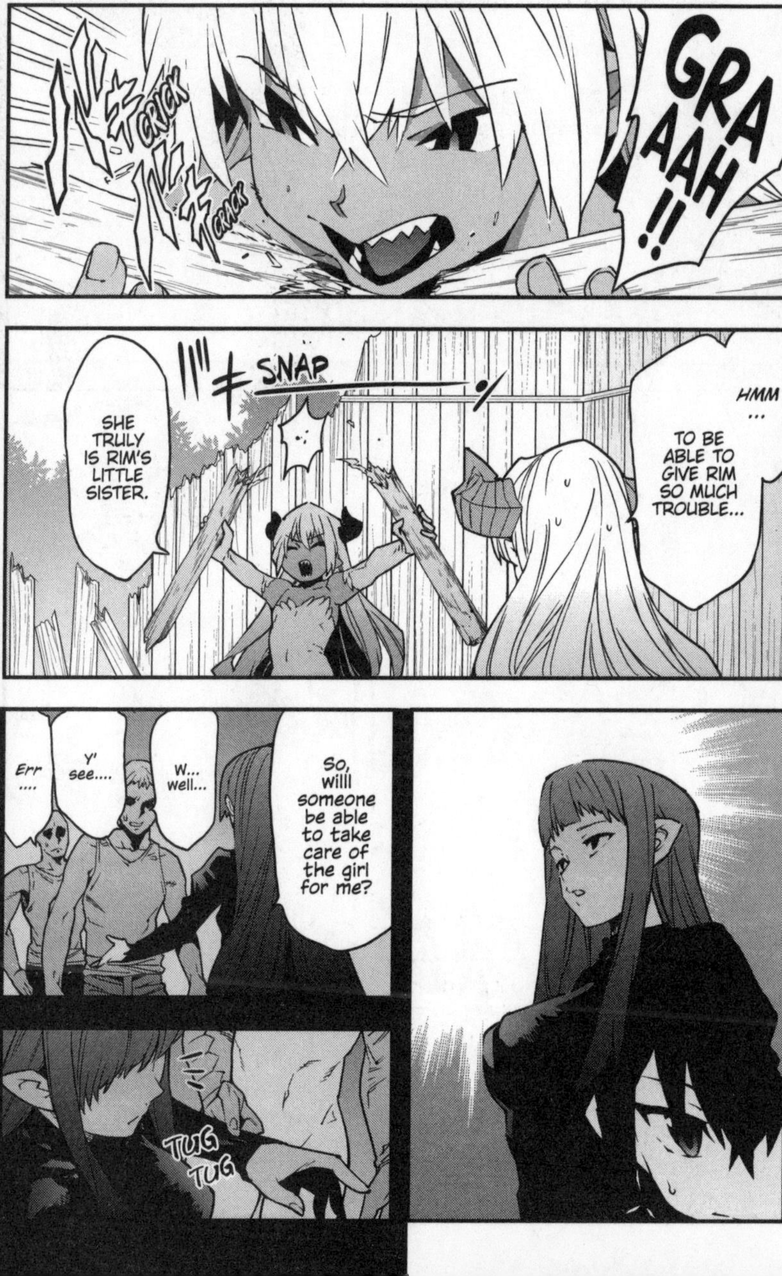

GRAAAH!!
CRICK
CRACK
HMM...
TO BE ABLE TO GIVE RIM SO MUCH TROUBLE...
SNAP
SHE TRULY IS RIM'S LITTLE SISTER.
So, willl someone be able to take care of the girl for me?
W... well...
Y' see....
Err ....
TUG TUG

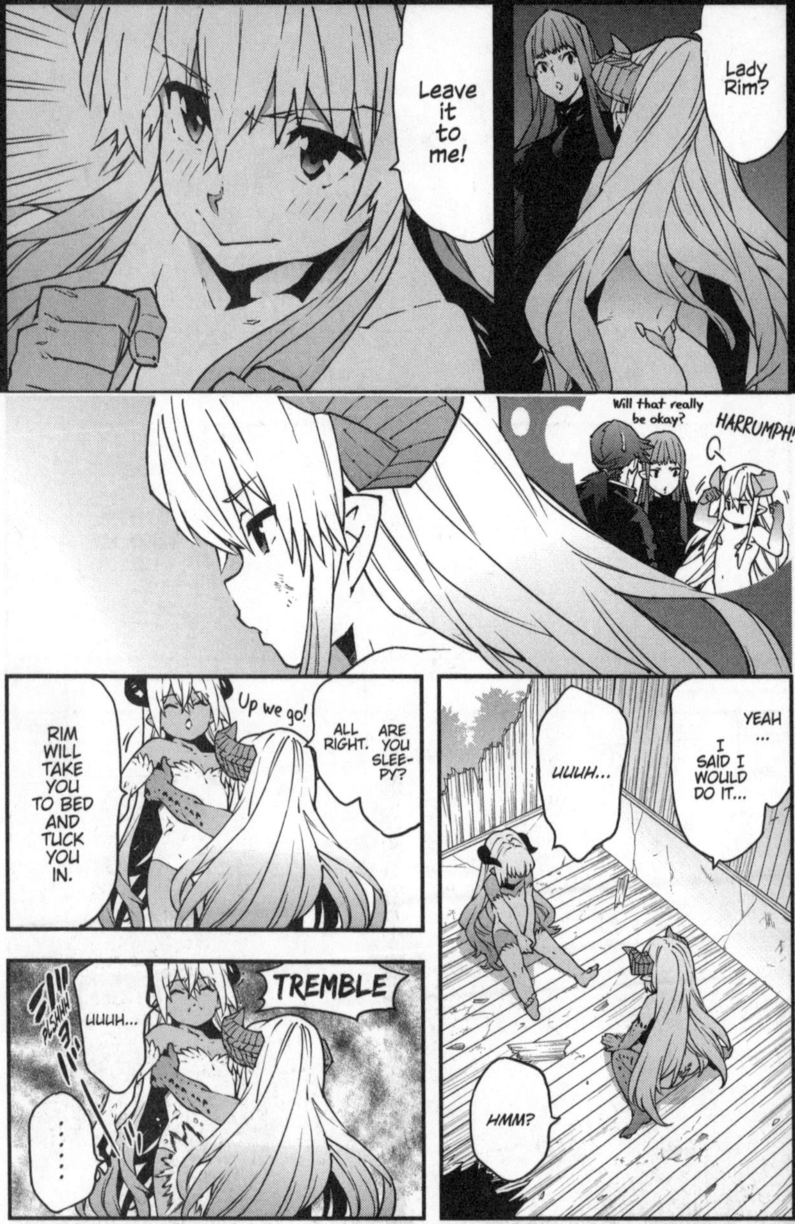
Lady Rim?
Leave it to me!
Will that really be okay?
HARRUMPH!
YEAH ... I SAID I WOULD DO IT...
UUUH...
HMM?
ARE YOU SLEEPY?
ALL RIGHT.
Up we go!
RIM WILL TAKE YOU TO BED AND TUCK YOU IN.
TREMBLE
UUUH...
PLSHHH
......

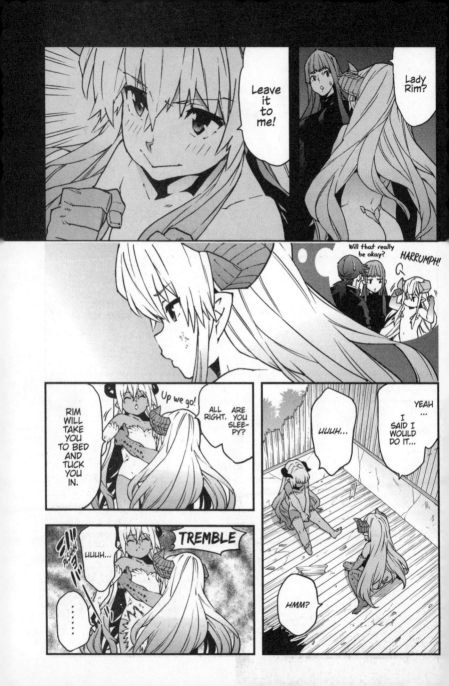

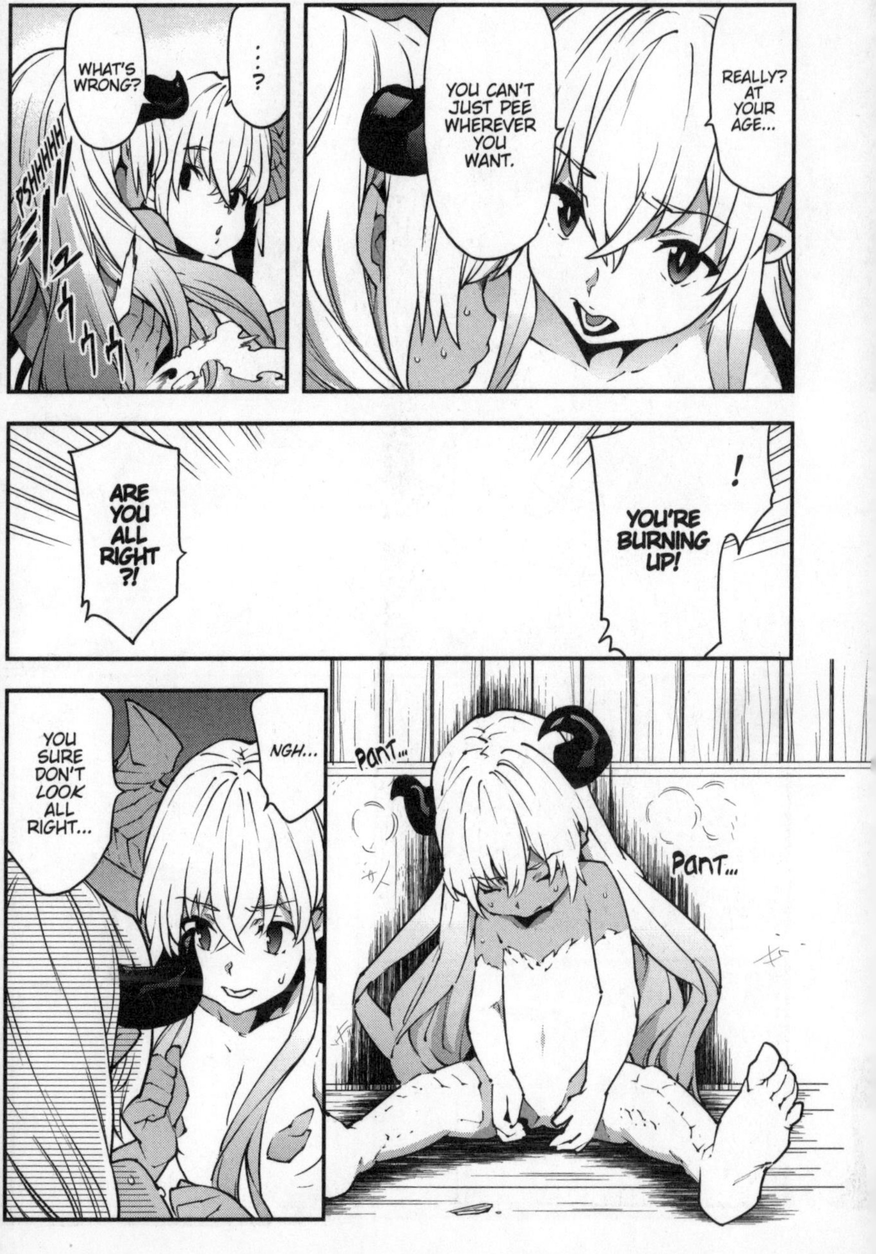
REALLY? AT YOUR AGE...
YOU CAN'T JUST PEE WHEREVER YOU WANT.
...?
WHAT'S WRONG?
PSHHHHH
!
YOU'RE BURNING UP!
ARE YOU ALL RIGHT?!
PANT...
PANT...
NGH...
YOU SURE DON'T LOOK ALL RIGHT...

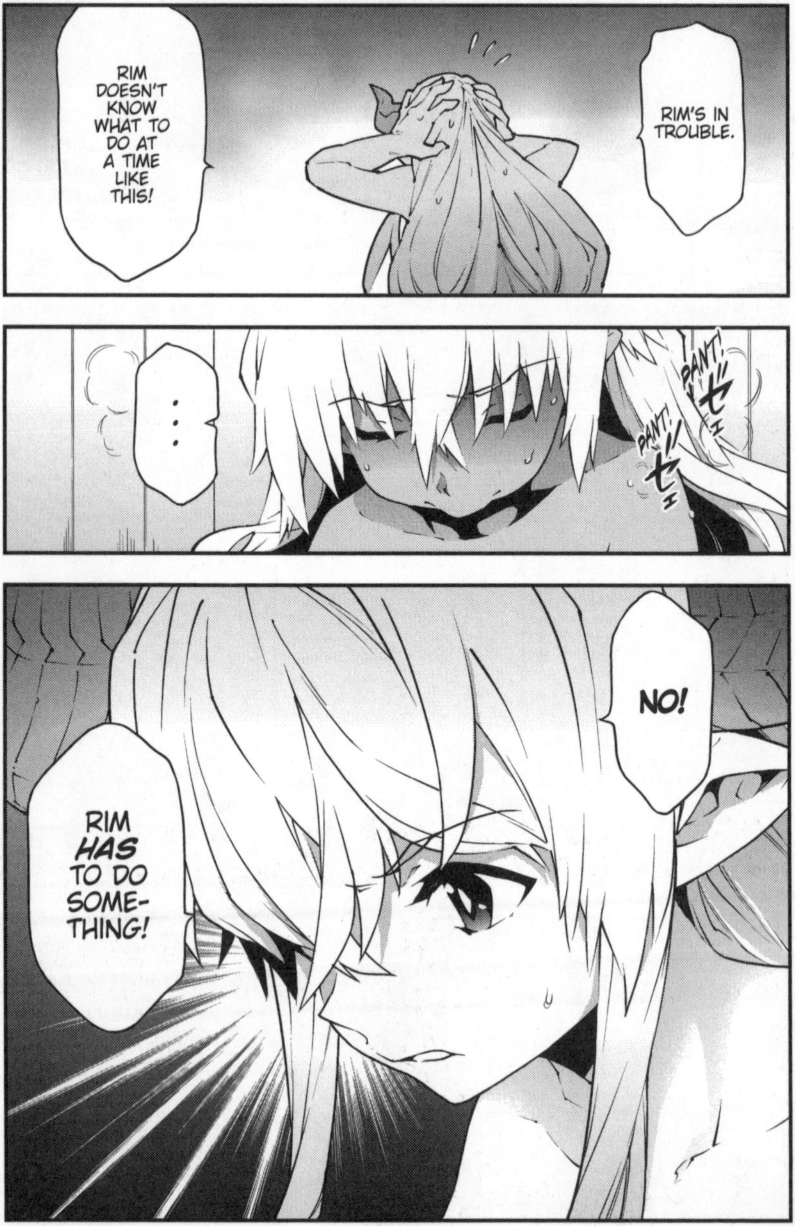
RIM'S IN TROUBLE.
RIM DOESN'T KNOW WHAT TO DO AT A TIME LIKE THIS!
PANT!
PANT!
...
NO!
RIM HAS TO DO SOMETHING!

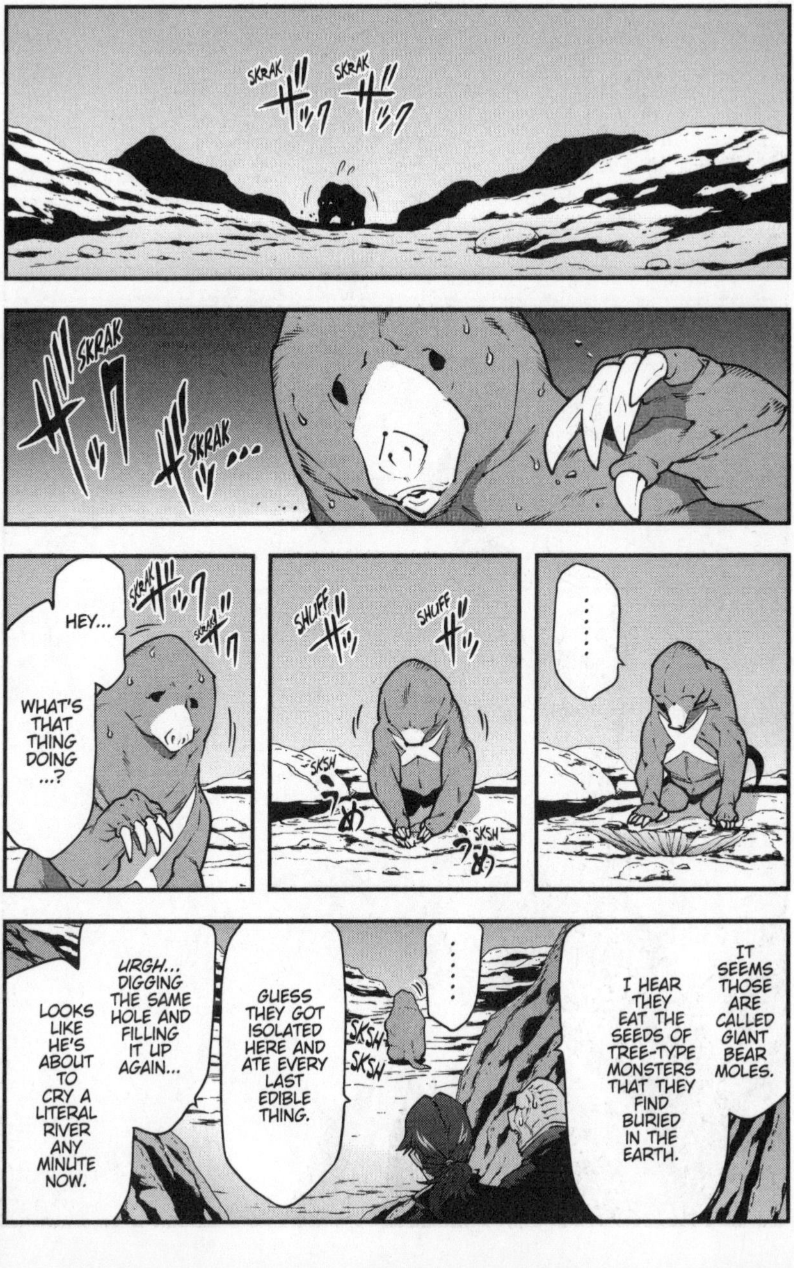
SKRAK
ザック
SKRAK
ザック
SKRAK
ザック
SKRAK...
ザッ
......
SHUFF
ザッ
SHUFF
ザッ
SKSH
SKSH
HEY...
SKRAK
ザック
SKRAK
ザク
WHAT'S THAT THING DOING ...?
IT SEEMS THOSE ARE CALLED GIANT BEAR MOLES.
I HEAR THEY EAT THE SEEDS OF TREE-TYPE MONSTERS THAT THEY FIND BURIED IN THE EARTH.
......
SKSH
SKSH
GUESS THEY GOT ISOLATED HERE AND ATE EVERY LAST EDIBLE THING.
URGH... DIGGING THE SAME HOLE AND FILLING IT UP AGAIN...
LOOKS LIKE HE'S ABOUT TO CRY A LITERAL RIVER ANY MINUTE NOW.

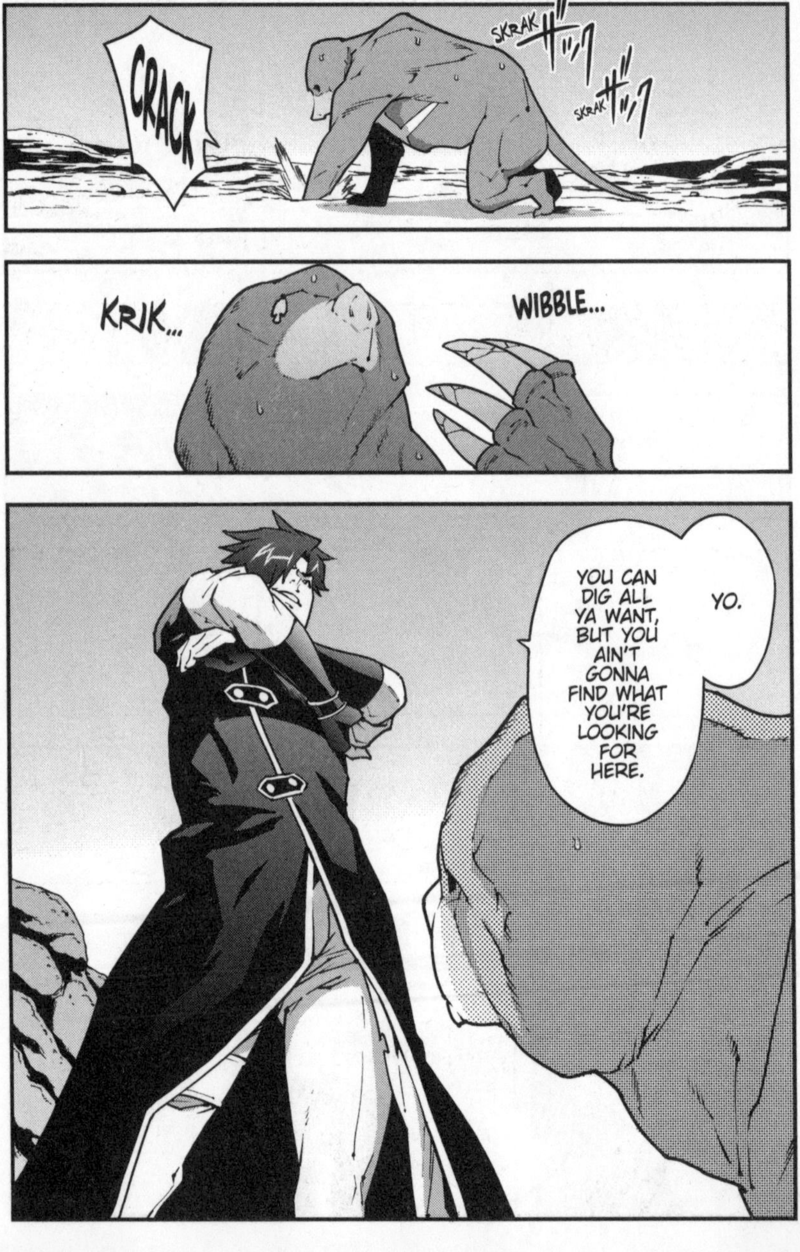
SKRAK
ザック
SKRAK
ザック
CRACK
WIBBLE...
KRJK...
YO.
YOU CAN DIG ALL YA WANT, BUT YOU AIN'T GONNA FIND WHAT YOU'RE LOOKING FOR HERE.

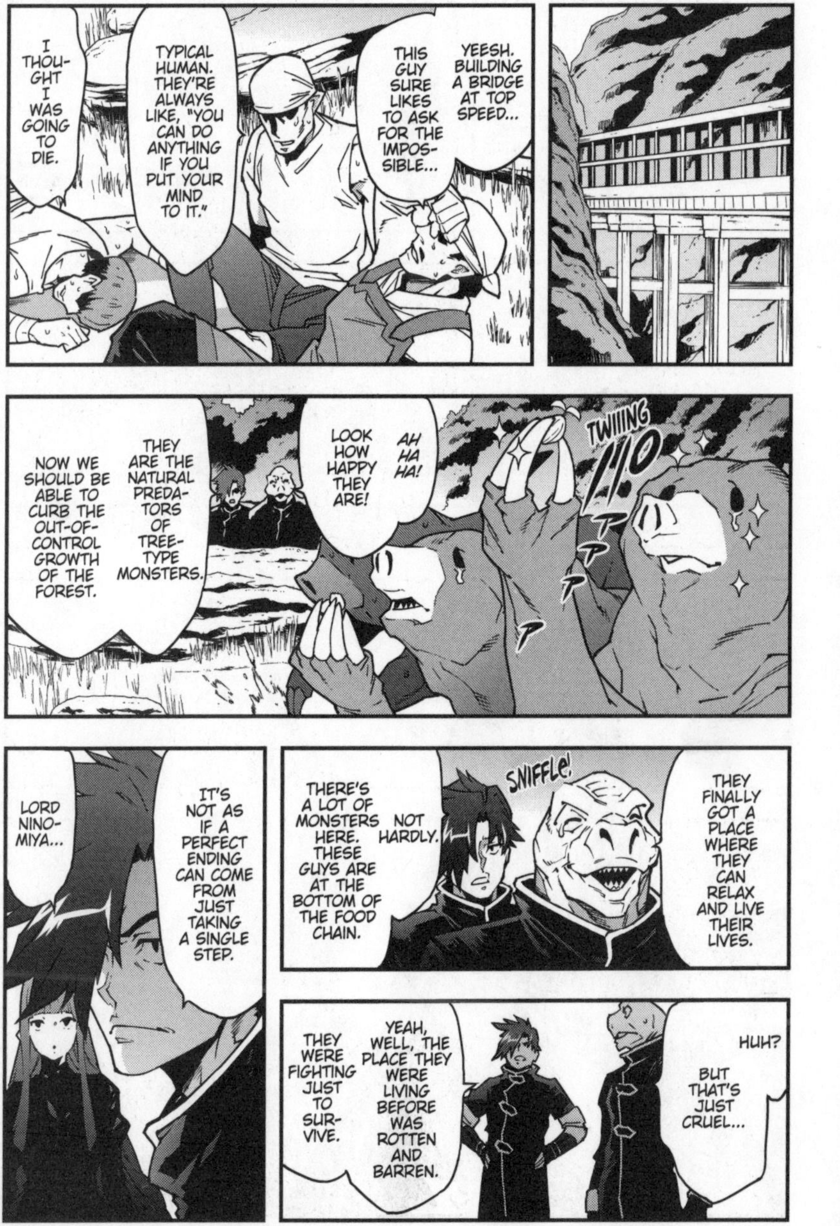
YEESH. BUILDING A BRIDGE AT TOP SPEED...
THIS GUY SURE LIKES TO ASK FOR THE IMPOSSIBLE...
TYPICAL HUMAN. THEY'RE ALWAYS LIKE, "YOU CAN DO ANYTHING IF YOU PUT YOUR MIND TO IT."
I THOUGHT I WAS GOING TO DIE.
TWIIING
AH HA HA!
LOOK HOW HAPPY THEY ARE!
THEY ARE THE NATURAL PREDATORS OF TREE-TYPE MONSTERS.
NOW WE SHOULD BE ABLE TO CURB THE OUT-OF-CONTROL GROWTH OF THE FOREST.
THEY FINALLY GOT A PLACE WHERE THEY CAN RELAX AND LIVE THEIR LIVES.
SNIFFLE!
NOT HARDLY.
THERE'S A LOT OF MONSTERS HERE. THESE GUYS ARE AT THE BOTTOM OF THE FOOD CHAIN.
HUH?
BUT THAT'S JUST CRUEL...
YEAH, WELL, THE PLACE THEY WERE LIVING BEFORE WAS ROTTEN AND BARREN.
THEY WERE FIGHTING JUST TO SURVIVE.
IT'S NOT AS IF A PERFECT ENDING CAN COME FROM JUST TAKING A SINGLE STEP.
LORD NINOMIYA...

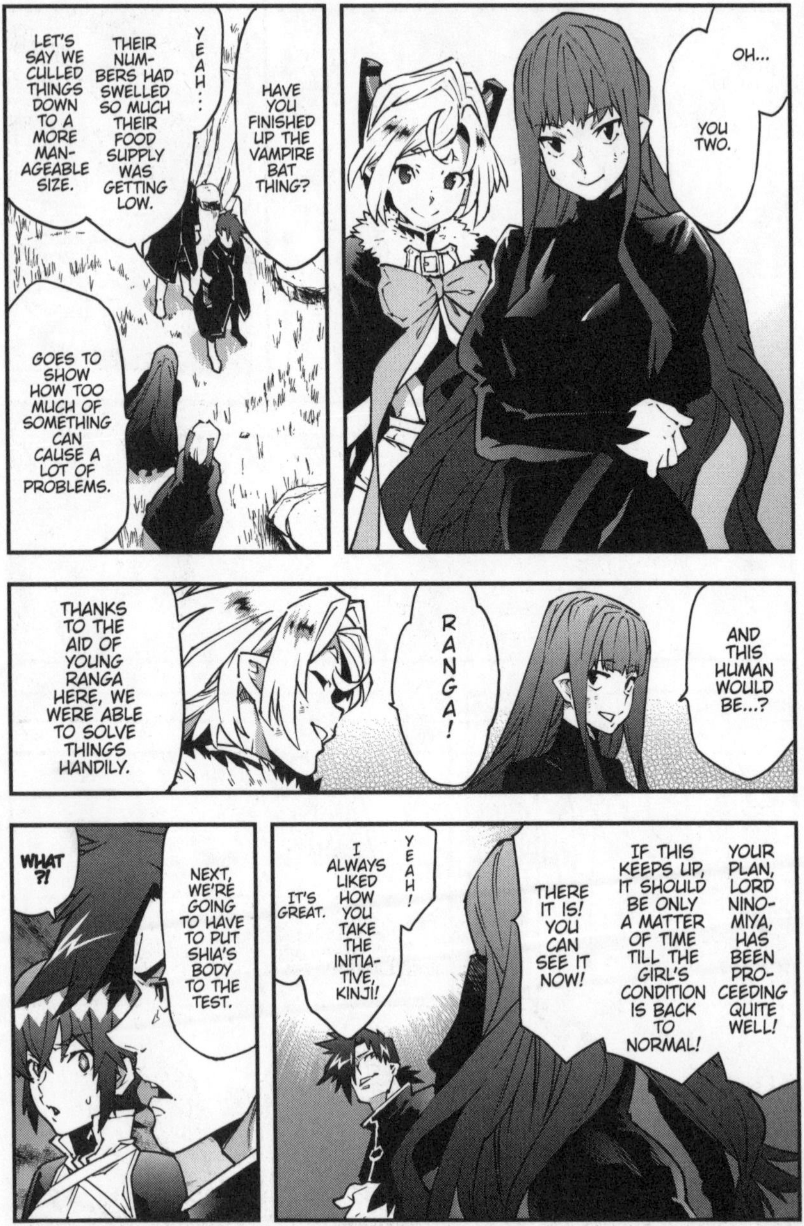
OH...
YOU TWO.
HAVE YOU FINISHED UP THE VAMPIRE BAT THING?
YEAH...
THEIR NUMBERS HAD SWELLED SO MUCH THEIR FOOD SUPPLY WAS GETTING LOW.
LET'S SAY WE CULLED THINGS DOWN TO A MORE MANAGEABLE SIZE.
GOES TO SHOW HOW TOO MUCH OF SOMETHING CAN CAUSE A LOT OF PROBLEMS.
AND THIS HUMAN WOULD BE...?
RANGA!
THANKS TO THE AID OF YOUNG RANGA HERE, WE WERE ABLE TO SOLVE THINGS HANDILY.
YOUR PLAN, LORD NINOMIYA, HAS BEEN PROCEEDING QUITE WELL!
IF THIS KEEPS UP, IT SHOULD BE ONLY A MATTER OF TIME TILL THE GIRL'S CONDITION IS BACK TO NORMAL!
THERE IT IS! YOU CAN SEE IT NOW!
YEAH!
I ALWAYS LIKED HOW YOU TAKE THE INITIATIVE, KINJI!
IT'S GREAT.
NEXT, WE'RE GOING TO HAVE TO PUT SHIA'S BODY TO THE TEST.
WHAT?!

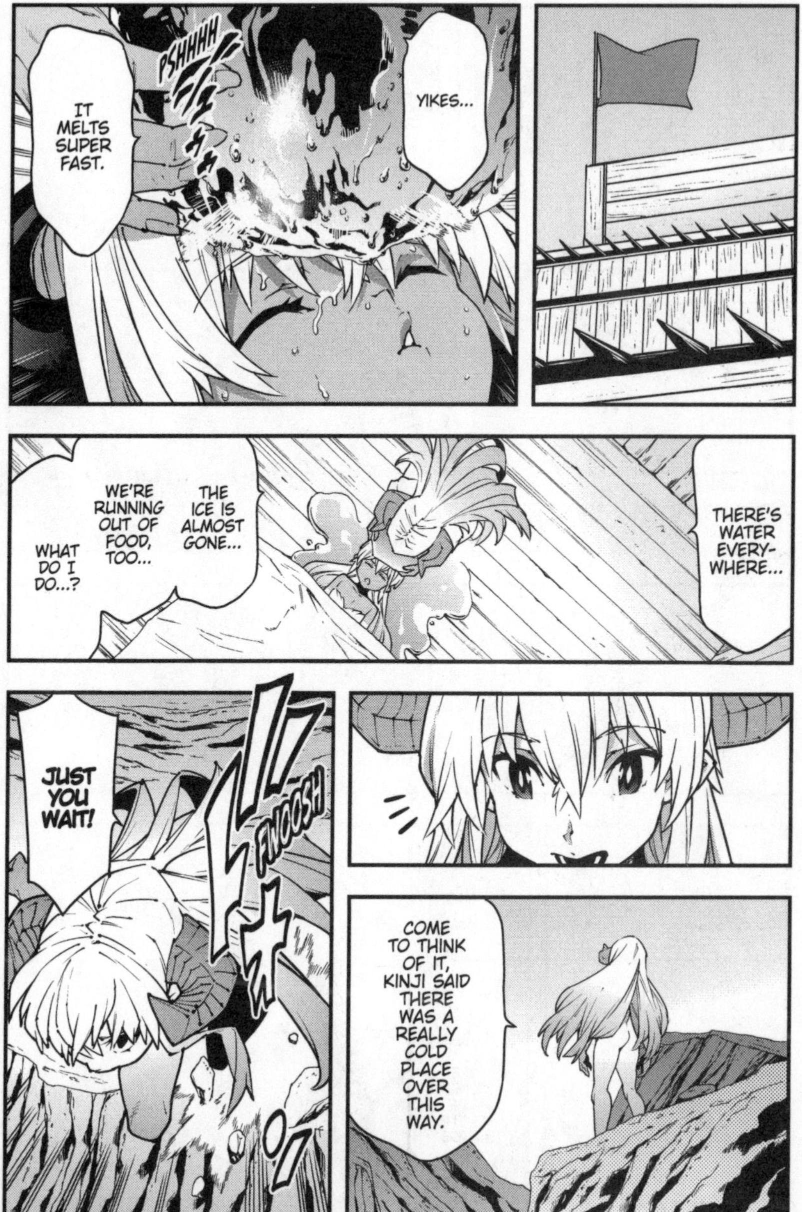
YIKES...
PSHHHH
IT MELTS SUPER FAST.
THERE'S WATER EVERY-WHERE...
THE ICE IS ALMOST GONE...
WE'RE RUNNING OUT OF FOOD, TOO...
WHAT DO I DO...?
COME TO THINK OF IT, KINJI SAID THERE WAS A REALLY COLD PLACE OVER THIS WAY.
JUST YOU WAIT!
FWOOSH

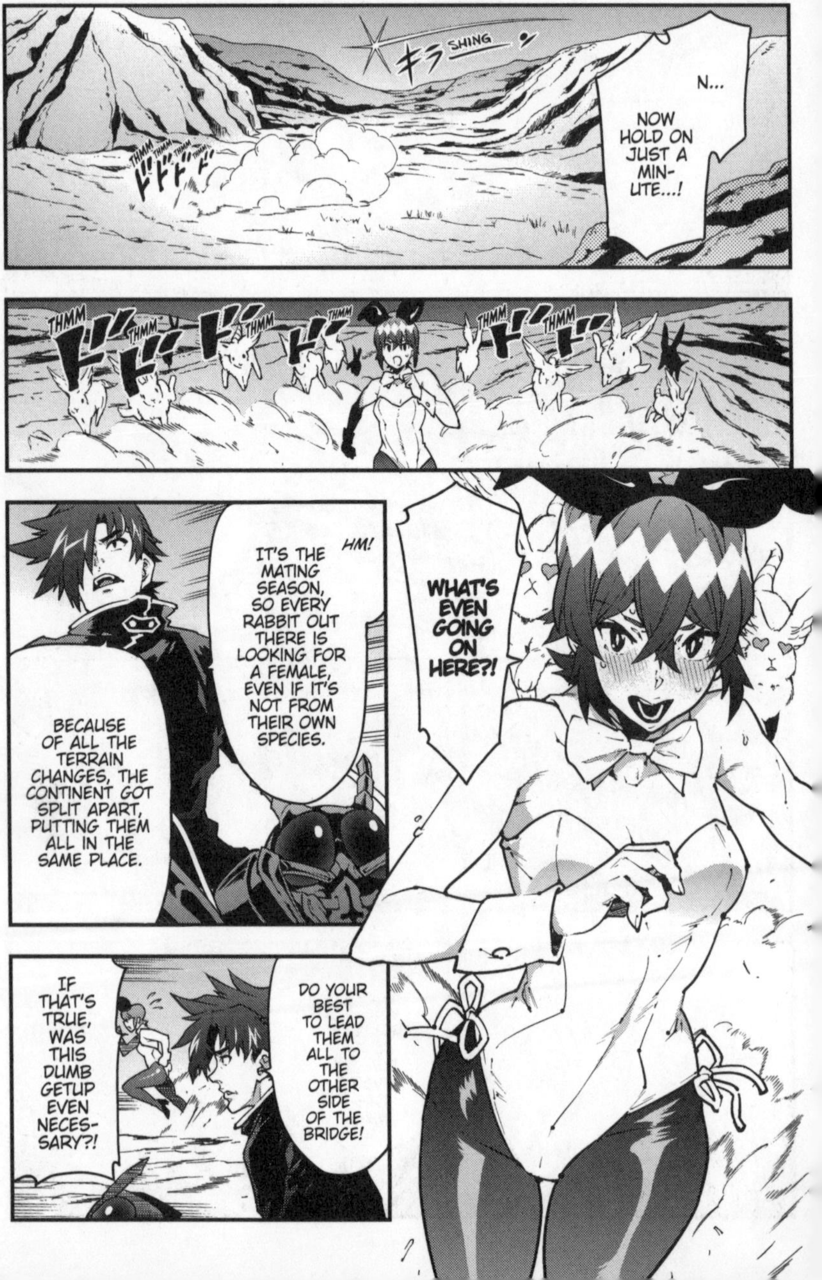
N...
NOW HOLD ON JUST A MIN-UTE...!
キラ SHING
THMM THMM THMM THMM
ドドドド
THMM THMM THMM THMM THMM THMM
WHAT'S EVEN GOING ON HERE?!
HM!
IT'S THE MATING SEASON, SO EVERY RABBIT OUT THERE IS LOOKING FOR A FEMALE, EVEN IF IT'S NOT FROM THEIR OWN SPECIES.
BECAUSE OF ALL THE TERRAIN CHANGES, THE CONTINENT GOT SPLIT APART, PUTTING THEM ALL IN THE SAME PLACE.
DO YOUR BEST TO LEAD THEM ALL TO THE OTHER SIDE OF THE BRIDGE!
IF THAT'S TRUE, WAS THIS DUMB GETUP EVEN NECES-SARY?!

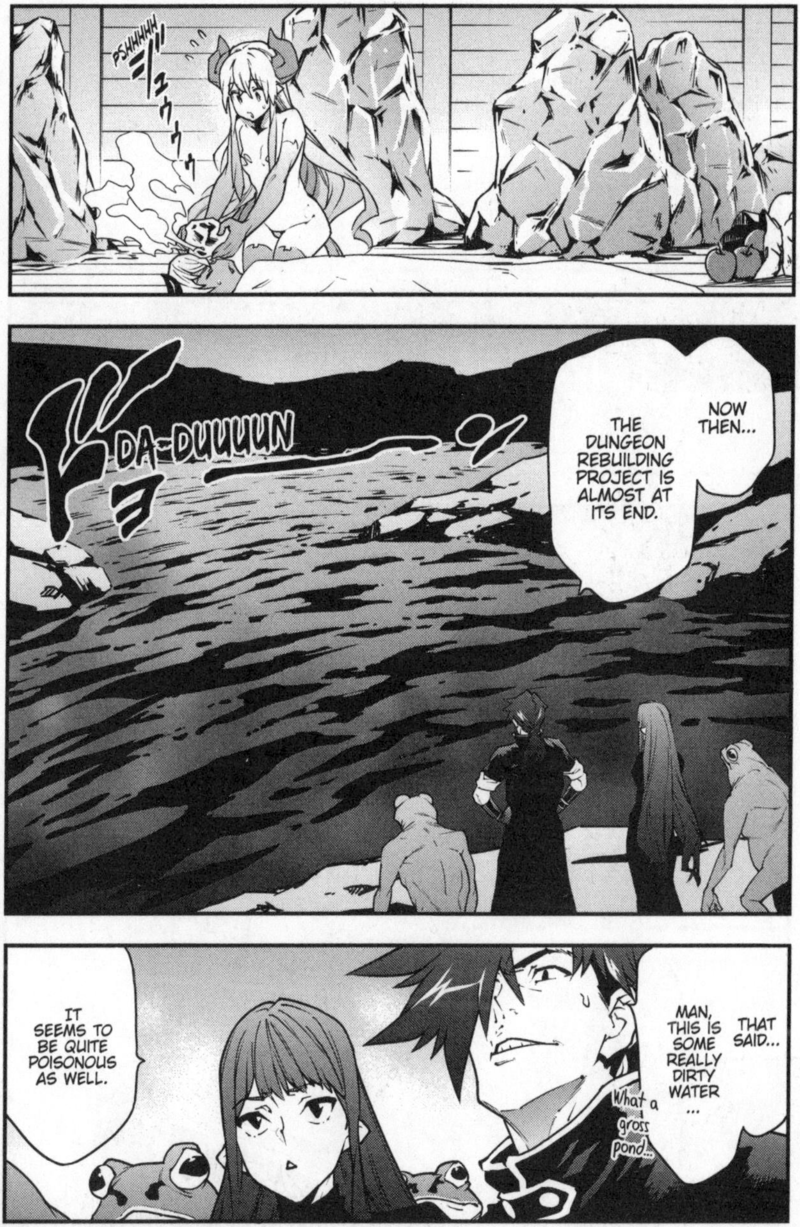
PSHHHHH
DA-DUUUUN
NOW THEN...
THE DUNGEON REBUILDING PROJECT IS ALMOST AT ITS END.
THAT SAID...
MAN, THIS IS SOME REALLY DIRTY WATER ...
What a gross pond...
IT SEEMS TO BE QUITE POISONOUS AS WELL.

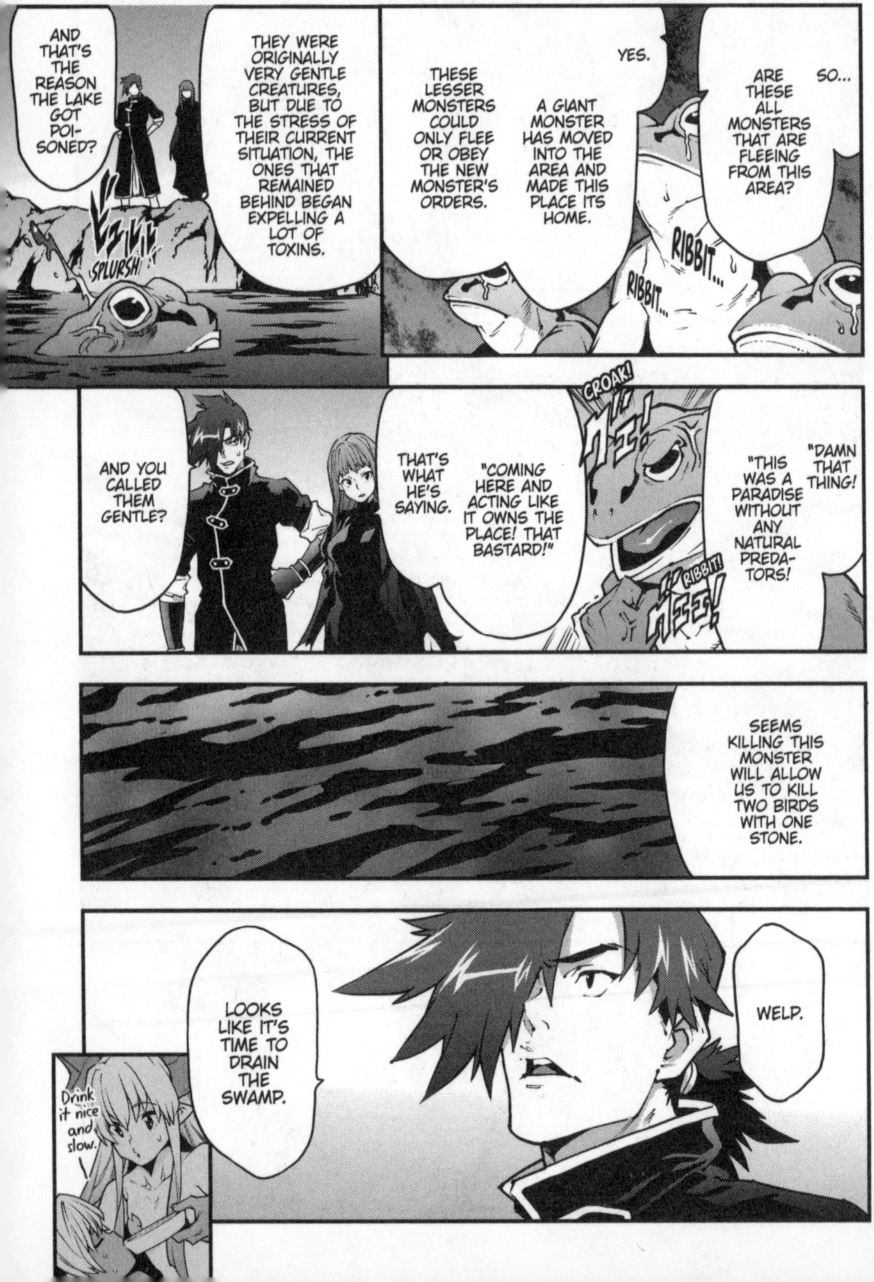
SO...
ARE THESE ALL MONSTERS THAT ARE FLEEING FROM THIS AREA?
YES.
A GIANT MONSTER HAS MOVED INTO THE AREA AND MADE THIS PLACE ITS HOME.
THESE LESSER MONSTERS COULD ONLY FLEE OR OBEY THE NEW MONSTER'S ORDERS.
RIBBIT...
RIBBIT...
THEY WERE ORIGINALLY VERY GENTLE CREATURES, BUT DUE TO THE STRESS OF THEIR CURRENT SITUATION, THE ONES THAT REMAINED BEHIND BEGAN EXPELLING A LOT OF TOXINS.
AND THAT'S THE REASON THE LAKE GOT POI-SONED?
SPLURSH
CROAK!
"DAMN THAT THING!
"THIS WAS A PARADISE WITHOUT ANY NATURAL PREDA-TORS!
RIBBIT!
"COMING HERE AND ACTING LIKE IT OWNS THE PLACE! THAT BASTARD!"
THAT'S WHAT HE'S SAYING.
AND YOU CALLED THEM GENTLE?
SEEMS KILLING THIS MONSTER WILL ALLOW US TO KILL TWO BIRDS WITH ONE STONE.
WELP.
LOOKS LIKE IT'S TIME TO DRAIN THE SWAMP.
Drink it nice and slow.

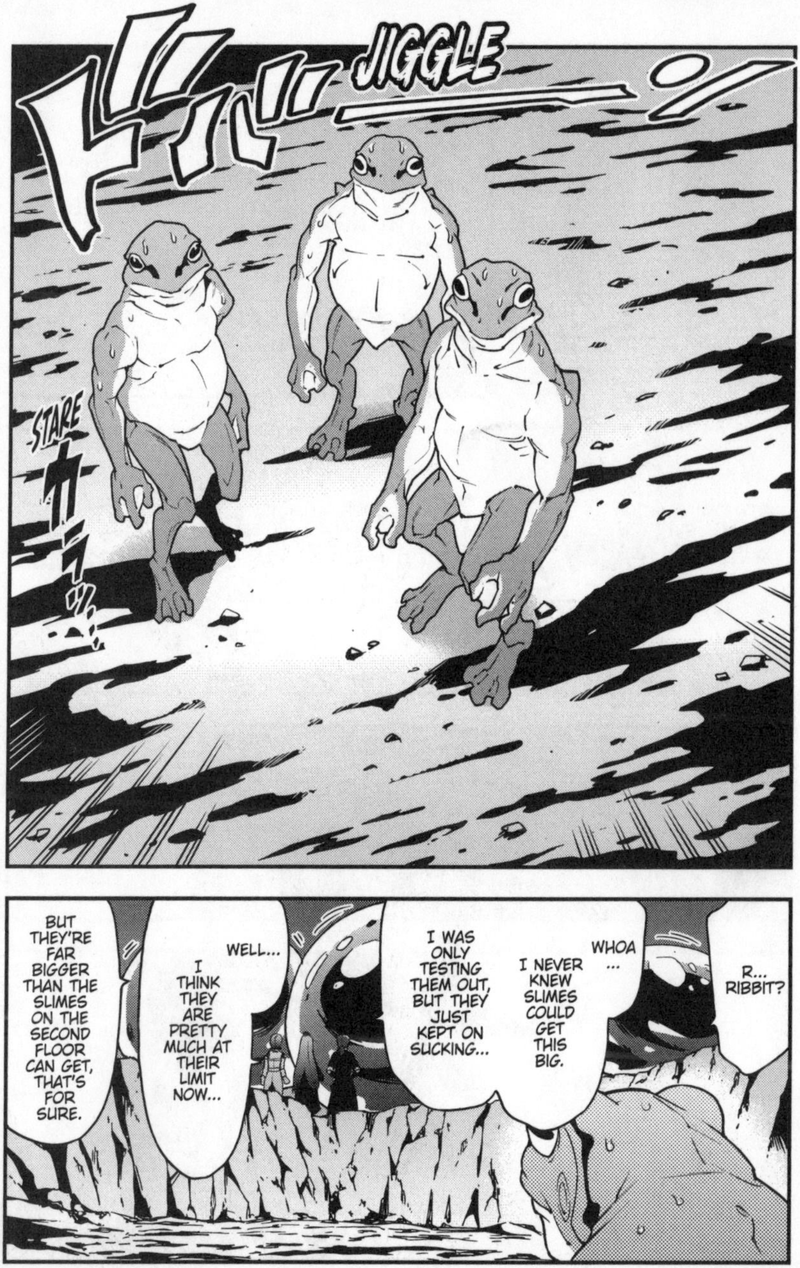
JIGGLE
STARE
R... RIBBIT?
WHOA ...
I NEVER KNEW SLIMES COULD GET THIS BIG.
I WAS ONLY TESTING THEM OUT, BUT THEY JUST KEPT ON SUCKING...
WELL...
I THINK THEY ARE PRETTY MUCH AT THEIR LIMIT NOW...
BUT THEY'RE FAR BIGGER THAN THE SLIMES ON THE SECOND FLOOR CAN GET, THAT'S FOR SURE.

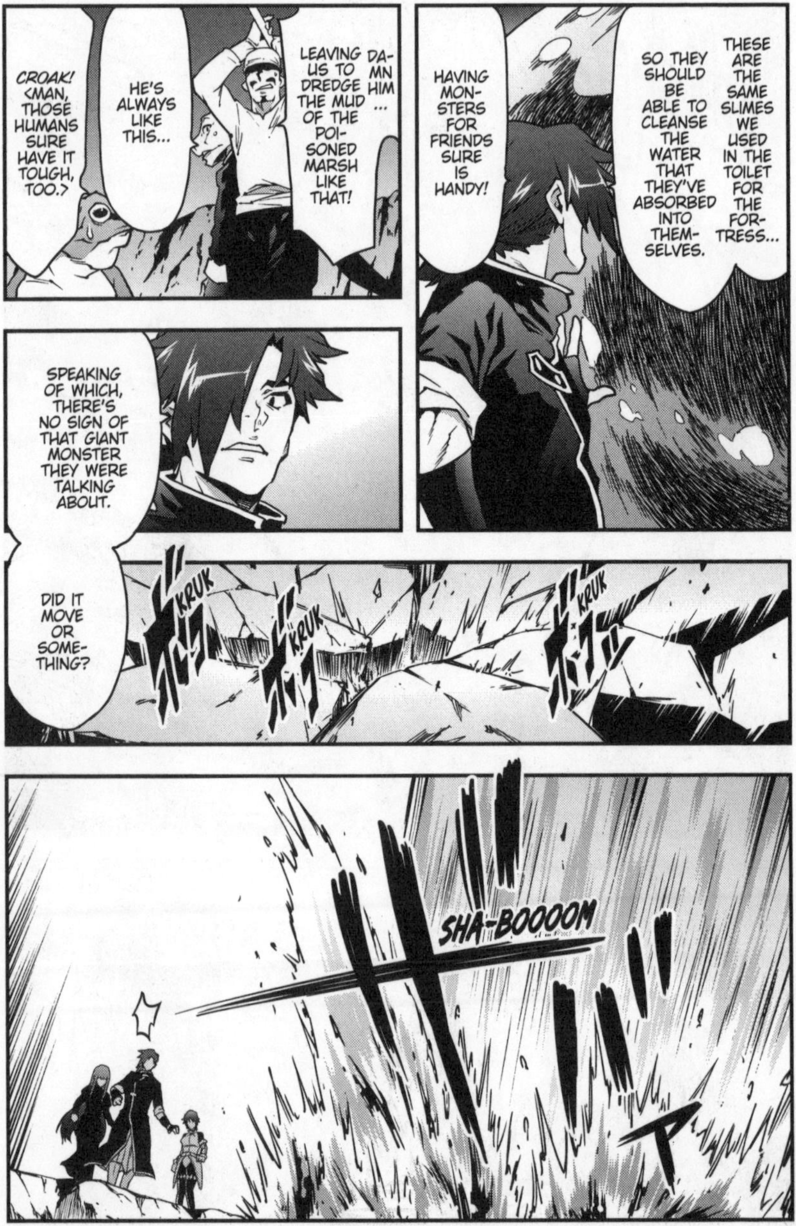
THESE ARE THE SAME SLIMES WE USED IN THE TOILET FOR THE FORTRESS...
SO THEY SHOULD BE ABLE TO CLEANSE THE WATER THAT THEY'VE ABSORBED INTO THEMSELVES.
HAVING MONSTERS FOR FRIENDS SURE IS HANDY!
DAMN HIM...
LEAVING US TO DREDGE THE MUD OF THE POISONED MARSH LIKE THAT!
HE'S ALWAYS LIKE THIS...
CROAK! <MAN, THOSE HUMANS SURE HAVE IT TOUGH, TOO.>
SPEAKING OF WHICH, THERE'S NO SIGN OF THAT GIANT MONSTER THEY WERE TALKING ABOUT.
KRUK
KRUK
KRUK
DID IT MOVE OR SOMETHING?
SHA-BOOOOM

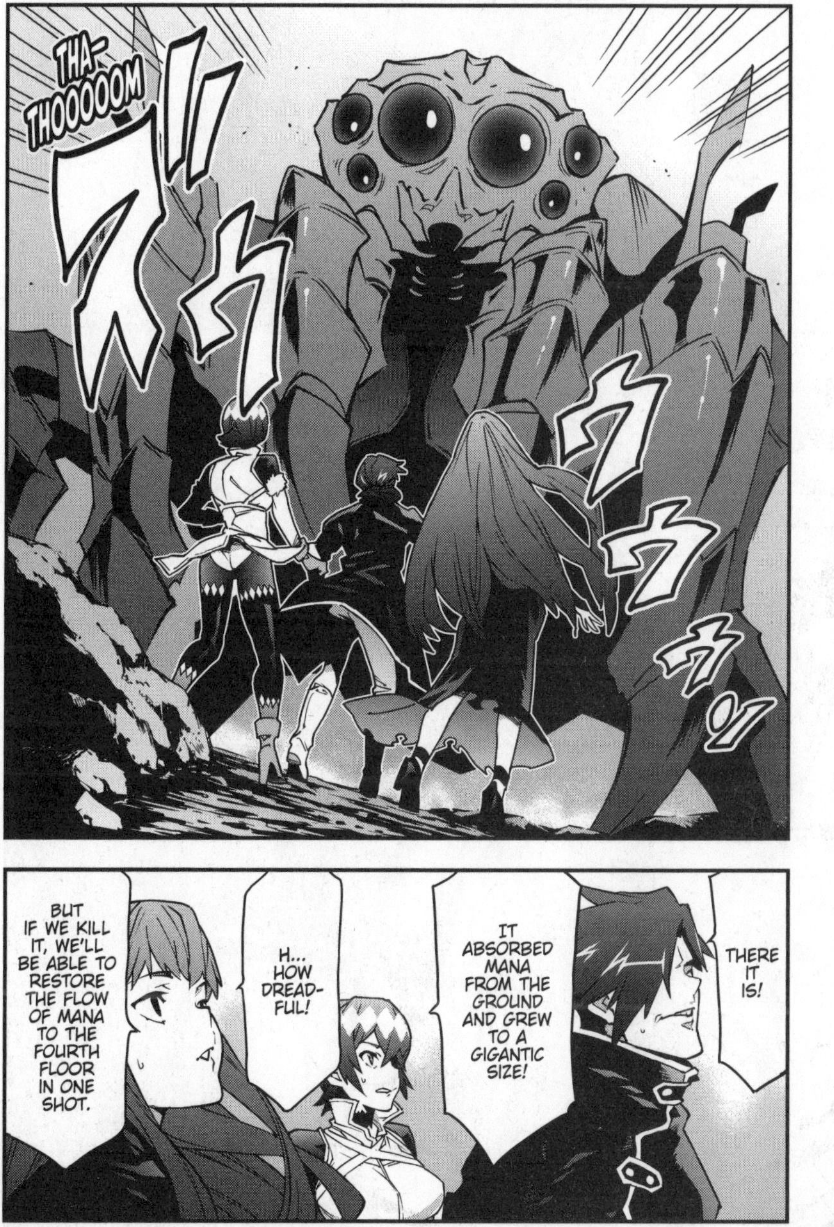
THA-THOOOOOM
THERE IT IS!
IT ABSORBED MANA FROM THE GROUND AND GREW TO A GIGANTIC SIZE!
H... HOW DREAD-FUL!
BUT IF WE KILL IT, WE'LL BE ABLE TO RESTORE THE FLOW OF MANA TO THE FOURTH FLOOR IN ONE SHOT.

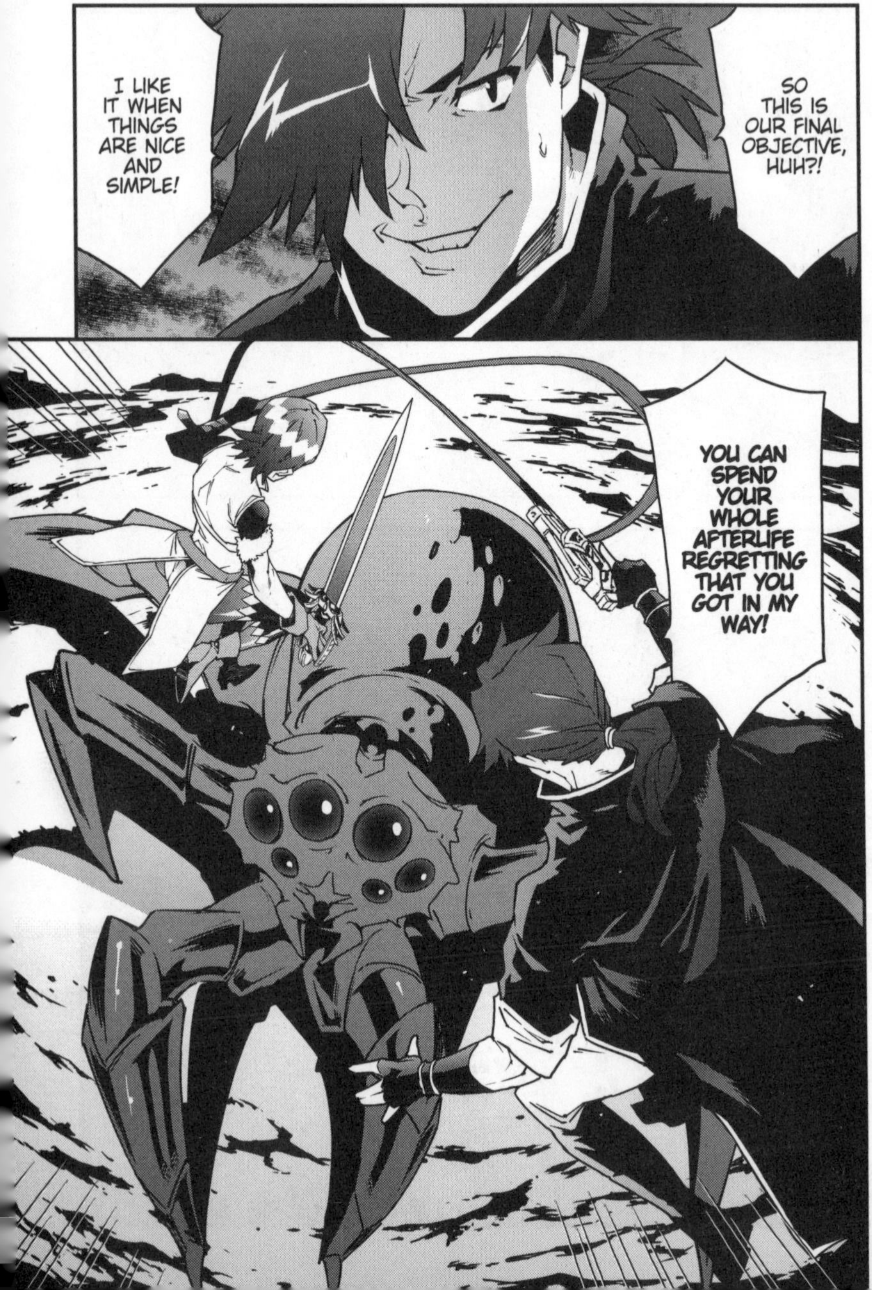
SO THIS IS OUR FINAL OBJECTIVE, HUH?!
I LIKE IT WHEN THINGS ARE NICE AND SIMPLE!
YOU CAN SPEND YOUR WHOLE AFTERLIFE REGRETTING THAT YOU GOT IN MY WAY!

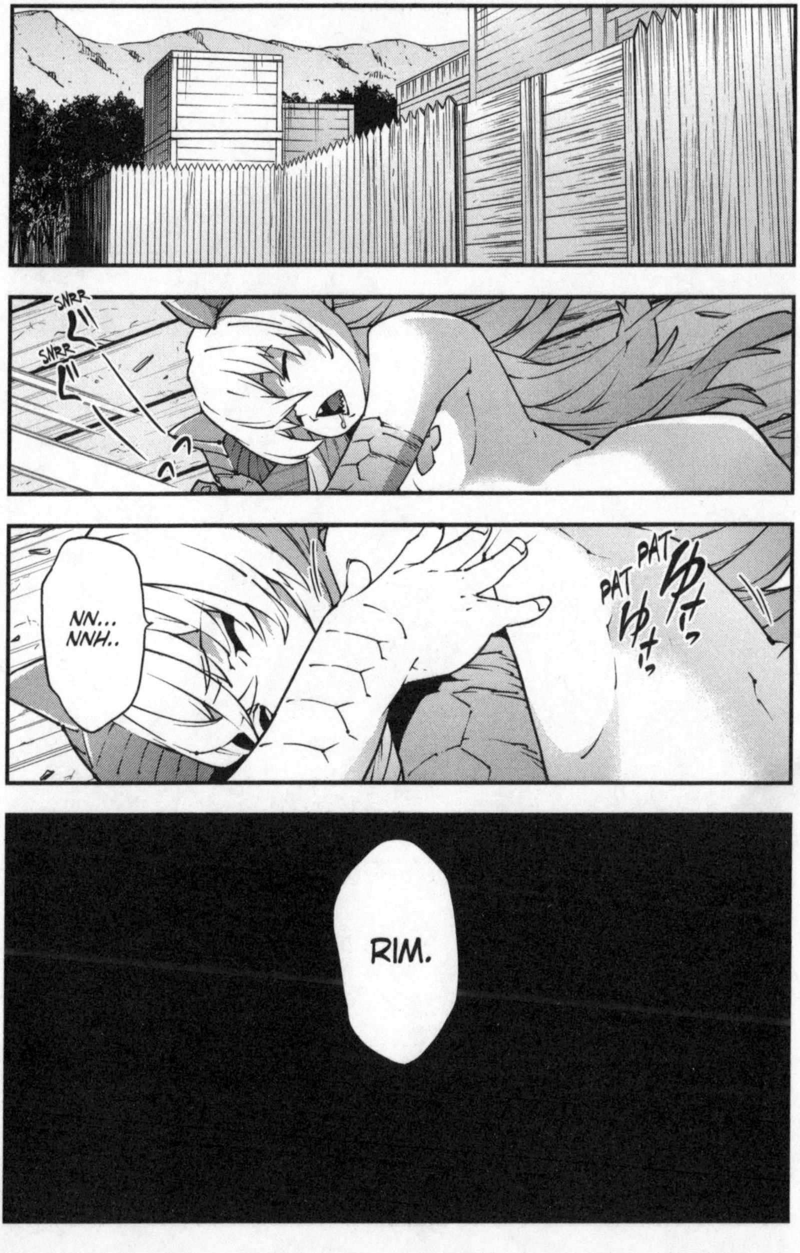
SNRR
SNRR
NN... NNH..
PAT PAT
RIM.

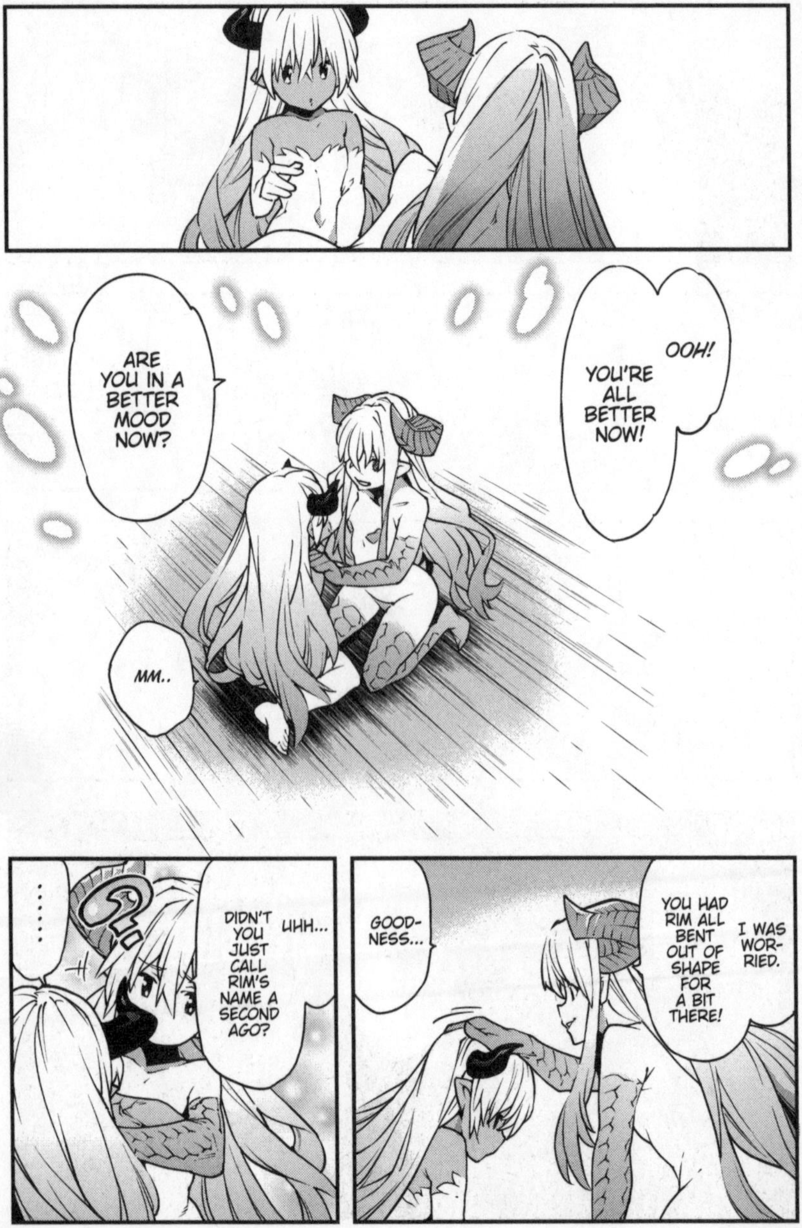
OOH!
YOU'RE ALL BETTER NOW!
ARE YOU IN A BETTER MOOD NOW?
MM..
I WAS WOR-RIED.
YOU HAD RIM ALL BENT OUT OF SHAPE FOR A BIT THERE!
GOOD-NESS...
UHH...
DIDN'T YOU JUST CALL RIM'S NAME A SECOND AGO?
......

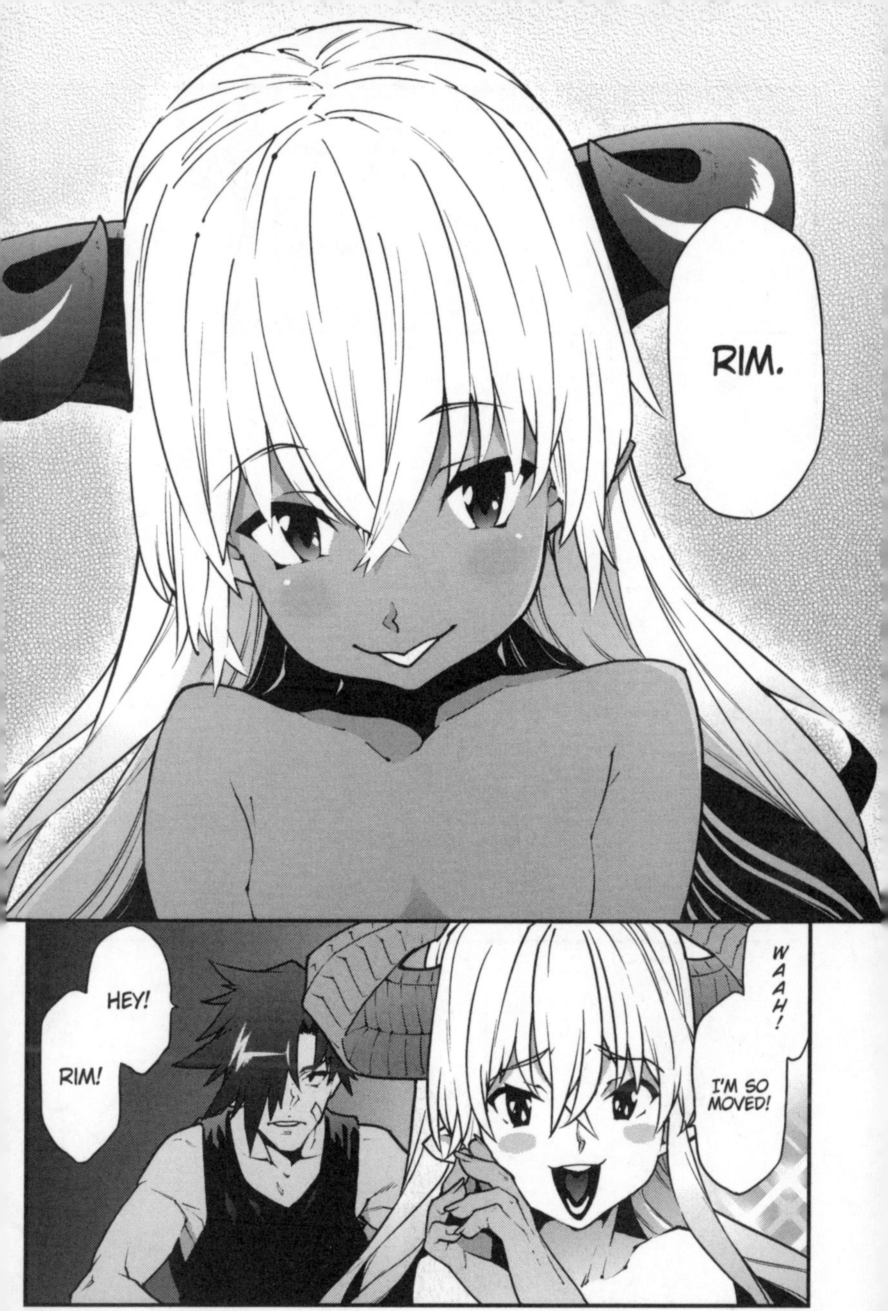
RIM.
WAAH!
I'M SO MOVED!
HEY!
RIM!

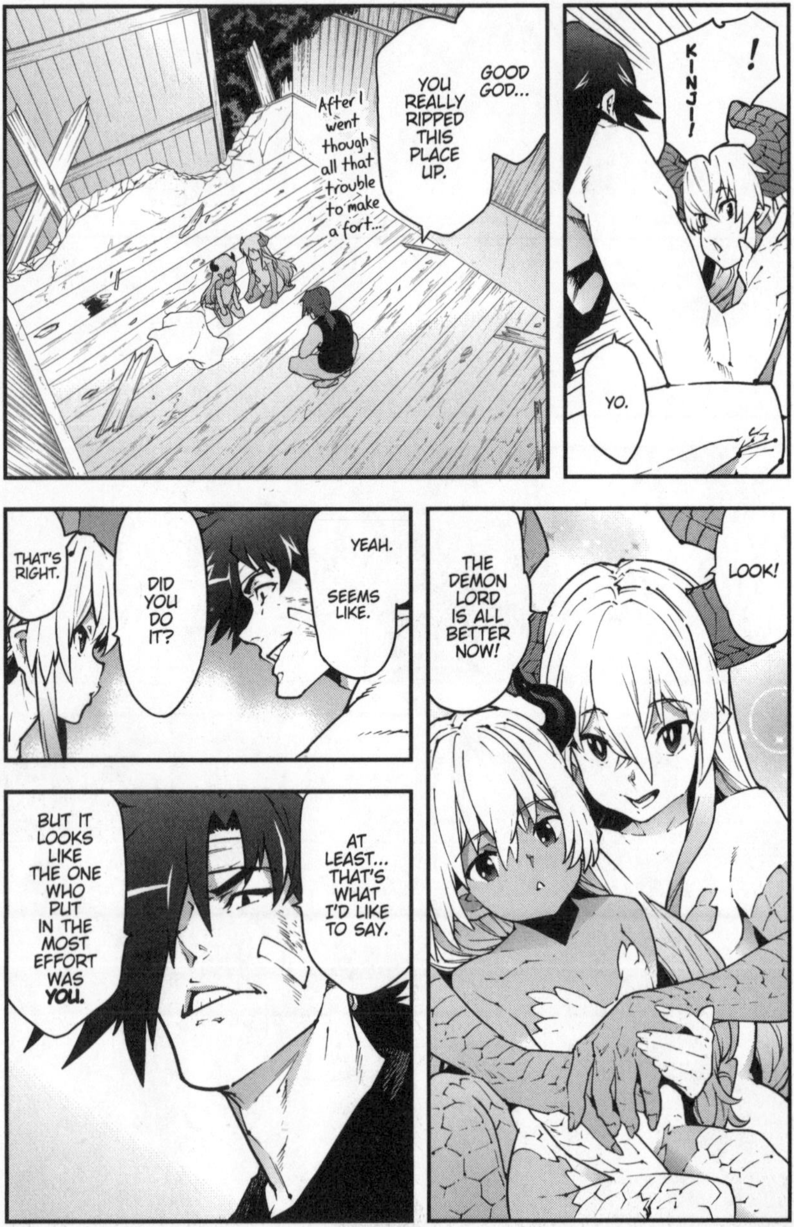
!
KINJI!
YO.
GOOD GOD...
YOU REALLY RIPPED THIS PLACE UP.
After I went though all that trouble to make a fort...
LOOK!
THE DEMON LORD IS ALL BETTER NOW!
YEAH.
SEEMS LIKE.
DID YOU DO IT?
THAT'S RIGHT.
AT LEAST... THAT'S WHAT I'D LIKE TO SAY.
BUT IT LOOKS LIKE THE ONE WHO PUT IN THE MOST EFFORT WAS **YOU.**

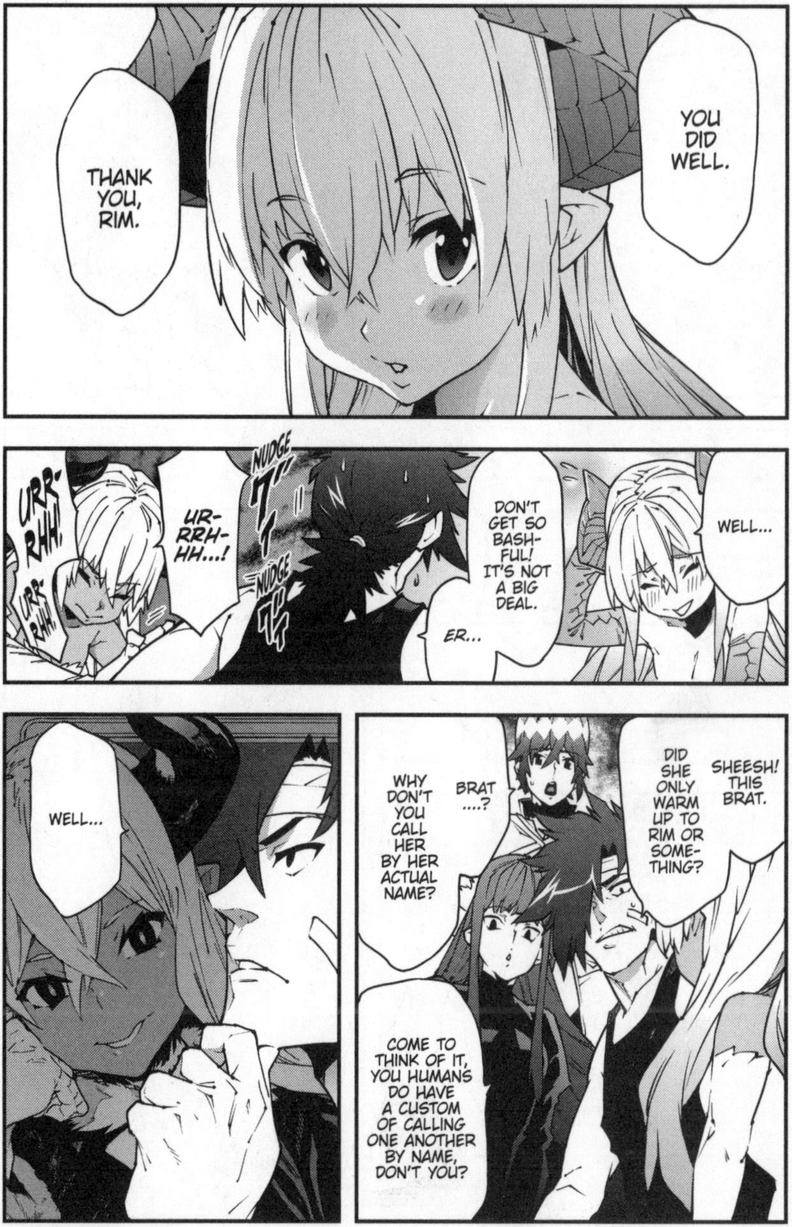
YOU DID WELL.
THANK YOU, RIM.
WELL...
DON'T GET SO BASHFUL! IT'S NOT A BIG DEAL.
ER...
NUDGE
NUDGE
URR-RRH-HH...!
URR-RHH!
URR-RHH!
SHEESH! THIS BRAT.
DID SHE ONLY WARM UP TO RIM OR SOMETHING?
BRAT ....?
WHY DON'T YOU CALL HER BY HER ACTUAL NAME?
COME TO THINK OF IT, YOU HUMANS DO HAVE A CUSTOM OF CALLING ONE ANOTHER BY NAME, DON'T YOU?
WELL...

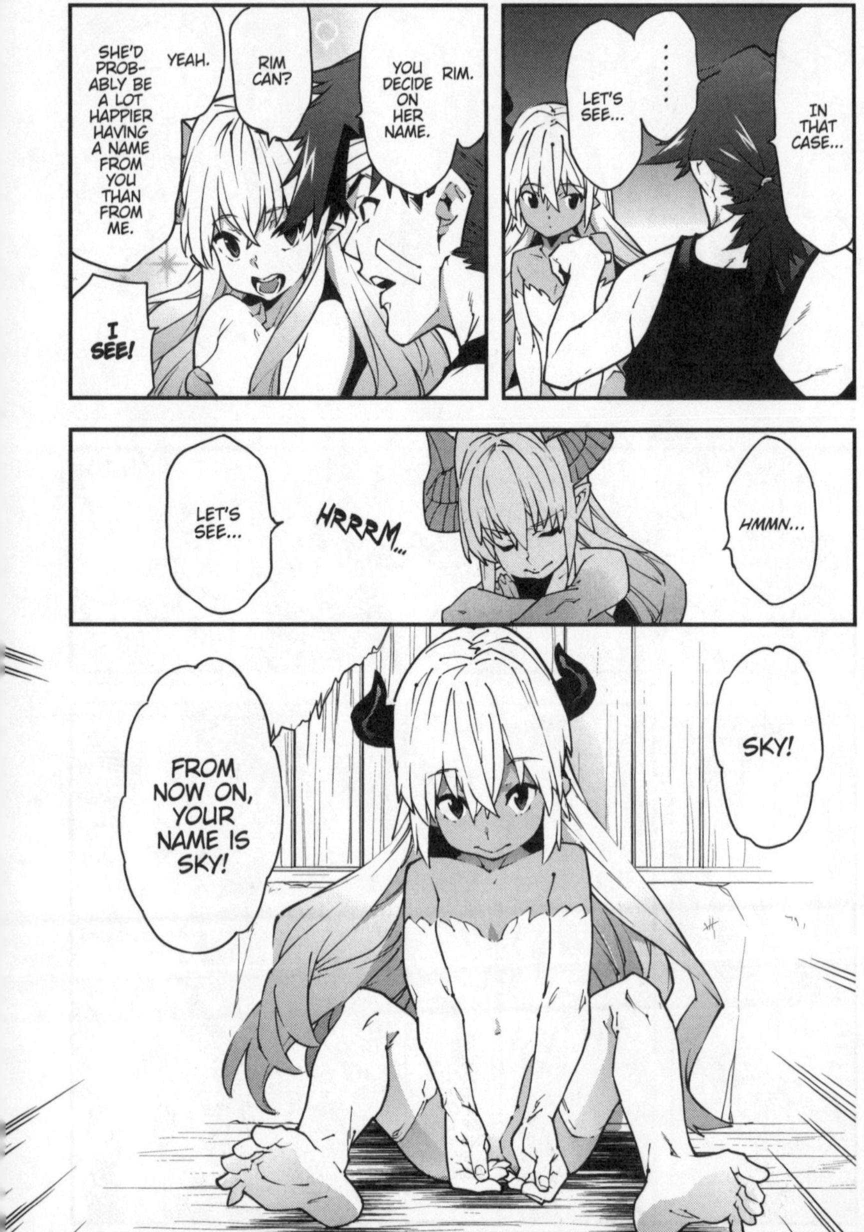
IN THAT CASE...
......
LET'S SEE...
RIM.
YOU DECIDE ON HER NAME.
RIM CAN?
YEAH.
SHE'D PROBABLY BE A LOT HAPPIER HAVING A NAME FROM YOU THAN FROM ME.
I SEE!
HMMN...
HRRRM...
LET'S SEE...
FROM NOW ON, YOUR NAME IS SKY!
SKY!

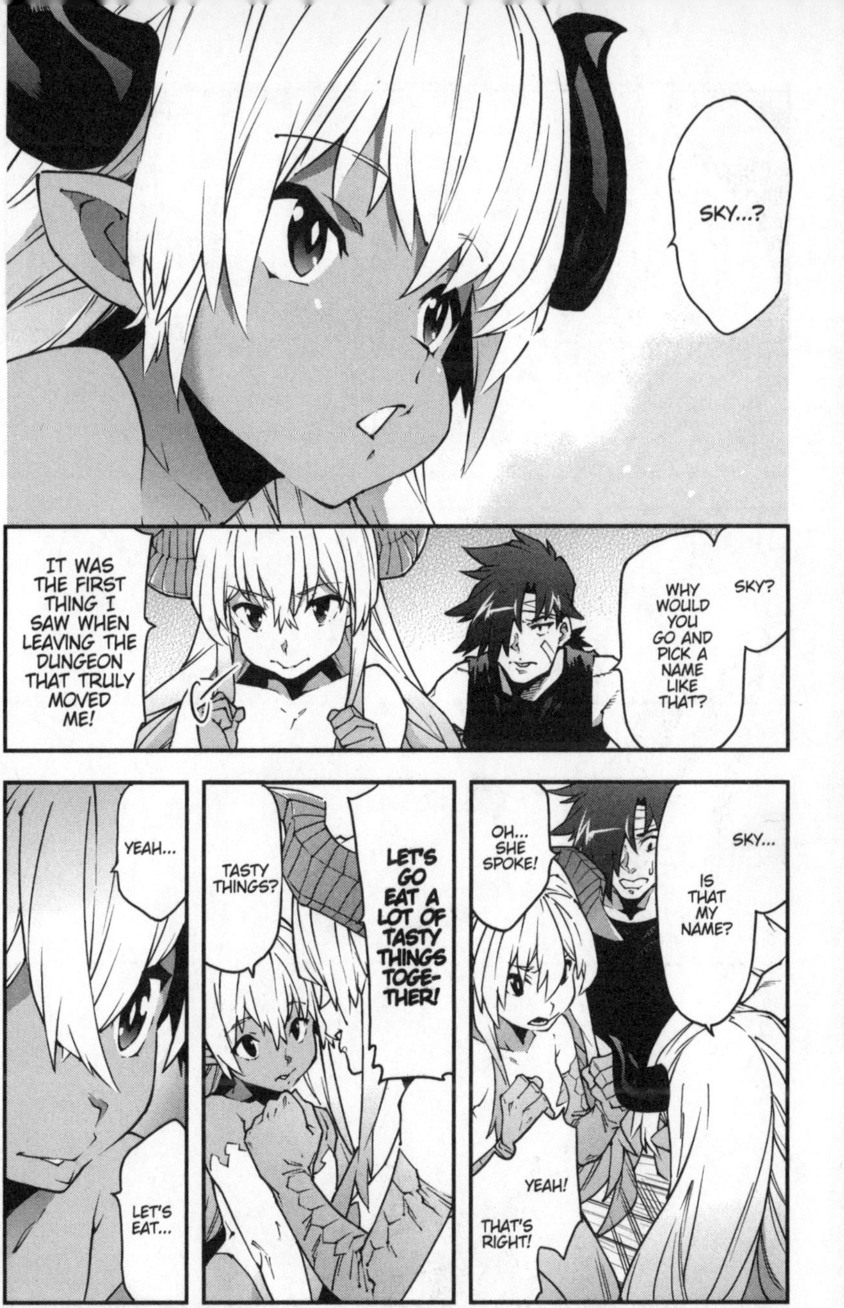
SKY...?
SKY?
WHY WOULD YOU GO AND PICK A NAME LIKE THAT?
IT WAS THE FIRST THING I SAW WHEN LEAVING THE DUNGEON THAT TRULY MOVED ME!
SKY...
IS THAT MY NAME?
OH... SHE SPOKE!
YEAH!
THAT'S RIGHT!
LET'S GO EAT A LOT OF TASTY THINGS TOGE-THER!
TASTY THINGS?
YEAH...
LET'S EAT...

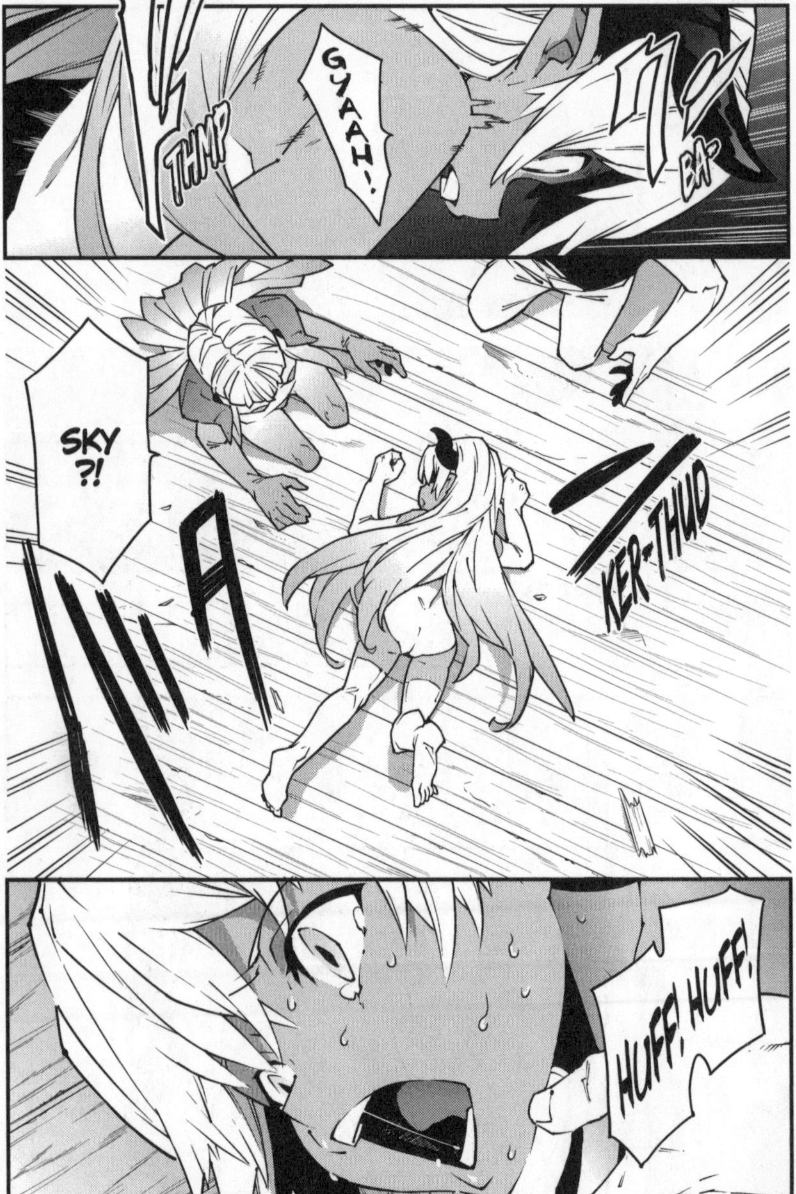
BA-
GYAAH!
THMP
KER-THUD
SKY ?!
HUFF! HUFF!

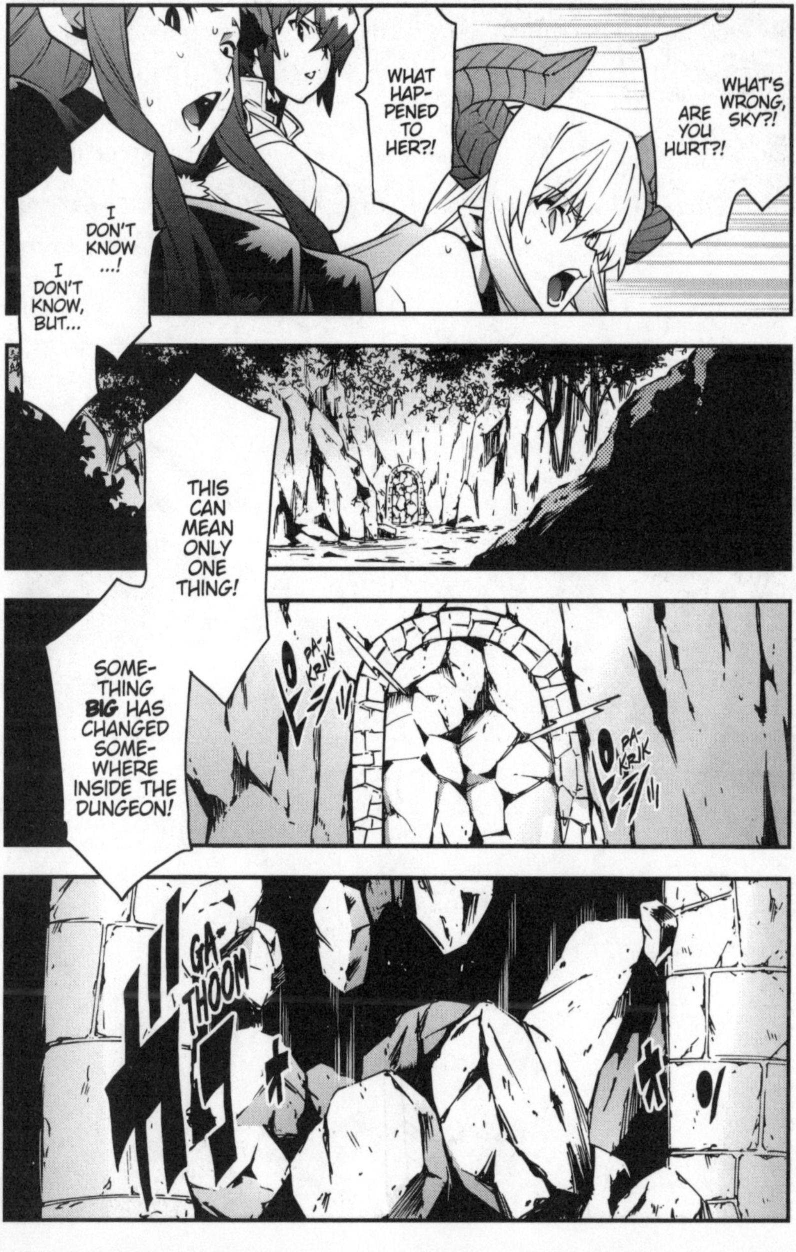
WHAT'S WRONG, SKY?!
ARE YOU HURT?!
WHAT HAPPENED TO HER?!
I DON'T KNOW...!
I DON'T KNOW, BUT...
THIS CAN MEAN ONLY ONE THING!
SOMETHING BIG HAS CHANGED SOMEWHERE INSIDE THE DUNGEON!
PA-KRIK
PA-KRIK
GA-THOOM

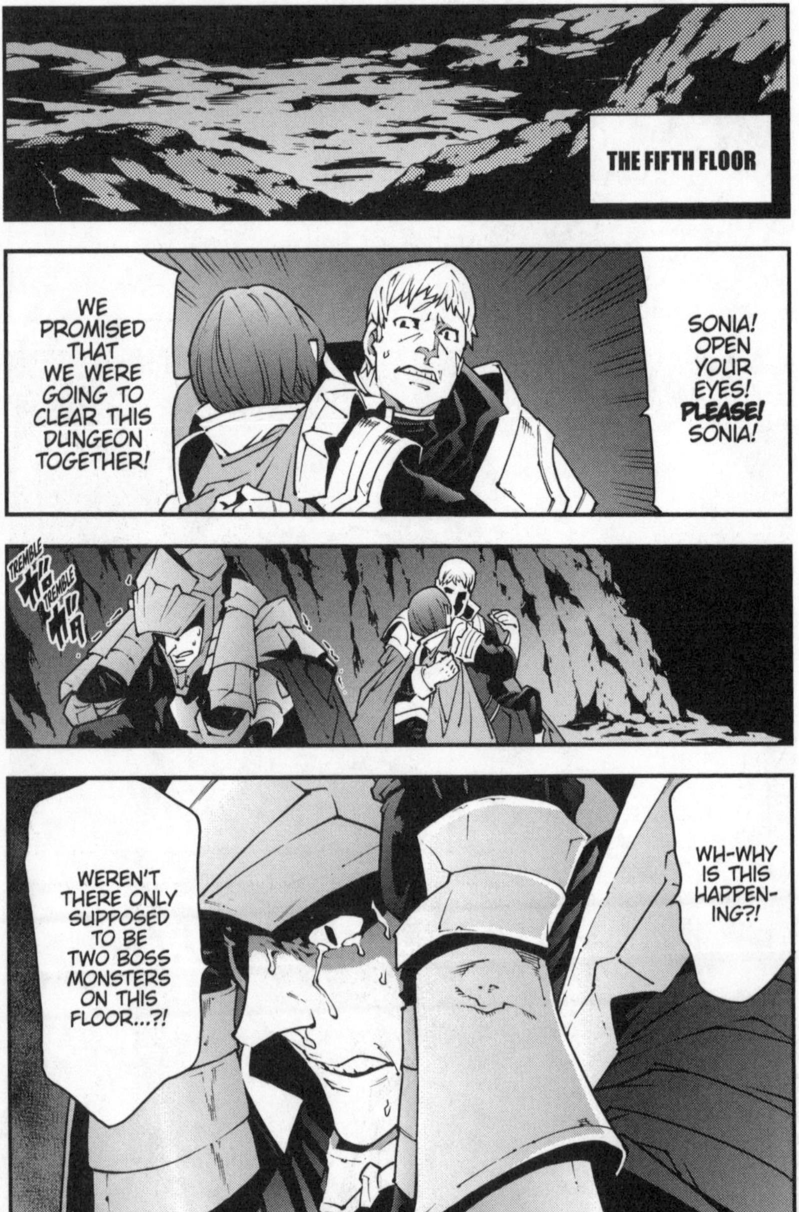
THE FIFTH FLOOR
SONIA! OPEN YOUR EYES! PLEASE! SONIA!
WE PROMISED THAT WE WERE GOING TO CLEAR THIS DUNGEON TOGETHER!
TREMBLE TREMBLE
WH-WHY IS THIS HAPPENING?!
WEREN'T THERE ONLY SUPPOSED TO BE TWO BOSS MONSTERS ON THIS FLOOR...?!

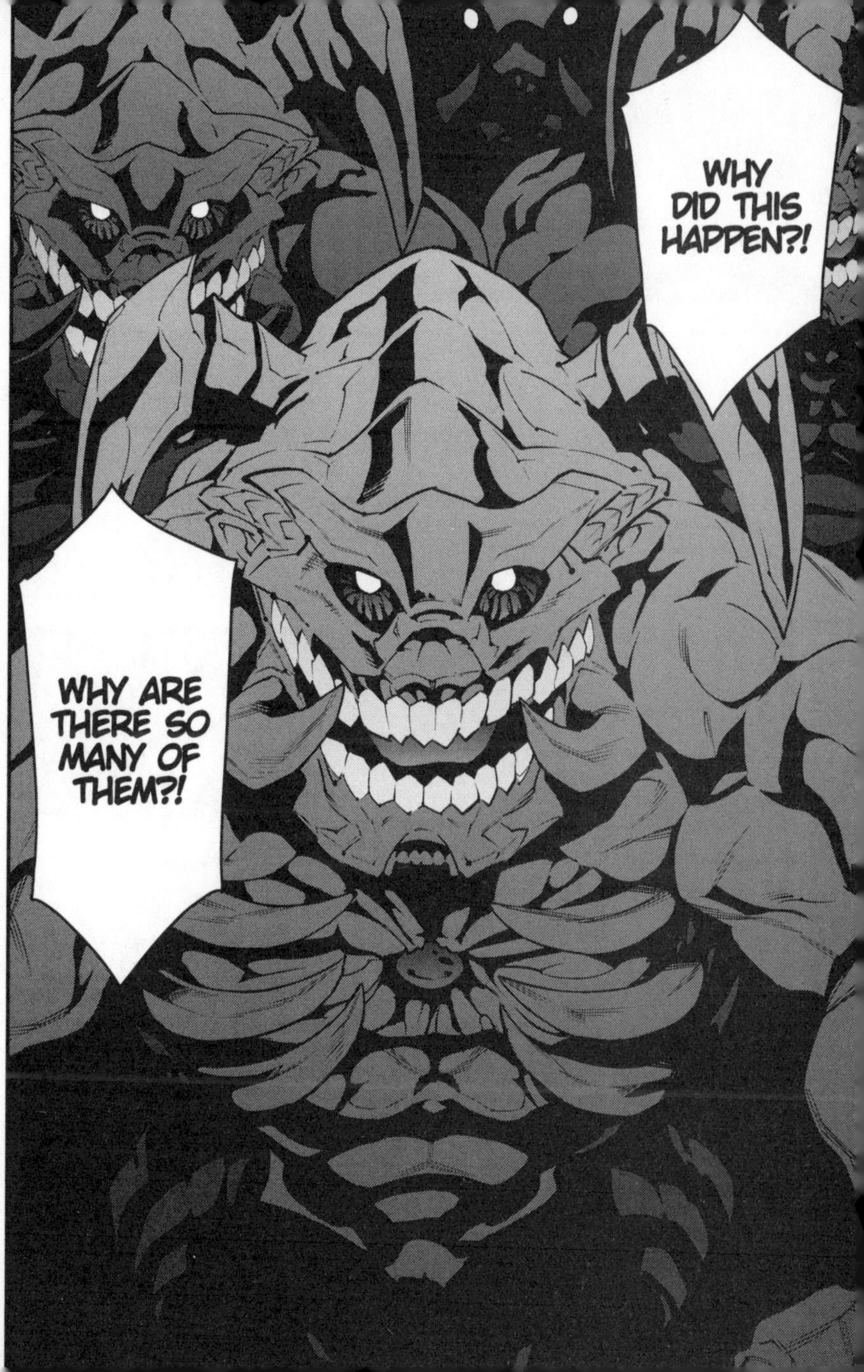
WHY DID THIS HAPPEN?!
WHY ARE THERE SO MANY OF THEM?!

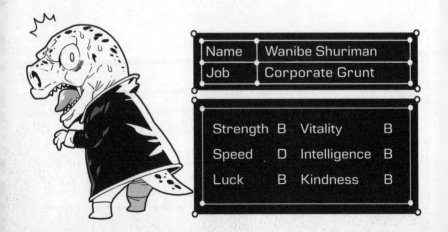

Name	Wanibe Shuriman
Job	Corporate Grunt

Strength	B	Vitality	B
Speed	D	Intelligence	B
Luck	B	Kindness	B

THE DUNGEON OF
BLACK COMPANY

Bonus Story: A Day in the Life of Rim

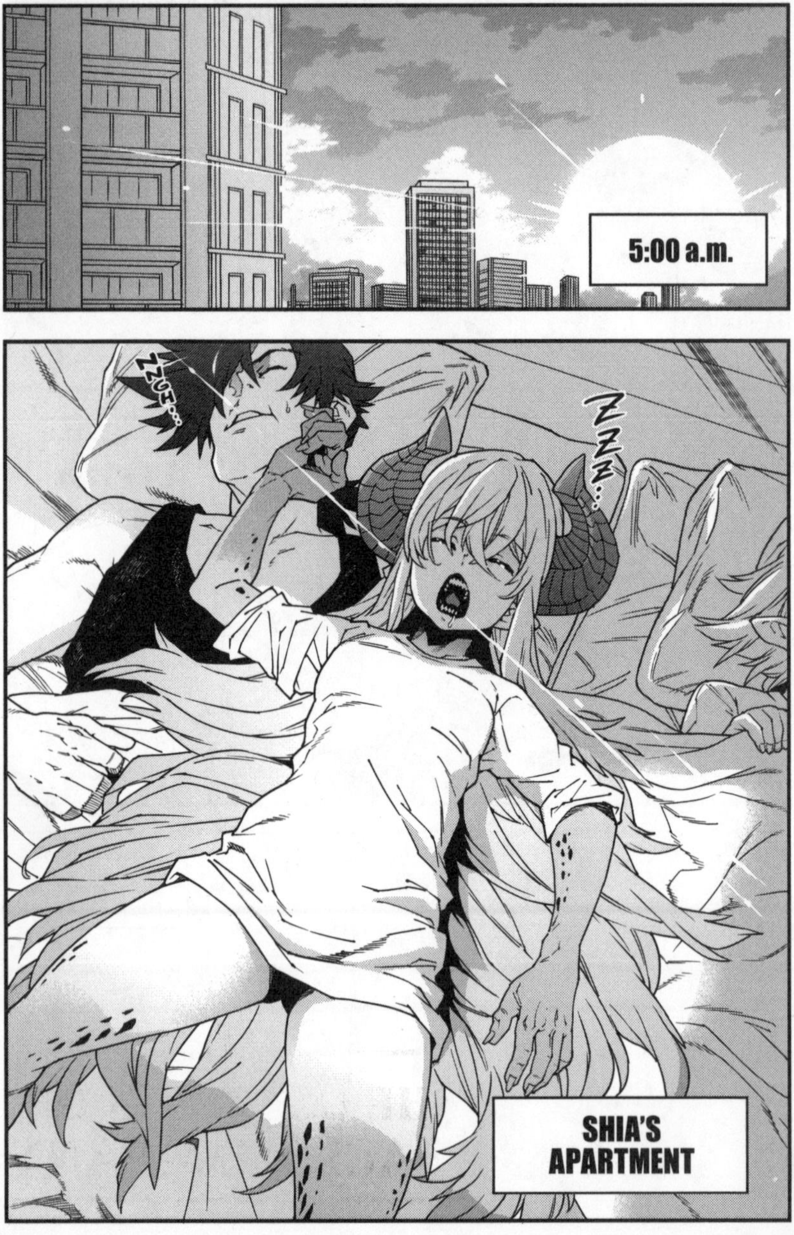
5:00 a.m.
ZZZ...
NNGH...
SHIA'S APARTMENT

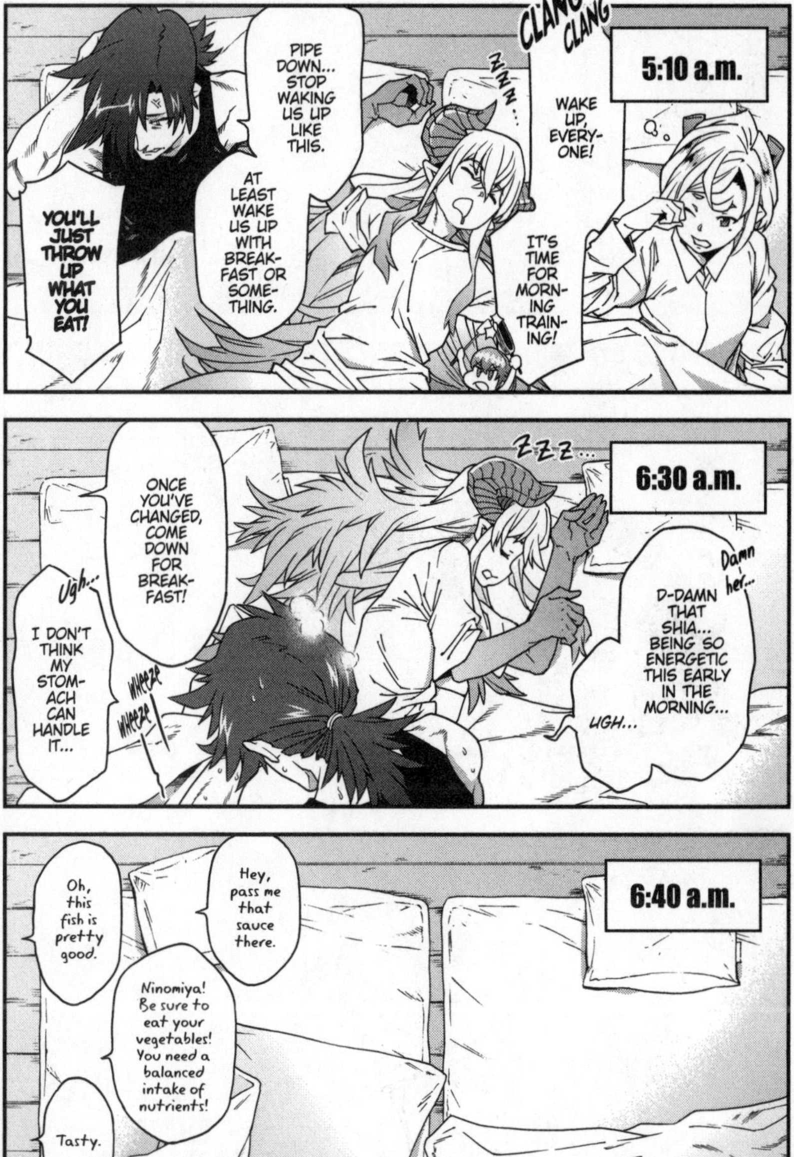
5:10 a.m.
CLANG CLANG
ZNN...
WAKE UP, EVERYONE!
IT'S TIME FOR MORNING TRAINING!
PIPE DOWN... STOP WAKING US UP LIKE THIS.
AT LEAST WAKE US UP WITH BREAKFAST OR SOMETHING.
YOU'LL JUST THROW UP WHAT YOU EAT!
6:30 a.m.
Z Z Z ...
Damn her...
D-DAMN THAT SHIA... BEING SO ENERGETIC THIS EARLY IN THE MORNING...
UGH...
ONCE YOU'VE CHANGED, COME DOWN FOR BREAKFAST!
wheeze wheeze
Ugh...
I DON'T THINK MY STOMACH CAN HANDLE IT...
6:40 a.m.
Hey, pass me that sauce there.
Oh, this fish is pretty good.
Ninomiya! Be sure to eat your vegetables! You need a balanced intake of nutrients!
Tasty.

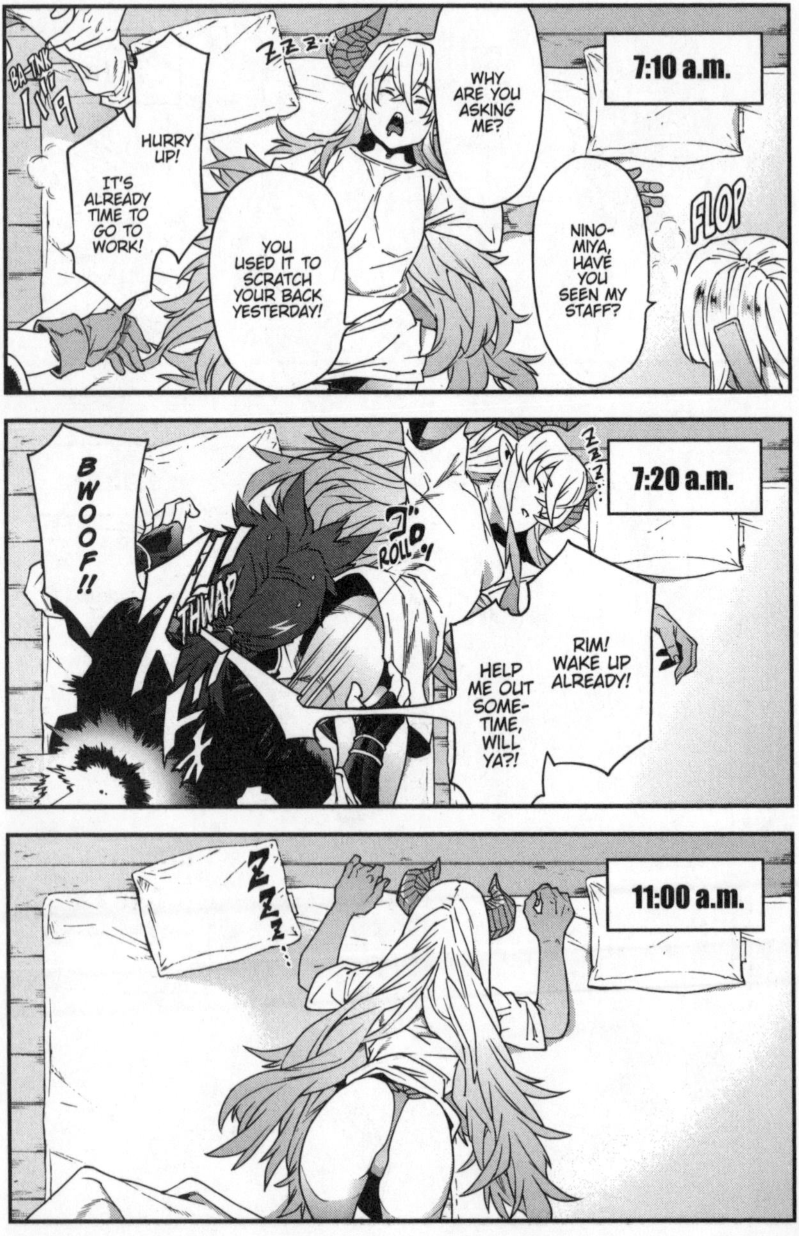
7:10 a.m.
FLOP
NINO-MIYA, HAVE YOU SEEN MY STAFF?
WHY ARE YOU ASKING ME?
YOU USED IT TO SCRATCH YOUR BACK YESTERDAY!
ZZZ...
HURRY UP!
IT'S ALREADY TIME TO GO TO WORK!
BA-TNK
7:20 a.m.
ZZZ
RIM! WAKE UP ALREADY!
HELP ME OUT SOMETIME, WILL YA?!
ROLL
THWAP
BWOOOF!!
11:00 a.m.
ZZZ...

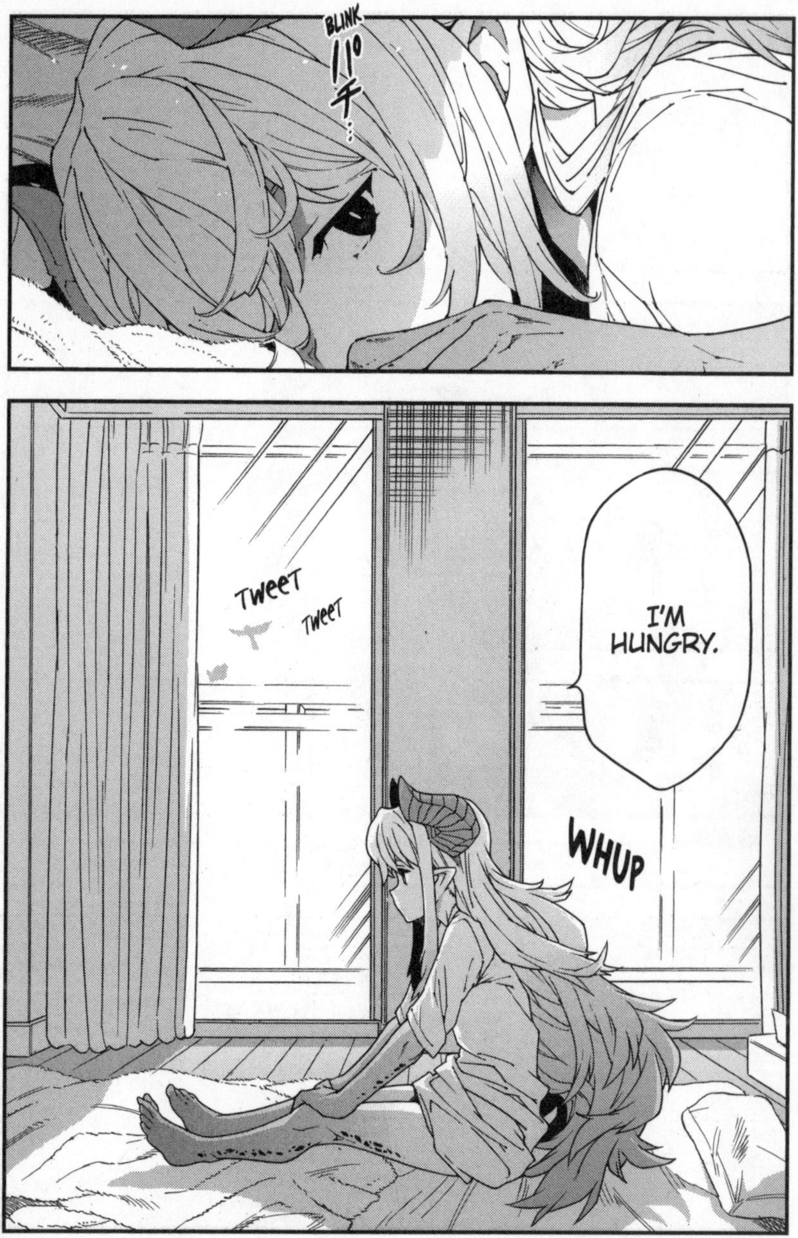
BLINK
パチ…
I'M HUNGRY.
TWEET
TWEET
WHUP

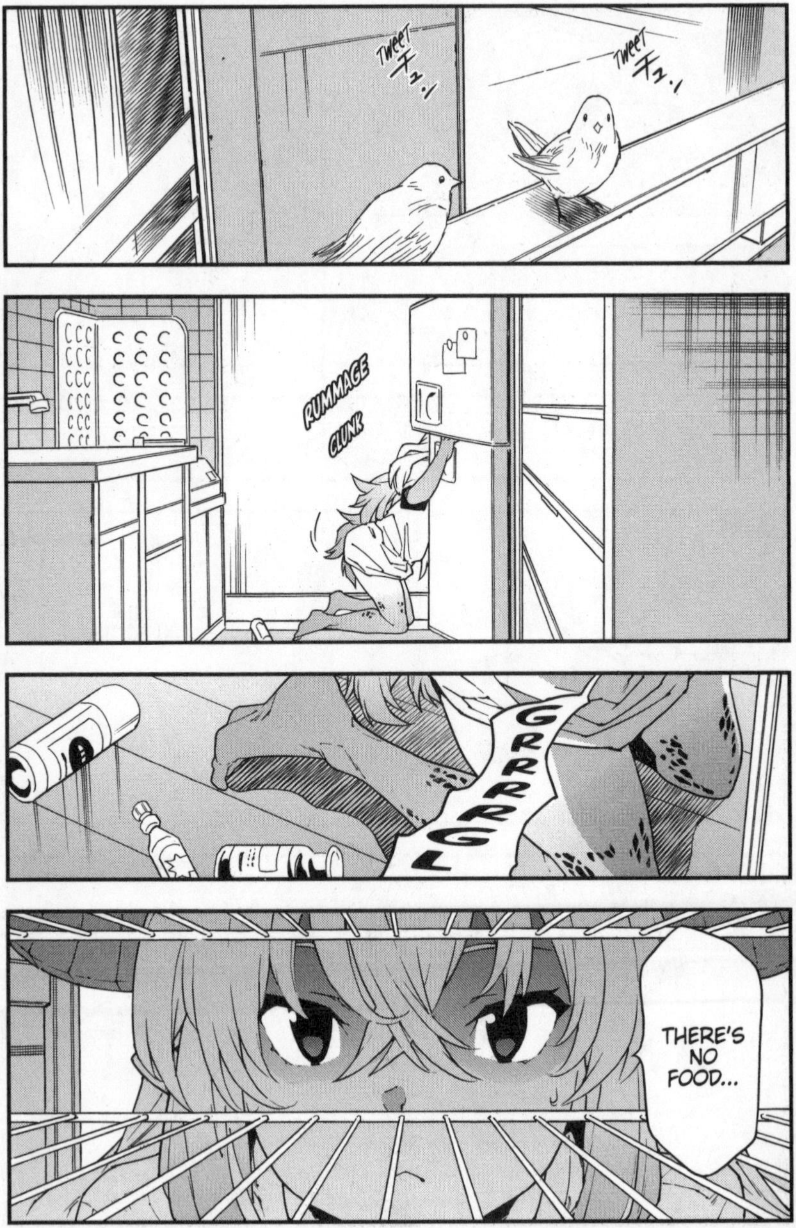
TWEET
TWEET
RUMMAGE
CLUNK
GRRRRGL
THERE'S NO FOOD...

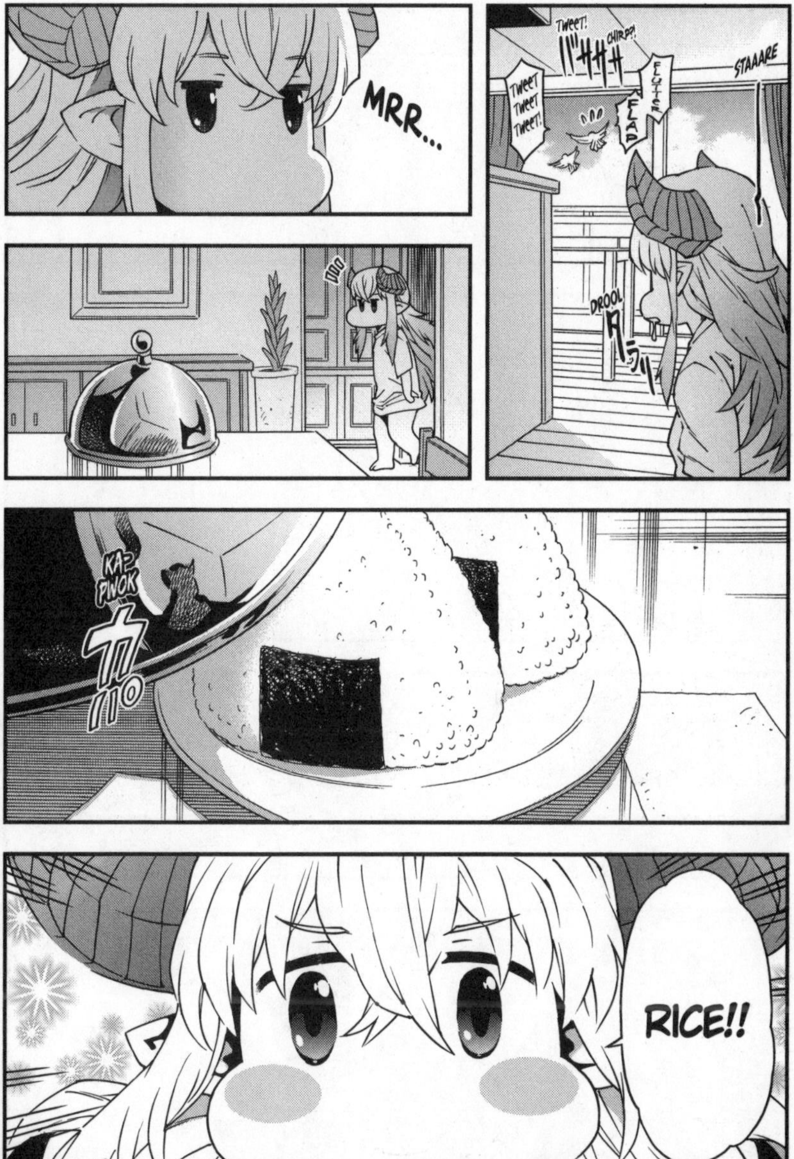
STAAARE
CHIRP?!
TWEET!
FLUTTER
FLAP
TWEET TWEET TWEET!
DROOL
MRR...
KAP PWOK
RICE!!

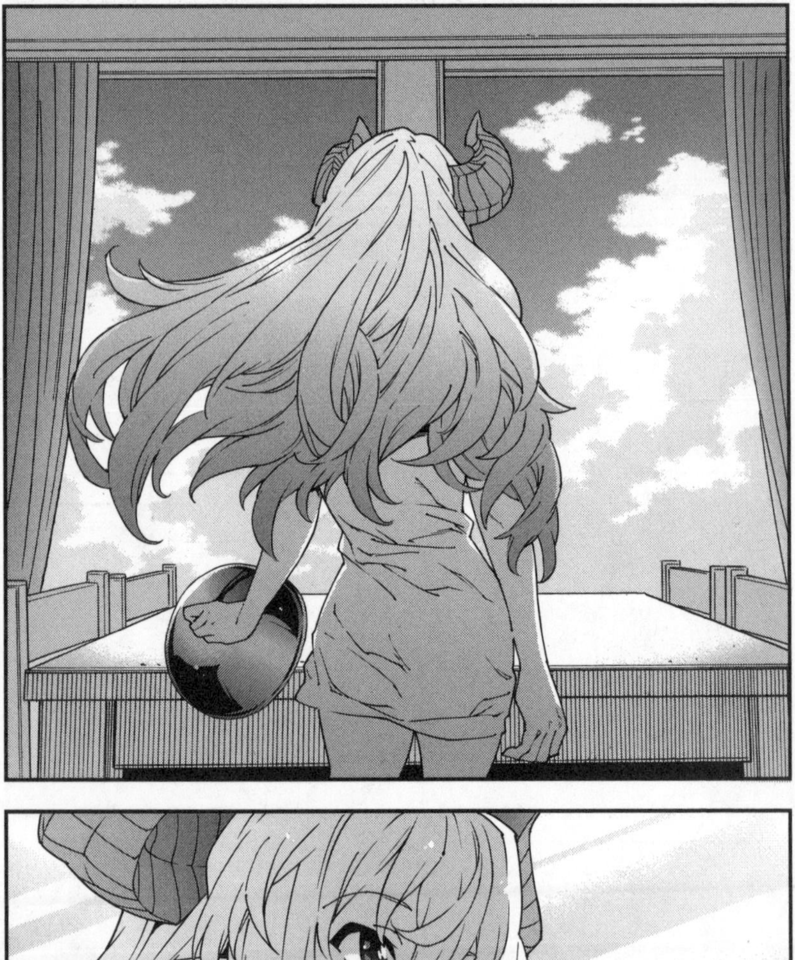
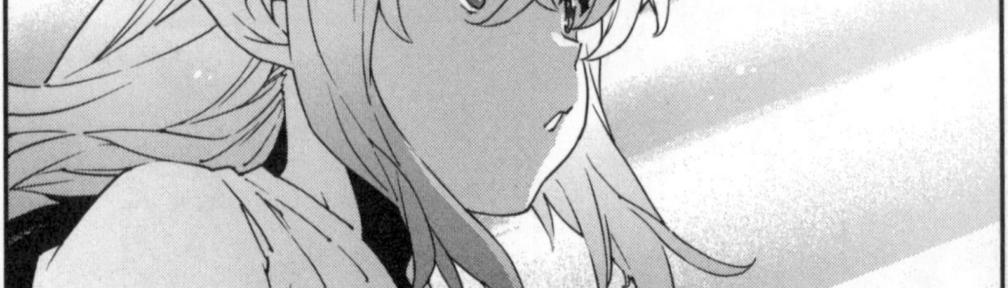

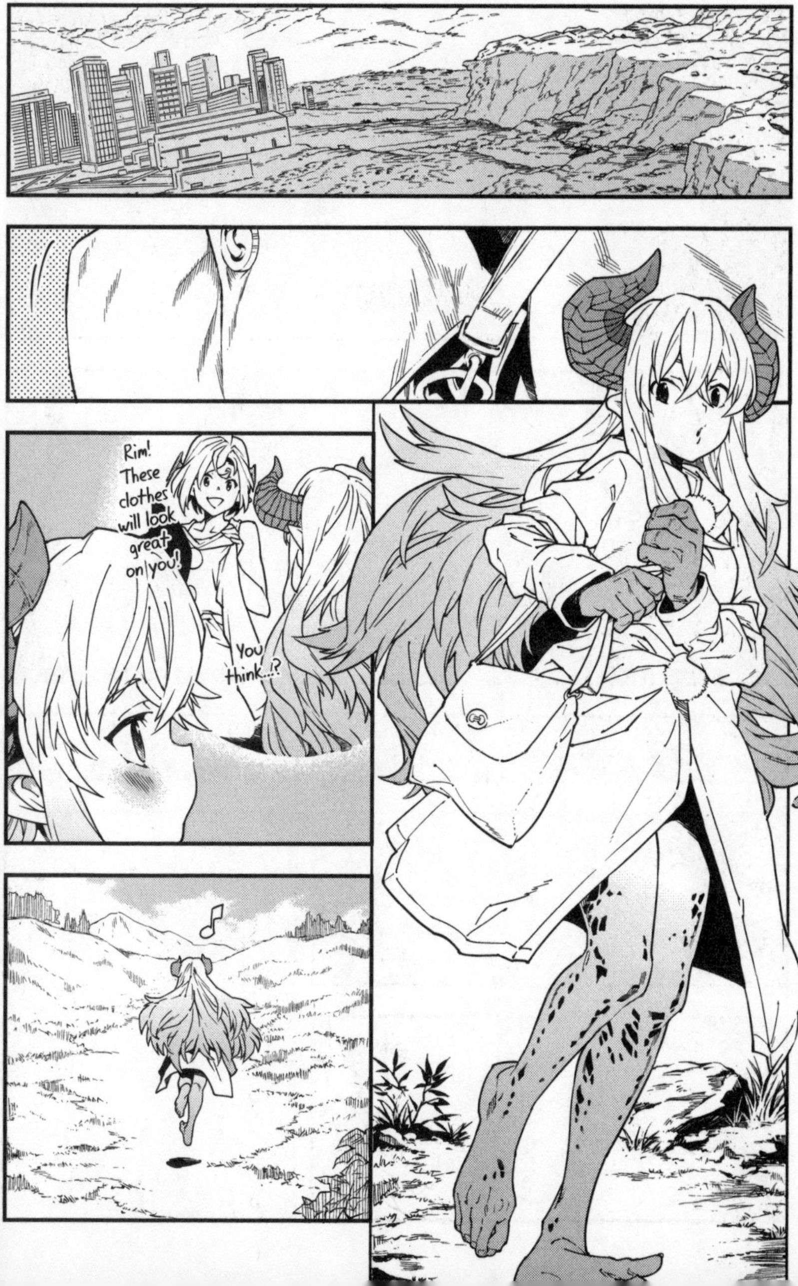
Rim! These clothes will look great on you!
You think...?
♪

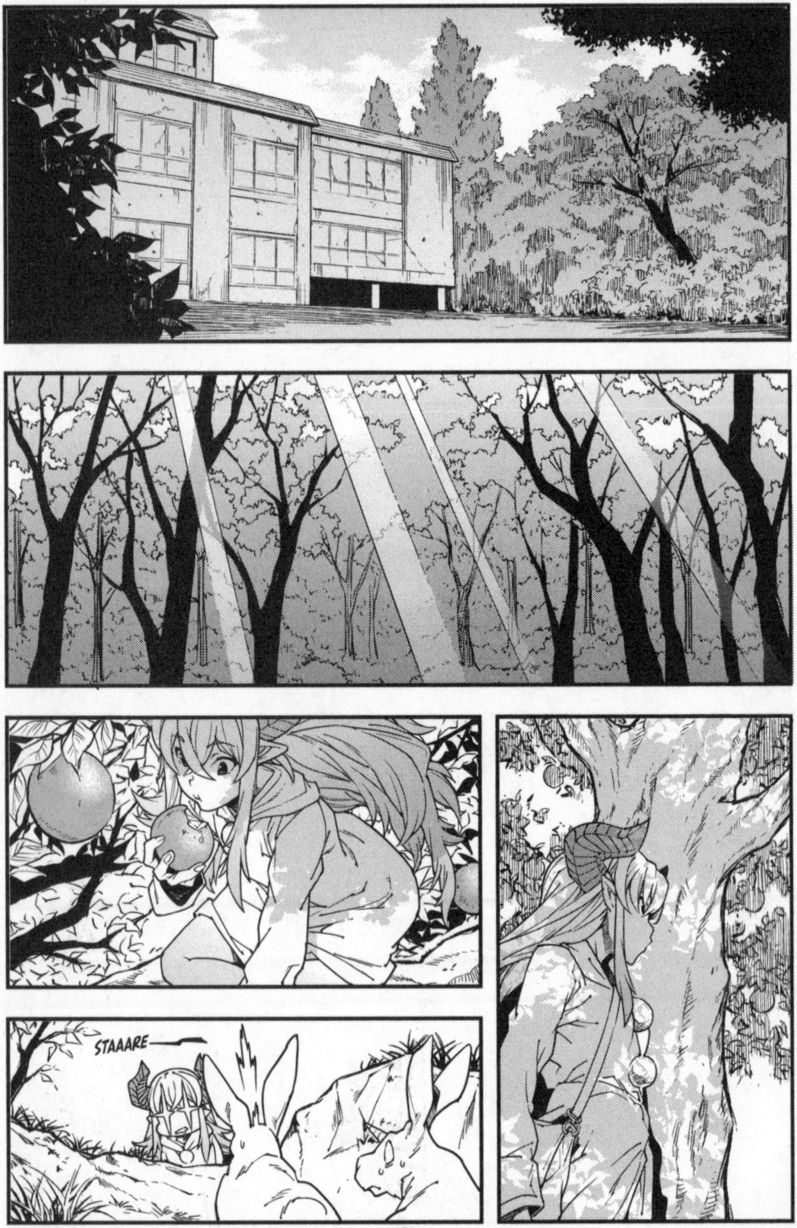
STAAARE—

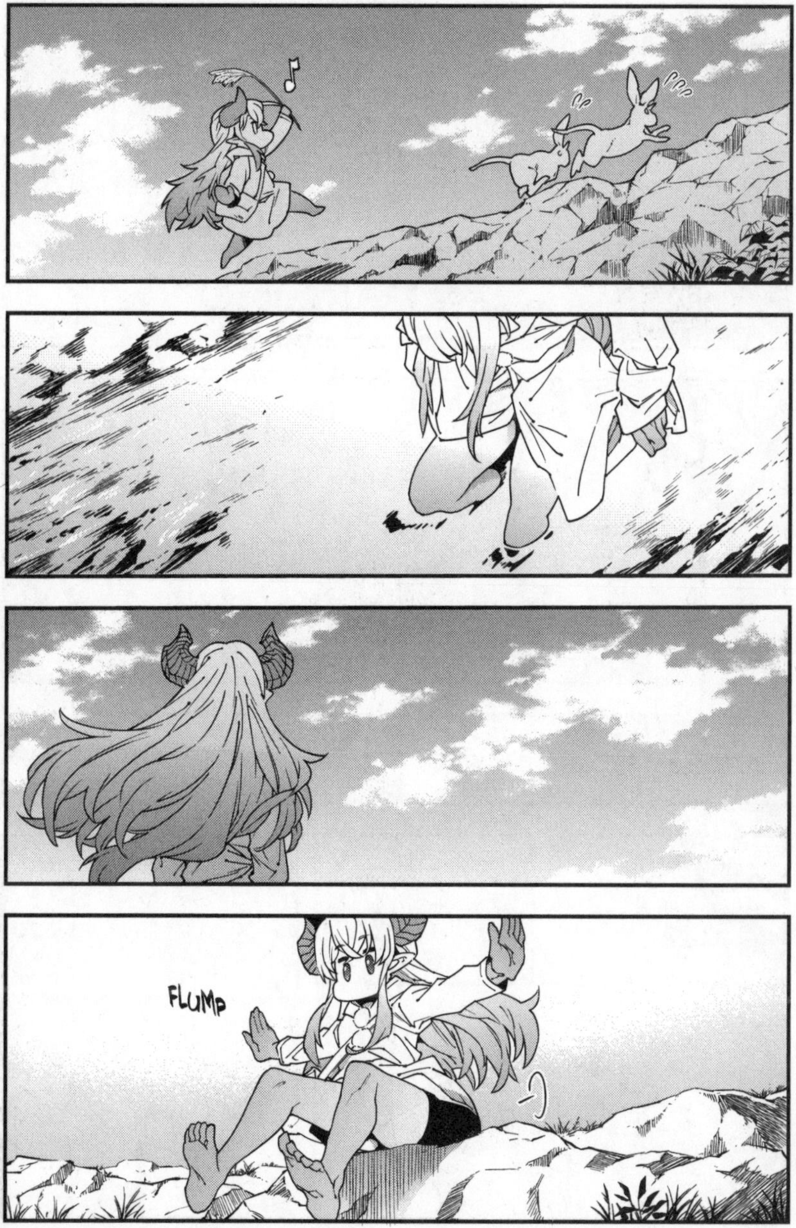
FLUMP

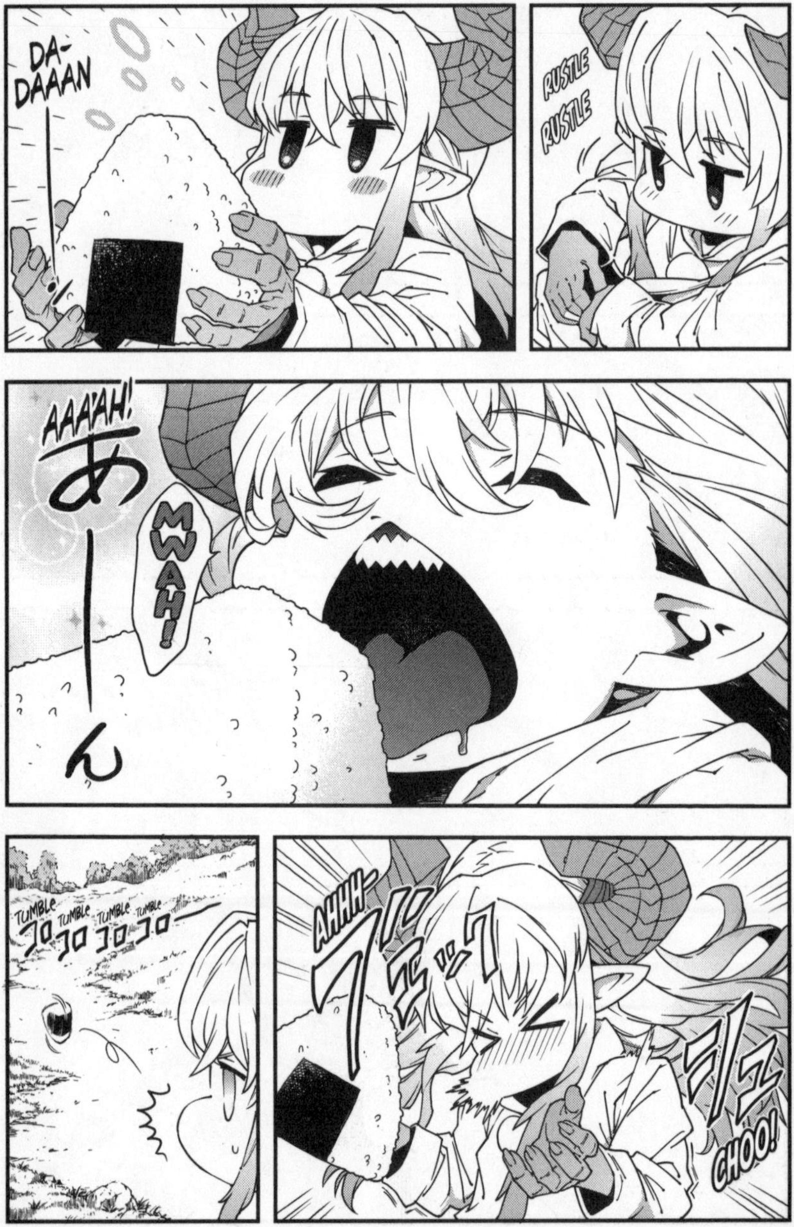
RUSTLE RUSTLE
DA-DAAAN
AAA'AH!
あーん
MWAH!
AHHH-
CHOO!
TUMBLE TUMBLE TUMBLE TUMBLE
コロコロコロコロ—

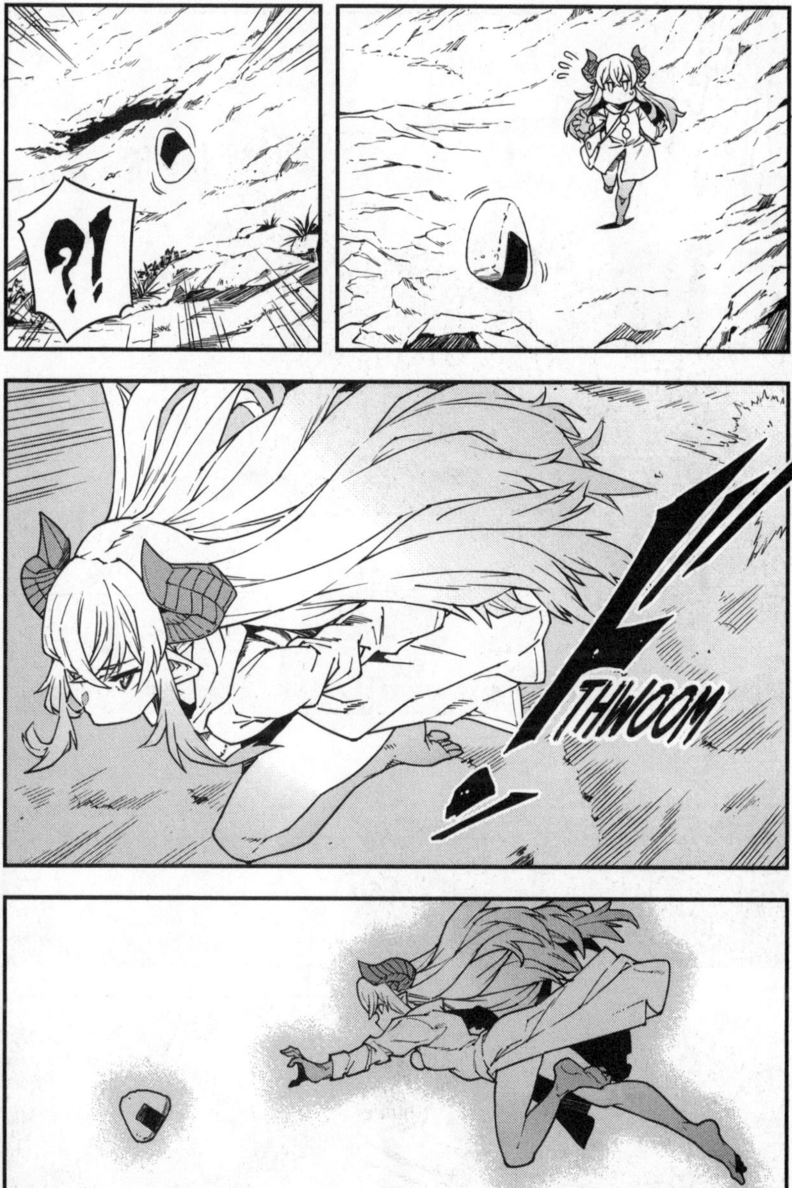
?!
THWOOM

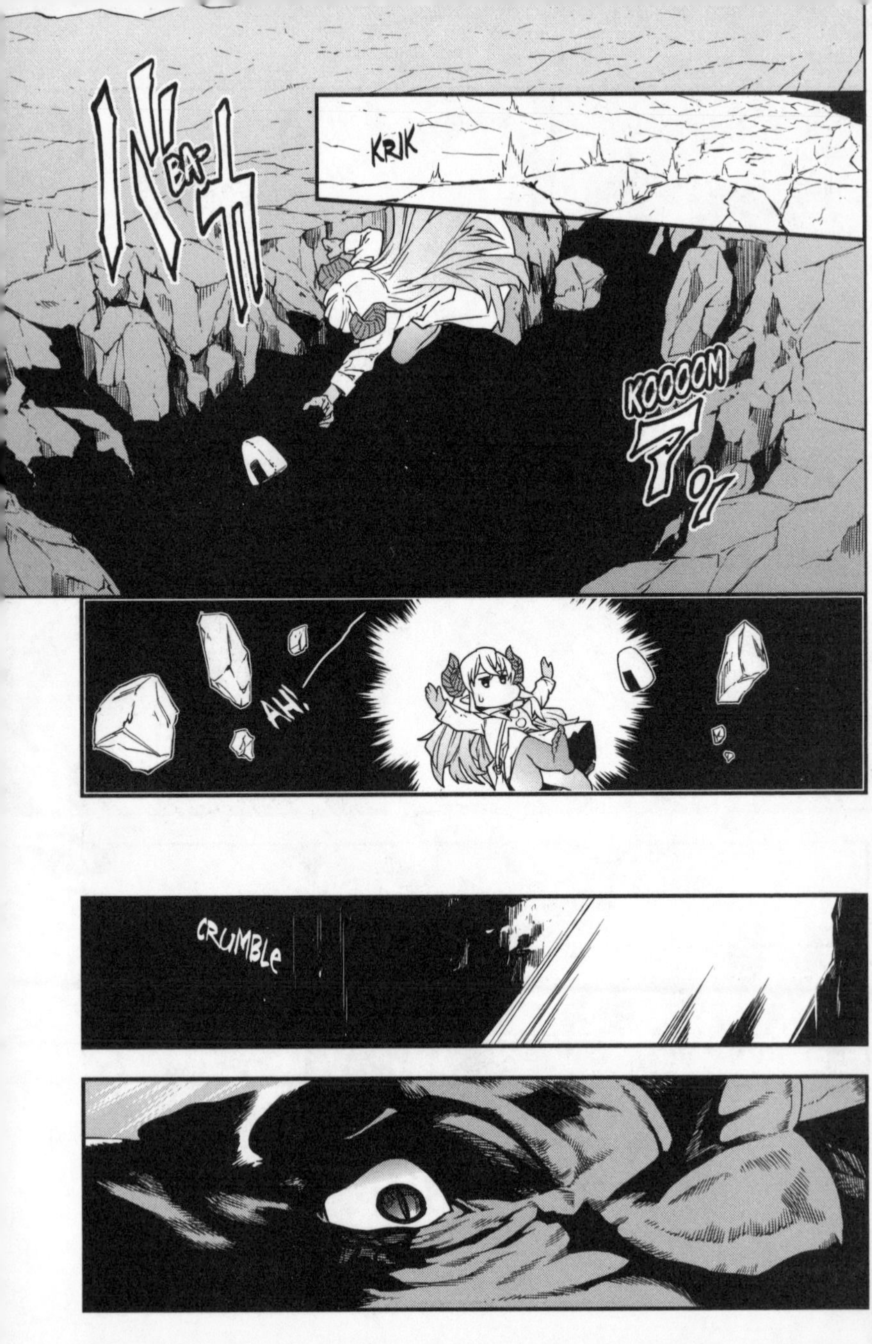
KRIK
KOOOOM
BAP
AH!
CRUMBLE

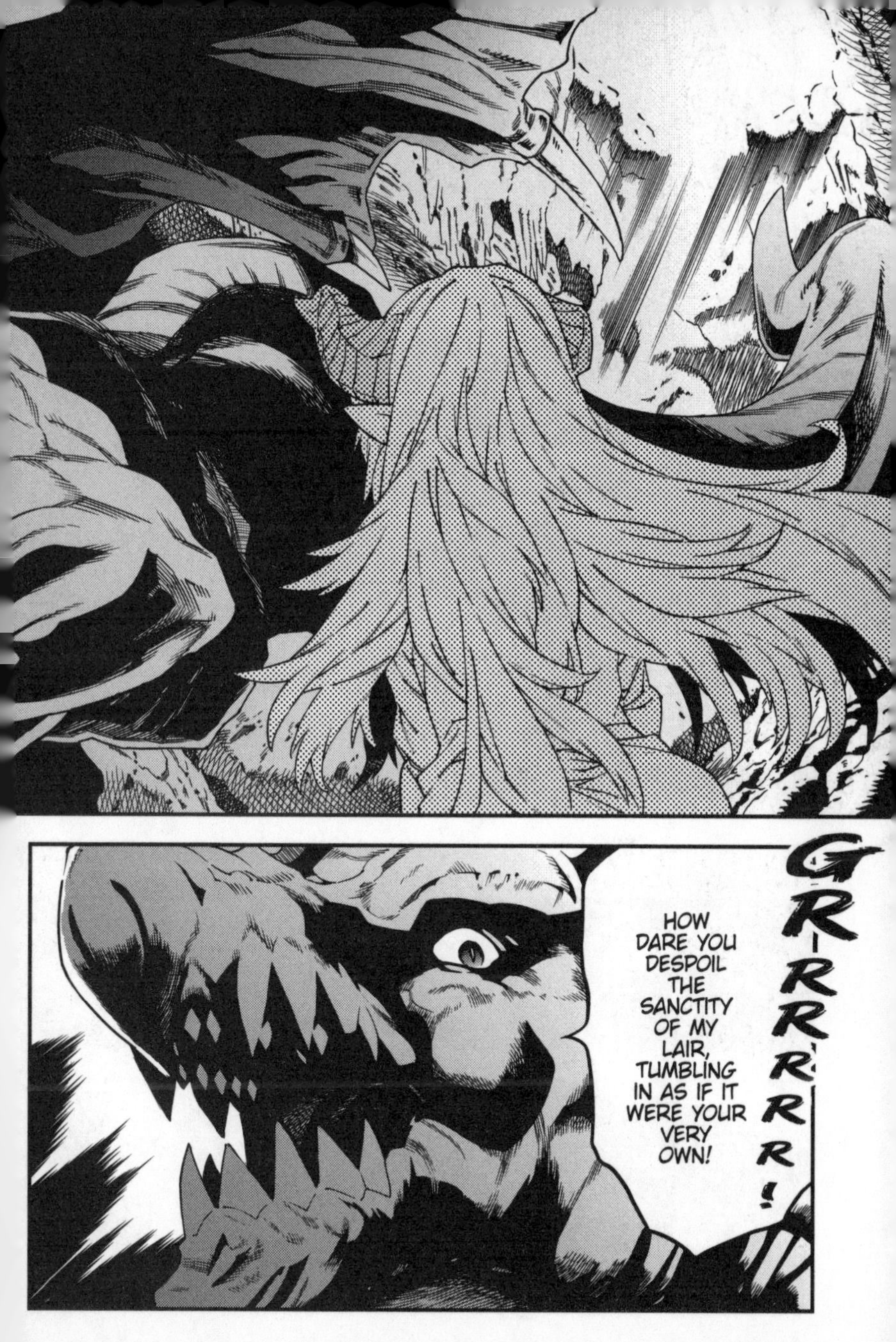
HOW DARE YOU DESPOIL THE SANCTITY OF MY LAIR, TUMBLING IN AS IF IT WERE YOUR VERY OWN!
GRRRRRR!

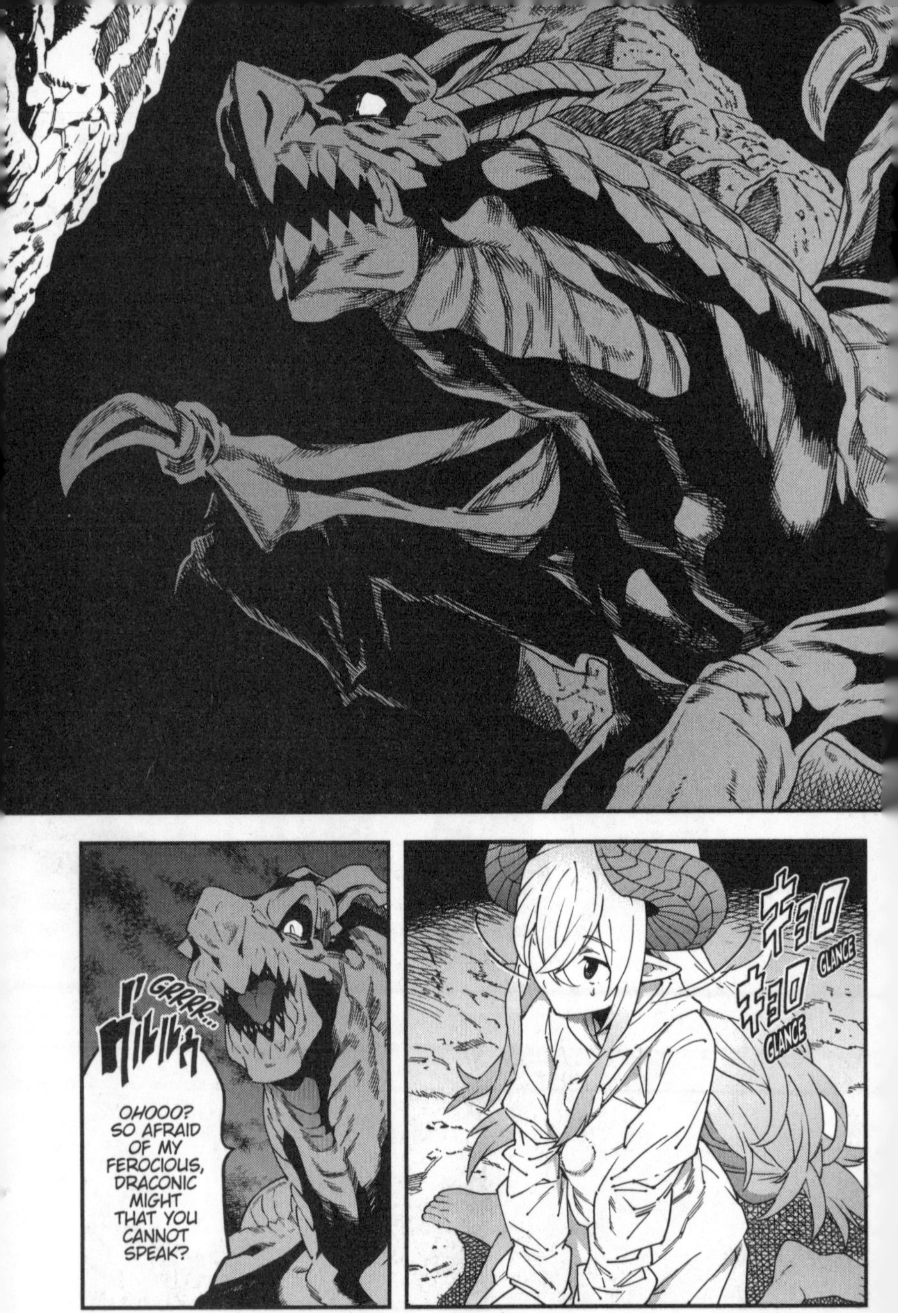
キョロ
GLANCE
キョロ
GLANCE
GRRRR...
OHOOO? SO AFRAID OF MY FEROCIOUS, DRACONIC MIGHT THAT YOU CANNOT SPEAK?

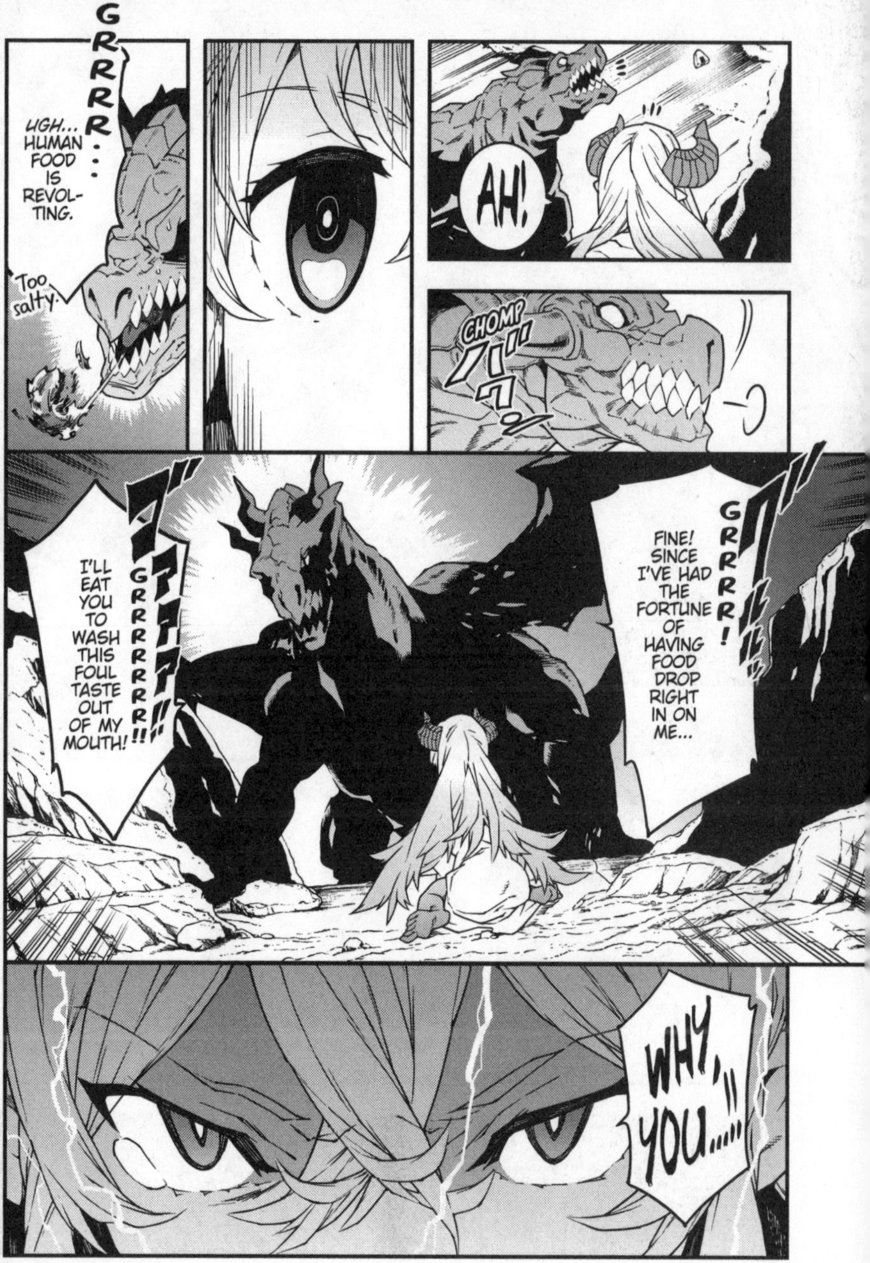
AH!
CHOMP
GRRRR...
UGH... HUMAN FOOD IS REVOLTING.
Too salty.
GRRRR!
FINE! SINCE I'VE HAD THE FORTUNE OF HAVING FOOD DROP RIGHT IN ON ME...
GRRRRRRR!!
I'LL EAT YOU TO WASH THIS FOUL TASTE OUT OF MY MOUTH!
WHY, YOU...!!!

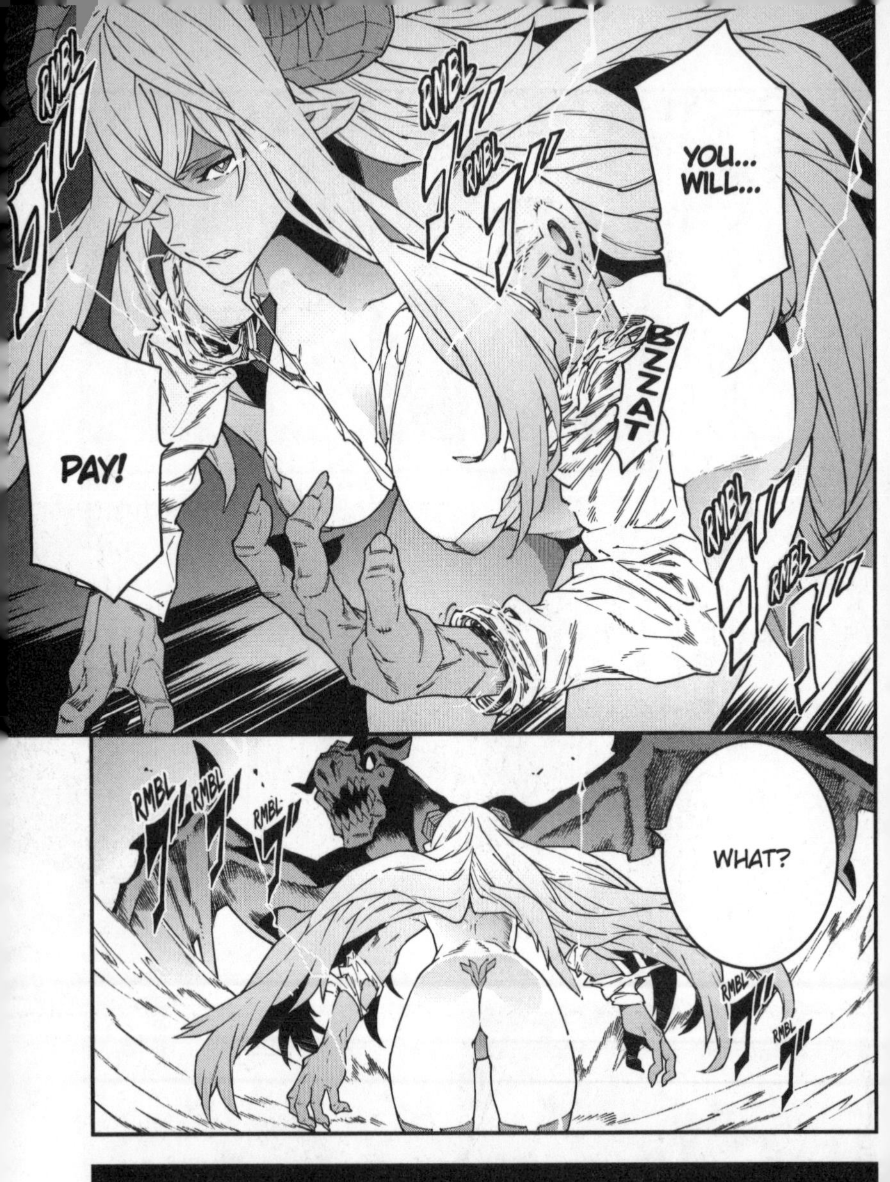
RMBL
RMBL
RMBL
YOU... WILL...
BZZAT
PAY!
RMBL
RMBL
WHAT?
RMBL
RMBL
RMBL
RMBL
RMBL

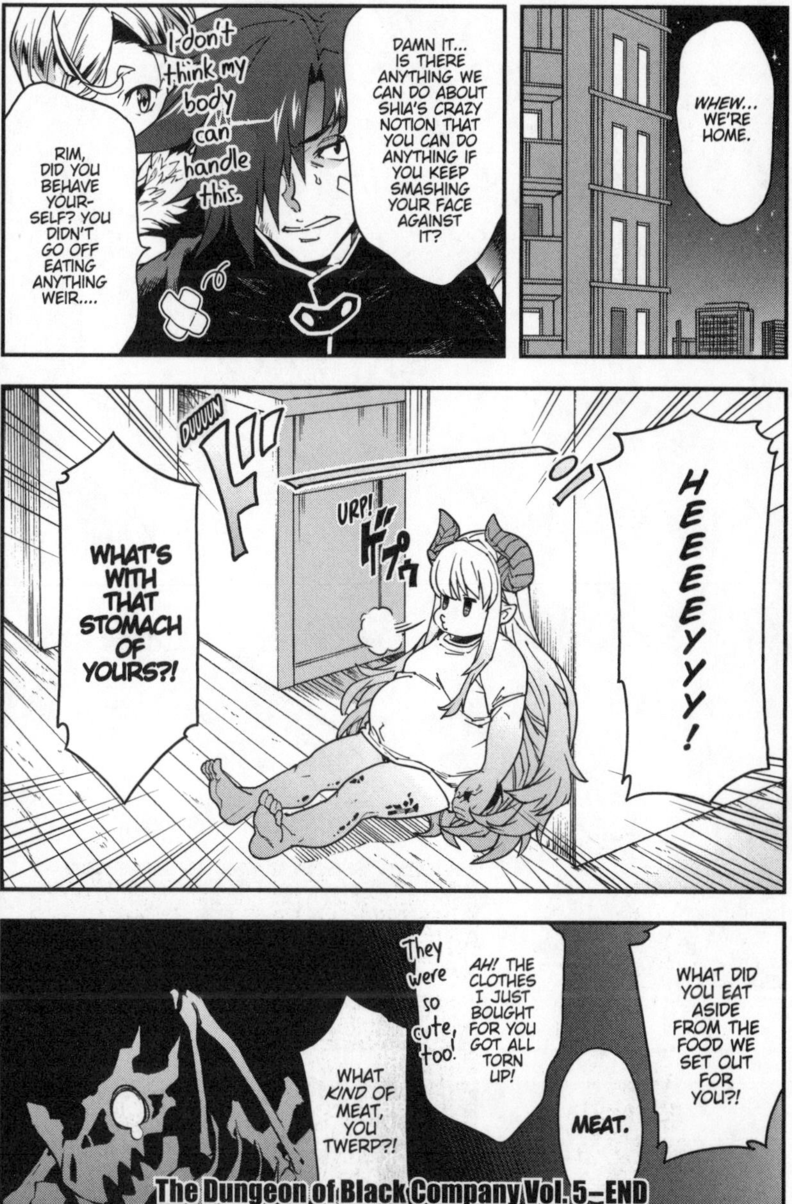
WHEW... WE'RE HOME.
DAMN IT... IS THERE ANYTHING WE CAN DO ABOUT SHIA'S CRAZY NOTION THAT YOU CAN DO ANYTHING IF YOU KEEP SMASHING YOUR FACE AGAINST IT?
I don't think my body can handle this.
RIM, DID YOU BEHAVE YOUR-SELF? YOU DIDN'T GO OFF EATING ANYTHING WEIR....
HEEEEEYYYY!
URP!
DUUUUN
WHAT'S WITH THAT STOMACH OF YOURS?!
WHAT DID YOU EAT ASIDE FROM THE FOOD WE SET OUT FOR YOU?!
MEAT.
AH! THE CLOTHES I JUST BOUGHT FOR YOU GOT ALL TORN UP!
They were so cute, too!
WHAT KIND OF MEAT, YOU TWERP?!
The Dungeon of Black Company Vol. 5–END

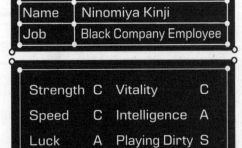

| Name | Ninomiya Kinji |
| Job | Black Company Employee |

Strength	C	Vitality	C
Speed	C	Intelligence	A
Luck	A	Playing Dirty	S

THE DUNGEON OF
BLACK COMPANY

THE DUNGEON OF BLACK COMPANY

CHARACTER

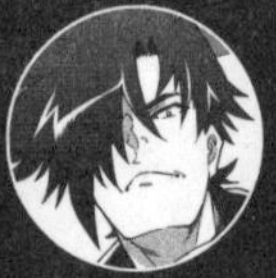

NINOMIYA KINJI
A man that was somehow, for some reason, transported to another world and forced to work at a ruthless company. A conceited man who works using cunning and underhanded means.

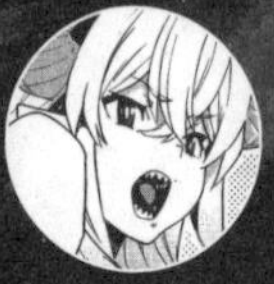

RIM
A monster girl with an insatiable appetite. So long as Ninomiya keeps her fed, she follows him. The most powerful good-for-nothing.

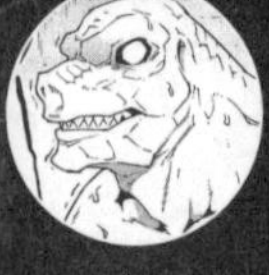

WANIBE
A lizardman who suffers from a severe lack of backbone. Having roomed with Ninomiya in the past, he's been used by him time and time again.

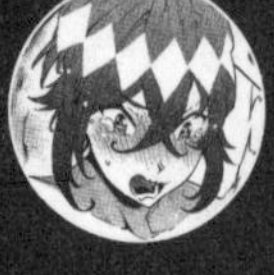

SHIA
A workaholic who rose from the ranks of mere livestock to attain the title of Hero. She has proven herself quite useful.

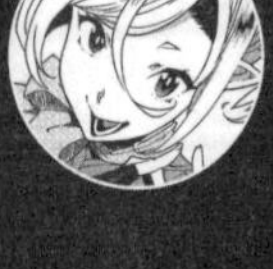

RANGA
An effeminate male mage. He followed Ninomiya from a messed-up future in order to knock some sense into his ancestor from current times.

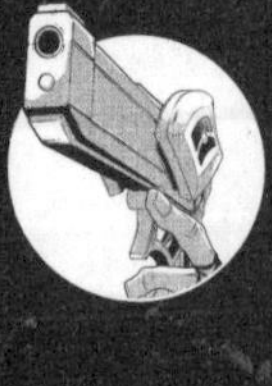

BLADE WING
Ninomiya's gun from the future. It has a needy, desperate, stalker-y personality. It's very powerful, but it consumes a ridiculous amount of energy.

STORY

Ninomiya Kinji was summoned to another world and forced into indentured servitude as corporate livestock. It turns out that a secret technology is hidden within the dungeon owned by his twisted company—one strong enough to control the whole world. Kinji is determined to find its power before management does. After obtaining some firepower in the form of a magic gun, vanquishing a floor covered in traps, and freeing a fortress from a vengeful spirit, he now prepares to confront the fourth floor of the dungeon.

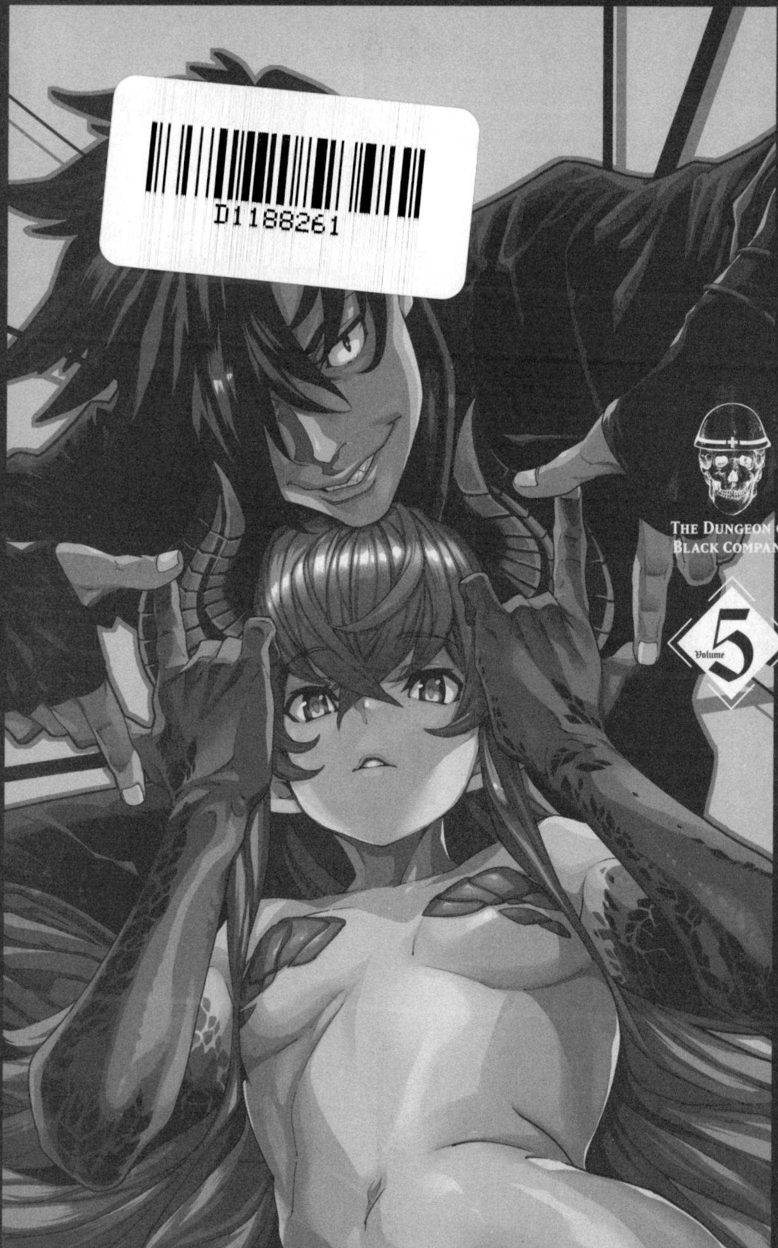
THE DUNGEON OF
BLACK COMPANY
Volume
5